From the Jesuit Fathers of the
Missouri Province
Xavier Jesuit Center
Denver, Colorado
2004

A Gift to
St. John Vianney Seminary

THE PHILOSOPHY OF MORALITY

SCIENCE AND CULTURE SERIES
JOSEPH HUSSLEIN, S.J., PH.D., GENERAL EDITOR

THE
PHILOSOPHY *of*
MORALITY

HENRI RENARD, S.J.

PROFESSOR OF PHILOSOPHY

CREIGHTON UNIVERSITY

PREFACE BY

JACQUES MARITAIN

THE BRUCE PUBLISHING COMPANY
MILWAUKEE

IMPRIMI POTEST:

DANIEL H. CONWAY, S.J.

NIHIL OBSTAT:

JOHN A. SCHULIEN, S.T.D.

Censor librorum

IMPRIMATUR:

✠ MOYSES E. KILEY

Archiepiscopus Milwauchiensis

February 17, 1953

171
R 394
83983

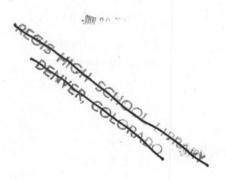

PATRI MATRIQUE DILECTISSIMIS

QUI

GESTIS MAGIS QUAM DICTIS

CHRISTIANAE VITAE MORES

MIHI

PRAESTITERUNT

PREFACE

It is a privilege to know Father Henri Renard and to come in contact with his alert and eloquent wisdom and the philosophical fire which animates him. It is a privilege also to read his books and use them either to teach or to study perennial philosophy. I should like to avail myself of the opportunity offered by the publication of his PHILOSOPHY OF MORALITY to express my high esteem and appreciation for the series of textbooks — *The Philosophy of Being, The Philosophy of Man, The Philosophy of God,* and now, THE PHILOSOPHY OF MORALITY — in which he has presented to us a remarkably systematic and articulate synthesis of Thomas Aquinas' philosophic thought. Quickened as they are by a living unity of insight and purpose, these various *Philosophies* appear to me as a choir of Aquinas Muses whose erudite and scholarly gowns have no doubt a certain quality of austerity, but whose faces are colored by eternally young blood and who move their fairy hands with the agility of faultless logic; their voices sing in perfect harmony an intelligible hymn to the basic truths that can be brought out of the existence of things by philosophy, and which human reason, under God, is able to discover and establish.

This latest book, on human acts, is, like the preceding ones, a testimony given to St. Thomas' perennial wisdom with a sure and penetrating pedagogical art which brings this wisdom, without diminishing it, within the understanding of the minds of the students. The relationship of moral philosophy to speculative philosophy, the field which is its own and the object which specifies it, its speculative-practical character, the way in which the moral order fundamentally presupposes, and is essentially distinct from, the order of nature, the central problems with

vii

which ethics has to deal and the central notions it has to discuss —
end, subjective and objective morality, moral obligation, law, moral
virtues — all this vast matter has been elucidated by Father Henri
Renard with exceptional clarity and mastery. I do not know
whether I would always agree with him on certain of the particular issues about which the disciples of the Angelic Doctor
usually have a fondness for controversy. What I do know, and
what I am especially happy to stress in this Preface, is that
Father Renard's books, and this book on moral philosophy in
particular, not only epitomize in the most helpful manner, but
clarify with outstanding penetration the various organic parts
of Thomistic philosophy, and that he puts at the service of this
philosophy an indefatigable energy, a fervor and fidelity, an intellectual penetration, perspicacity, and power of synthesis for which
I feel toward him deep gratitude and affectionate admiration.

JACQUES MARITAIN

FOREWORD

THE PHILOSOPHY OF MORALITY represents an effort to propose to undergraduate students the moral philosophy of St. Thomas. In the language of the modern educator, this little work might be called a course in general ethics. The book is intended to give a fundamental view of the metaphysics of the moral act according to the doctrine proposed principally in the *Prima Secundae* of the *Summa Theologica*.

Did St. Thomas write a "philosophy" of morality? Yes and no. The Angelic Doctor is primarily a Christian theologian, not a philosopher; he is, therefore, a realist who examines man as he exists in the present order of grace and not as he might have been in an order of pure nature. Because he is a Christian theologian, St. Thomas accepts the fact of the elevation of human nature to a supernatural end. The existential moral act of man which he studies in the *Summa Theologica* (especially in the *Secunda Secundae*) is not one placed by the pure nature of man but by a nature elevated to an end which is the vision of the Divine Essence, by a nature which has been wounded by sin and redeemed by the Man-God. This nature is made capable — by means of habitual grace and infused habits — of placing existential acts that are meritorious of a supernatural end. Obviously, a science which is concerned with such an existential act must accept the revealed data. Such a science could never be a mere philosophy; it is a moral theology or at best could be called a philosophy of Christian conduct.

We believe, however, that it is possible to discover in this Christian moral theology of St. Thomas a purely philosophical foundation, a substratum. For man, even though elevated to a supernatural order, possesses a nature — a created, limited, rational nature. Now grace, as Thomas himself has aptly remarked, supposes and perfects nature; grace does not destroy nature. For, the Angelic Doctor explains, neither grace nor sin can change radically the principles of nature; the elevated nature of man is still a nature; the human act is still the act of human nature. That is why we are able to examine the human act in the light of reason and infer principles of right living that are absolute. Such inferences, we believe, have been proposed by St. Thomas in the *Prima Secundae*. THE PHILOSOPHY OF MORALITY endeavors to examine, explain, and evolve these principles into an undergraduate course of moral philosophy.

This little book is not controversial. It does not pretend to supplant several excellent textbooks in the field of ethics. The author is aware that moral philosophy has undergone considerable development since the Middle Ages. The scope of the book is merely to propose and explain the moral philosophical principles of Aquinas. The author believes that a faithful presentation of these principles will help the student to read and to understand the writings of the Angelic Doctor with greater profit. If it proves to be such a help, THE PHILOSOPHY OF MORALITY will have accomplished its purpose.

The author is indebted to Father F. J. Moriarty, S.J., to Mother M. L. Martinez, R.S.C.I., and to Mrs. R. J. Childress for their valuable criticisms and suggestions. In a special manner, the author wishes to thank Father M. O. Vaske, S.J., without whose generous help and constant encouragement the book would not have been written.

—H. R.

CONTENTS

CONTENTS

THE PHILOSOPHY OF MORALITY

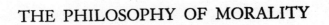

INTRODUCTION

Man is a rational being. Because of his intellectual nature, he is endowed with freedom of judgment and of choice. Man alone, in the world of corporeal beings, is able to choose,[1] that is, to use or to reject the means necessary to attain his last end. The possibility of a choice between operations which dispose his nature to his last end, and actions which cause him to deviate from that end, brings to focus the moral problem.

Three Fundamental Truths: Before definitely stating the moral problem, we should recall briefly three fundamental truths: (1) the existence of God and the complete dependence of all limited reality upon Him, (2) the rationality of man's nature from which results his freedom of judgment and of choice, and (3) man's ordination to God, his ultimate end. Although these truths were established in the basic courses of the philosophy of being, of man, and of God, we shall find it useful to restate the reasons for accepting them. For without a clear understanding of these philosophical inferences the moral problem is meaningless.

1. Necessity of the Existence of God,[2] Pure Act, Absolute Goodness:

a) A limited being, because it is not its act of existing, is not intelligible without a First Cause which is its own "to be" (*esse*). For without the existence of such a First Cause which here and now causes existence in its effects, there would be no sufficient reason for the actual existing of any limited being. This First Cause, whom we call God, is Pure Act, precisely because being first cause, its existence

---

[1] *"Per se potestativum"* (*S. Th.,* I–II, *Proemium*).

[2] Cf. Henri Renard, S.J., *The Philosophy of God* (Milwaukee: Bruce, 1951), p. 26, and *The Philosophy of Being* (Milwaukee: Bruce, 1946), p. 119.

cannot be limited by a distinct potency. For if the act of existing were limited, it would need to be caused by another.

b) God, the Pure Act, is the Absolute Good because goodness, which consists in the plenitude of existence, is unqualifiedly perfect in a pure act of existing.

2. **Because of his rational nature, man enjoys freedom of judgment and choice as regards the particular good:**[3] A nature which knows being as such, and on this account is capable of becoming all things by knowledge, is intellectual. Its form is subsisting, that is, independent of matter in its existence as well as in its operation. Such a form is spiritual and therefore immortal. Because it is capable of knowing all things, the rational nature is in potency (intellectual capacity) to know even God who is absolute truth. Moreover, an operative potency of knowledge ordered to absolute truth demands a proportionate appetite (will) ordered to the absolute good; for being, truth, and good are convertible. Consequently, the absolute good is the necessitating object of the rational appetite. Now that which is necessitated to the absolute good cannot be necessitated to a particular good. Man, therefore, is free by a freedom of judgment (intellect) and of choice (will) as regards the particular good.

3. **Man is ordered to God as to his last end:**[4] Man by his highest appetite — an appetite which results from his rational nature — is ordered to the absolute good. God is the absolute good. Therefore, man is ordered to God by his highest appetite. Now the necessitating object of a nature's highest appetite is its last end; for such an object when attained will necessarily actuate the most radical potency of that nature. Therefore, man is ordered to God as to his last end.

Having established the existence of the Pure Act without whom the world of limited beings is meaningless and contradictory, and having shown that God's most perfect creature, man, is ordered to his Maker, the Absolute Good, as to his last end, we now endeavor to understand how man, a rational supposit and therefore a prin-

---

[3] Cf. Henri Renard, S.J., *The Philosophy of Man* (Milwaukee: Bruce, 1948), p. 176.
[4] Cf. *The Philosophy of Man*, p. 228.

ciple of his own operations, must act in order to reach this end. We are now prepared to propose the moral problem.

The Problem: The problem of morality may be thus stated: Why is a human, a free act good or evil morally?[5] Why does such an action dispose man's nature toward or away from his last end? THE PHILOSOPHY OF MORALITY will endeavor to give an adequate answer to that question, by examining the nature of the moral act and its relation to the last end of human nature.

Object of Moral Philosophy: Obviously, the subject matter, which philosophers call the *material object,* will be for THE PHILOSOPHY OF MORALITY the free acts of man, the human acts. These operations, however, will not be examined in this treatise in their ontological reality. This was done in *The Philosophy of Man* where the freedom of judgment and of choice was analyzed. Now we shall study the free acts of man from a different point of view, from a different formality, which will distinguish the science of ethics from the other branches of philosophy. We shall view these human acts in so far as they are *moral acts,* that is, *in their relation to the last end of human nature,* which is the attainment of the Absolute Good.[6] The formal object of our study is, therefore, the human act *as moral.*

Place of Ethics Among Intellectual Habits: St. Thomas explains[7] that the science of ethics belongs to a rational being in a special manner. It is indeed proper to a man of wisdom to put order into things. Now as the intellect of man observes this world of things, it discovers and establishes four distinct orders[8] which are the basis

---

[5] In this life all free acts are moral, and all moral acts are free. Freedom and morality, however, are distinct formalities. Freedom refers the act to its principle which is the rational subject. It implies that the subject, because it is a rational supposit, is not necessitated to such an operation. Morality, on the other hand, looks to the end; it indicates the direction of the act toward the attainment of that end.

[6] *"Subiectum moralis philosophiae est operatio humana ordinata in finem, vel homo prout est voluntarie agens propter finem"* (In I Eth., lect. 1).

[7] The following is a paraphrase of a basic text of Thomas' commentary on the *Nichomachean Ethics* (cf. In I Eth., lect. 1).

[8] Order is a term difficult to define because of its analogous usage. St. Thomas explains that order is had by reference to some common principle. " . . . *ordo semper*

for classifying human knowledge, for forming both speculative habits of science (speculative intellect) and practical habits of art (practical intellect).

1. The first is the order of existing realities. Obviously, human reason does not cause this order but merely examines it. The intellectual knowledge obtained from such observation is, in its ultimate analysis, the foundation for the habit of metaphysics and of the philosophy of nature.

2. The second order is caused (efficient causality) by human reason as it considers its intellectual operations: definitions, enunciations, argumentations. Reason is able to establish relations between these operations. In doing this it forms second intentions which are the object of the science of logic.

3. The third order is caused (formal causality) by reason as it freely specifies (freedom of judgment) those operations which issue from a free will (freedom of choice). The philosophy of morality views the relation of these actions to their active principle, which is human nature in so far as it is rational, and, consequently, perceives their relation to the end of that nature. From this study, the moralist is able to infer certain definite moral principles which should govern human actions if these are to be properly ordered to the last end of man. The philosophy of morality, therefore, embraces a study of the relations discovered between human operations and their active principle, and, as a result, it obtains a definite knowledge of the relation of these acts to the end of man.

4. The fourth order is caused (exemplarity) by reason. It is the world of artifacts. These are the objects of the various arts, as, for example, building a house. The true knowledge of this order, that is to say, of the order of things to be made (*recta ratio factibilium*), is the habit of the practical intellect called art.

---

dicitur per comparationem ad aliquod principium" (*S. Th.*, I, 42, 3, *c*). Order implies a unit composed of things which have something in common. An order, therefore, embraces beings whether real or logical, whether natural or moral, which are viewed under the same formal aspect. Hence, it implies unity and multiplicity: unity as to a common denominator, either intrinsic or extrinsic; multiplicity because of differences. Consequently, we may say that an order indicates mutual relations between those things which can be classified under the same formal type.

Speculative or Practical: From this discussion it appears that, although the philosophy of morality has a most practical purpose, that is, to help man in attaining his end, nevertheless, in itself, it belongs to the intellectual habit called science. Now science is a habit, not of the practical, but of the speculative intellect.[9] The science of ethics, therefore, although ordered to a *practical end,* is a *habit* of the *speculative intellect.* This inference can be shown in the following manner:

Speculative: In common with all true philosophical sciences, ethics is not confined to the consideration of a particular individual fact, but rises to the knowledge of universal truths. The moralist wants to discover the *universal what* and the *universal why* of the human act. Obviously, the knowledge obtained in such a philosophical reflection does not necessarily result in right living. Indeed, it is quite possible that a learned moralist be a wicked man, because knowledge of universal truth does not necessarily perfect man as man, but only as philosopher. The philosophy of morality, therefore, is in itself a habit of the speculative intellect; it is not a way of life. This conclusion is made evident when one considers that the science of morals is certainly distinct from the virtue of prudence which belongs to the practical intellect. For prudence which consists in the true knowledge of the things to be done — *recta ratio agibilium* — is not concerned with the knowledge of universals but with the specification of the individual will-act in accordance with right reason. Prudence looks immediately to the moral act; ethics immediately looks to knowledge and only mediately to action.

Practical: We should observe, however, that in sharp contrast with the other branches of philosophy, such as the philosophy of being, of God, and of nature, the ultimate purpose of the study of the science of morals is not merely the contemplation of truth. Rather, ethics presents us with a set of principles and laws which should direct man in his quest for his last end which is happiness. This science gives us an understanding of the foundations of the

---

[9] We have explained in *The Philosophy of Man* (p. 131) that the speculative and practical intellect are not distinct operative potencies but distinct functions of the same intellectual faculty.

good life; indeed, its true *raison d'être* is to help us live right-eously.[10] Moral philosophy, therefore, besides being in itself a habit of the speculative intellect, has an ultimate purpose which is wholly practical. And it is, indeed, because of this practical aim that we place so much importance on the study of this science. For, if the investigations undertaken in the philosophy of morality were pursued only for the sake of obtaining universal truths, the knowledge obtained would not be worth the effort. "It is not of great import, nor of great value to the human intellect, to know the variable truth of the contingent operables that are the object of virtue."[11]

We conclude: the philosophy of morality *in itself* is a speculative, intellectual habit; it belongs to the speculative intellect; it seeks universal truths. On the other hand, *by reason of its ultimate purpose,* which is to help man live a good life, it can be viewed as a practical science. It is, therefore, both speculative and practical; *speculative in itself, practical in its purpose and application.*

Realm of Morality: The science of morals examines the action of a rational nature, in so far as this nature is rational, and consequently in so far as such a nature determines itself freely to attain its ultimate end. Obviously, such a philosophical reflection will be on a level of intelligibility all its own; it will be concerned with that realm of reality which we call the *moral order.*[12] What do we mean by this moral order? First of all, we note that it is established by the human act. The moral order is discovered by referring a human

---

[10] Moral philosophy indirectly affects human action in this way: its universal conclusions, which are the precepts or judgments of the natural law, can be applied by conscience in the formation of prudential judgments. These prudential judgments, as we shall see, should specify the will-act in accord with right reason. Now any practical application of the natural law is in the order of action and therefore does not belong to the science of ethics as such but to a way of life. Such usage is the true practical knowledge of right living, of right doing; it pertains to the *recta ratio agibilium,* not to philosophy as such.

[11] *"Non enim magnum quid est, nec multum pertinens ad perfectionem intellectus, quod aliquis cognoscat variabilem veritatem contingentium operabilium, circa quae est virtus"* (*In II Eth.,* lect. 2).

[12] To express what we term the "moral order" St. Thomas uses these phrases: *"in genere morum"; "in rebus moralibus."*

action to its active principle, the rational nature viewed as rational. *The moral order may be defined as the order of actions which are referred to their rational active principle in so far as it is rational.* Because the active principle referred to is a rational nature, these actions will found relations to the last end of that nature; they will dispose man toward or away from his end.[13]

Moral Order and Order of Nature: This moral order is not opposed to the order of nature, the order of nonrational nature, but rather presupposes it and in a way includes it. In the order of nature, any action is referred to its active principle in so far as this active principle is not considered as rational. Let us beware of confusing nature with the order of nature and with the moral order. (*a*) We call a nature any principle of action necessarily seeking a definite end. (*b*) The order of nature, on the other hand, is established by an action whose active principle is not rational. (*c*) In addition to this, the moral order adds the note of rationality to the active principle to which the action is referred. Both orders, therefore, presuppose a nature which is the active principle. In the moral order, action is referred to an active principle in so far as it is rational. In the order of nature, the active principle, the nature to which action is referred, either is not rational or is not viewed as rational. An example will make this evident. Let us consider these three living beings: man, dog, tree. They are three distinct natures and like all natures must act for an end. Any vegetative operation, such as, for example, the act of growing, found in each of these natures belongs to the order of nature, since the action looks to an active principle in so far as it lives, not in so far as it is rational. On the other hand, the action of taking something which belongs to another, if referred to an active principle in so far as it is rational, that is, in so far as knowing and willing, belongs to the moral order. If referred to a dog or even to a man who is not in his right mind; or, to put it

---

13 We cannot really understand what a rational nature is without an implicit understanding of its last end which is absolute truth, absolute good. For the definition of such a nature — a nature made to understand being — necessarily connotes what the end must be. Hence, any action placed by such an active rational principle in so far as it is rational always establishes a new relation in the nature toward the last end or away from it.

philosophically, if referred to an active principle which is not viewed as rational, the very same action — in its objective reality — is not in the moral order, but in the order of nature, that is, of nonrational nature. This distinction, let us note in passing, will be found of importance in establishing the nature of objective morality, that is, the nature of the moral goodness or malice of the human act.

Morality: "Morality" is an abstract term. It is significant that St. Thomas never used it. "Morality" is of later vintage; it belongs to a day when philosophy began to be divorced from reality. Because of its abstract form, the word "morality" may seem to suggest that the moral order is a figment of the mind, a relation of reason, a second intention. Nothing could be farther from the truth. The moral order, we have explained, is that realm of reality in which a most perfect being, a rational supposit, a person, by exercising his highest powers, that is, his freedom of judgment and of choice, disposes himself toward or away from his last end.[14] The Angelic Doctor, we note, does speak of the moral order (*in genere morum*) on occasion; and he is especially fond of concrete expressions, such as "the human act," "the voluntary action"; he extols "right reason"; he discusses "the goodness and malice" of a given action; he envisages the "real relation" which such an action establishes between its principle, man, and his last end. All these terms express concrete realities which belong to this concrete order, the moral order.

The point we should like to make is that, although we accept and use the term "morality," it is not to be taken as an abstraction, nor is it a product of the imagination; rather it indicates a very real order. The moral order results from the action of a rational nature as rational and therefore as related to its last end. The human act which is placed by such a nature really disposes its principle, man, toward or away from his last end. It does so, not because of a categorical imperative, or any other subjective affirmation, but because of its own determined goodness or malice which is specified by an objective reality. Man, because he is rational, is necessarily ordered to a last end which is the absolute good, and his changing

---

[14] Moral actions either perfect (dispose toward) or harm (dispose away from) a rational nature with reference to the attainment of its last end.

disposition to this end of his nature results from his **human acts.** The order of morality, as we shall call it, is objectively **true; it** is real.

Division: Since the moral order is established by the action of a rational nature as related to the last end, in the first chapter we examine the relation of the moral act to the last end of man. Beginning with the consideration of the proximate end or object of the will-act, we rise to the necessity of a first final cause which is the last end of man "as desired," and without which the moral act is unintelligible. We proceed then to study the properties of the last end. Finally, after excluding the errors of man in his mistaken search for happiness in the possession of objects which can only give an ephemeral satisfaction, we present the nature of the act by which man attains the last end, true happiness, and the conditions necessary for its attainment.

The second chapter is concerned with the central problem of the course and its solution, to wit: What is the nature of the moral act? After an analysis of the structure of the human act, we establish, first, why an act is imputable to its author (subjective morality or voluntariness), and secondly, why an act is good or bad morally (objective morality and objective norm). To this we add some reflections on the influence of passions and habits upon the morality of the act in its objective constituents as well as in regard to its voluntariness.

The third chapter is entitled "Law." How does the question of law arise in a discussion of the moral problem? Law is a rule and measure of the human act and may, therefore, seem to be something extrinsic to the morality of the act. Nevertheless, in its most fundamental reality, law in a certain manner is radicated in the nature itself. For the obligation, the "must" which is expressed by a judgment of law, results from the necessary natural appetite of a nature to its last end, from the nature's finality. Let us explain. Nature as a principle of action is necessarily ordered to its last end. From such intrinsic finality there flows a "must," that is, a necessity to place those actions which dispose the nature toward its true end. This necessity is absolute in an irrational nature, necessarily determining such a nature in its operations. In man, however, the "must" of intrinsic finality results in a moral obligation, an obligation whose fulfillment depends upon man's power to determine himself, upon his freedom of judgment and choice. Clearly, then, a discussion of law is necessary to attain a complete solution of the moral problem. Such a discussion presupposes the conclusions of the first chapter which is concerned with the end. Moreover, law proposes a norm, a rule of the moral act. Now the moral act is examined and analyzed in the second chapter. It might, therefore, seem more logical if the division of this work would follow this sequence: (1) end, (2) law, and (3) moral act. We prefer, however, to accept the order of the *Summa Theologica* which to us seems a better pedagogical approach. The reason is that the complete meaning of law, and in a special manner, of the natural law, can only be realized after the constituents of the moral act have been carefully examined.

Our division, therefore, is in the following: (1) end, (2) moral act, and (3) law.

CHAPTER I

THE END OF MAN

"The principle of the entire moral order is the last end."[1]

Prologue

Purpose of Chapter: The aim of this chapter is to examine the finality of the human act. Such a study will make known to us the relation of dependence of any moral act upon man's natural desire for his last end. Because the attainment of the absolute good, happiness, is the last end of human nature, man cannot rest without it. In all his free actions he must always, directly or indirectly, rightly or wrongly, seek happiness.[2] For nature is a principle of action to an end, and is necessarily ordered to its last end by its natural appetite. This "to be desired"[3] of the last end, which is the radical tendency of rational nature, is the first final cause of every human action. Indeed the moral act is not intelligible, it cannot take place without an actual influx (here and now) of this first final cause.

In consequence of this actual dependence upon a natural desire for happiness, the human act, whenever morally good, establishes a disposition in the subject (rectitude of will) toward the last end; whenever morally evil, the human action causes a contrary disposition (lack of rectitude, disorder of the will) away from the last end of man. Such is the all-embracing finality of the human act.

---

[1] *S. Th.*, I–II, 72, 5, *c*. Because they do not connect morality with the last end of man, many modern philosophers propose ethical theories which admit of no absolutes.

[2] "Our heart is restless till it find repose in Thee" (*Inquietum est cor nostrum donec requiescat in Te*) (St. Augustine, *Confessions*, I. 1).

[3] "Influere causae finalis est *appeti* et *desiderari*" (*De Ver.*, XXII, 2, *c*).

The End: The end — we should recall[4] — is twofold: objective (*finis cuius*) and subjective (*finis quo*).[5] The objective end is the object itself, for example: food, money, God. The subjective end is the attainment, the possession of the object: eating the food, hoarding the money, being united with God. Obviously, that which is desired, that which moves the appetite to action by being desired, is not the object itself (objective end), but the attainment of the good, that is, the possession of the object (subjective end). Moreover, the subjective end is twofold. Viewed as the attainment, the possession of the desired good, the end is the effect, not the final cause of action, and consequently it exists in the order of execution. Viewed as the desire for the good to be possessed, the subjective end is a final cause of action; it has a direct influx upon an operation and determines its nature. Such a desire is obviously in the order of intention.[6]

Applying these distinctions to the last end of human nature, we note that the absolute good which is God is the objective end. The last subjective end of any rational nature is the attainment of this absolute good. This attainment of the absolute good which is the term of action is the happiness of man. It is therefore in the order of execution. On the other hand, the desire for happiness, that is to say, the natural desire of human nature for its last end, is the first final cause of man's action. This cause, this desire for happi-

---

[4] Cf. *The Philosophy of Being*, p. 157.

[5] Cf. *S. Th.*, I, 26, 3, ad 2ᵐ; I–II, 1, 8, *c*; 2, 7, *c*.

[6] A diagram may help the student to visualize these important distinctions between the various types of ends:

The end can be — objective — the thing itself, the good object, e.g., food, money, God.

or

subjective —

as attained it is the effect or term of action; it is in the order of execution, e.g., I actually eat the food, I own the money, I am united with God.

as desired it is the final cause of action; it is in the order of intention, e.g., I *desire* to eat the food, to acquire wealth, to be united with God.

Conclusion to be established: The final existential cause of any action is the *subjective end as desired.*

ness, in so far as it is communicated to the will through intellectual knowledge of the good, is in the order of intention. We shall prove that the causal influx of such a desire is necessarily required and actually found in every human act. Throughout this chapter we shall discuss the true relation between the human act and its first final cause which is the natural desire of man for happiness.

Human Acts: What is meant by the term, human acts? We shall the better understand what these actions are by distinguishing them from other operations of man which are not in the order of morality.

The *human acts* are those which are proper to man as man. Now man is man because he is rational and free. *Those operations,* therefore, *which proceed from a deliberate free will are called human acts.* These are the moral acts and they establish definite relations between a rational nature and its last end. Hence, human or moral acts are proper to man, for freedom is the property of a rational nature. On the other hand, man's nature, because it is corporeal, is capable of many nonrational operations, such as vegetative and spontaneous sentient actions. These are not peculiar to man alone but common to other living creatures as well. Such operations are sometimes called the *acts of man;* they are not human acts, for of themselves they do not pertain to the moral order. The reason is that they do not proceed from a deliberate will, and consequently they do not of themselves dispose man toward or away from his last end.

Elicited or Commanded Acts: Because of the unity of the human suppposit, it often happens that reason and will are able to control the operations of the other faculties of the soul, as well as of the members of the body. Accordingly, there is need of distinguishing between two classes of human acts: elicited acts and commanded acts. The *elicited acts* are the free acts of the deliberate will, as for example, the acts of intention and of choice. Evidently, these actions are always moral acts. On the other hand, the *commanded acts* designate the operations of the other faculties whenever these faculties act under the control of reason. It is, of course, quite possible that violence be exerted by an extrinsic cause upon external acts, doing away with the control of the will over them and thereby destroying their status of commanded acts.

In short, the actions of man as man, that is, the human acts, differ from those of irrational creatures in this, that human acts proceed from a deliberate will; man has power over them; he is master of these actions. They are moral acts.

Division: This chapter will contain three questions. In the first, we shall demonstrate the necessary dependence of the human act upon the last end, that is, upon man's natural desire for happiness. In the second, we shall refute some fundamental errors regarding the object of man's desire for happiness. In the third question, we shall consider the attainment of the last end, that is to say, the nature of the action by which man actually attains his happiness.

In short:
1. Necessity of actual influx (here and now) of the last end "as desired" (first final cause) upon each human act.
2. Refutation of some common errors regarding the object of man's happiness.
3. Nature of man's happiness.

Question I

NECESSITY OF AN ACTUAL INFLUX OF THE LAST END AS DESIRED UPON EACH HUMAN ACT[1]

Is the human act related to the last end of human nature? In order to answer this query, we institute an analysis of the human act from the viewpoint of its final cause (end). The human act is placed for a freely chosen end and which is the object of the will-act. Consequently, this object-end specifies the action; that is to say, it makes it good or evil morally.[8] This moral specification of the

---

[7] The end moves to action by being desired. The end as desired is the final existential cause. The causality of the end is "to be desired."

[8] The specific determination of an operation was explained in *The Philosophy of Man*, pp. 58, 59. Specification is the formal determination of the quiddity, the "whatness," of a being. As regards the moral act, specification makes it to be this kind

will-act is not intelligible; that is, it could not take place without a causal dependence here and now upon the last end as desired. For the freely chosen object-end of the will-act is a new actuation of the subject in the order of finality. Hence this new actuation must depend here and now upon a first final cause. Now, this first final cause, we shall explain, is an ever present desire for happiness. It is the natural appetite of rational nature constantly inclining man to his last end. It is not a new actuation, but is the nature itself as necessarily ordered to its end. This natural inclination in the order of finality is communicated to the highest appetite of man which is the will. Because of this necessary desire for happiness (the possession of absolute good), the will is able to choose freely the object-end (the particular good) of the moral act. The human act, therefore, must depend here and now upon the causal influx of the last end as desired. Finally, from the knowledge of this causal dependence, we shall infer four important properties of the last end.

Division: This question comprises three articles:

1. The human act is specified in the moral order by a freely chosen object-end.

---

of moral act; it establishes primarily the objective morality of the operation; that is to say, it causes the action to be objectively good or evil. St. Thomas explains (*S. Th.,* I, 77, 3, *c*) that every action is caused (efficiently) either by an active or a passive operative potency. A passive operative potency (faculty) must be actuated in order to act. The actuation, the formal determination of the operation, that is the specification of the act, is from the object. An example will prove helpful. Color is the formal determination of the operation called vision. Color is the formal object which determines the action of the operative faculty, to see this material object.

The will is an operative potency which needs to be actuated both in the order of exercise and of specification in order to place an action. God alone (cf. *The Philosophy of Man,* p. 194) can actuate the will efficiently. Consequently, in the order of exercise the will is moved by a divine motion to the good in general, in accordance with the nature of the rational appetite which tends necessarily to the absolute good. This inclination is called active indetermination (cf. *The Philosophy of Man,* p. 183). The will in order to place this or that operation will need to be actuated in the order of specification. This formal determination is from the object which, having been presented to the will (as a good) through intellectual knowledge, is freely chosen. The "to be desired" of the object-end is the influx which formally determines the act of the will. The object, therefore, is the cause of the specification of the will-act. It establishes its moral nature; it causes it to be good or evil.

2. This moral specification of the human act is not intelligible without an actual causal influx of the last end as desired. In other words, a moral act must depend existentially (here and now) upon the last end as desired, that is, upon the first final cause.

3. Some properties regarding the nature of the last end are inferred.

ARTICLE I: The Human Act Is Specified in the Moral Order by a Freely Chosen Object-end.

1. **Human acts are placed for definite (proximate) ends which are the objects of the will-acts.** Is every human act placed for an end? Yes, most assuredly. This can be easily proved thus: The nature of an action which proceeds from an operative potency (faculty) is determined and, therefore, in some manner (formally)[9] caused by the nature of its object. Now the object of the rational appetite, the will, which is the faculty from which proceeds the human act, is the good as desired.[10] But the good as desired has the nature of an end.[11] The object of the will-act, therefore, is an end (proximate),[12] a final cause of the operation. It follows that all human acts are for an end.

---

[9] "An action receives its species (specific determination) from its principle or from its end or term" (S. Th., I, 77, 3). Note that the subjective end is both principle and term of the will-act; principle in so far as by being desired it moves the will as the final cause, term in so far as it is the effect produced by the operation.

[10] The good (real or apparent), because desirable, is the object of the appetite. "Whatever is desired has the nature (rationem) of good" (S. Th., I, 6, 2, ad 2ᵐ).

[11] The good as desired, which is the object sought by an appetite, has the formal aspect of the end. The reason is that the nature of a final cause is "to be desired." In other words, the final cause has its influx by being desired.

[12] We note that this object-end of the will-act is a particular good. Hence it cannot be identical with the last end of man which is the absolute good. Moreover, this particular good is freely chosen, whereas human nature in common with all natures is necessarily determined to its last end. For this reason we shall call the object-end of the will-act the *proximate end* to distinguish it from the end of human nature which is the *last end* or simply the end of man.

2. **In placing a human action, man, the agent, acts in a manner proper only to a rational nature.** Every agent acts for an end.[13] There is, therefore, nothing peculiar, nothing proper to man in the fact that a human act is placed for an end. The manner, however, in which man acts for an end in his human actions is proper only to rational natures. For in the human act man determines himself to an end. He is not necessitated; he is free. "It is proper to a rational nature to seek the end as if by acting upon itself or moving itself to the end."[14] This statement may be explained in the following manner:

All creatures, man as well as nonrational beings, tend by action or motion to an end which is distinct from them. They tend to their respective ends, however, in a different manner, each in accordance with its own nature. The rational creature, being endowed with an intellect made to know being, and possessing a will necessarily ordered to the absolute good, is able to move itself freely to the particular good which is the object-end of the will-act. Man, then, is free to choose such an object-end. On the other hand, the creature which lacks reason and will is necessitated to the object of the act, whether known or not, by a natural inclination "as if acted upon and led by another." We conclude: In placing a human action, man acts for an object-end which is freely chosen; he acts freely, whereas every other agent below man is directed or necessitated to operation.

3. **The object-end specifies the will-act in the moral order.** This truth is, of course, a necessary consequence of the identification of end and object as regards an appetite. The formal object, we know, is the specifying factor of any operation.[15] But the object of the

---

[13] The principle of finality was established in metaphysics (cf. *The Philosophy of Being,* p. 144 ff.). The absolute necessity of the determination of the action of any agent by an intention to the end is stated thus by Aquinas: "If the agent were not determined to some particular effect, it would not do one thing rather than another" (*S. Th.,* I–II, 1, 2). This entire article should be read and studied.

[14] *S. Th.,* I–II, 1, 2, *c.*

[15] Because the act of the will can be compared to a motion, St. Thomas, in the *S. Th.,* I–II, 1, 3, *c.,* gives an analysis of the specification of motion viewed both as ac-

act of the will, which is a particular good as known and desired, is the end of the will-act. Therefore, this object-end must specify the act of the will. Now, the first specific determination of a human act, of a moral act, is that it be morally good or morally evil.[16] Consequently, the object-end of the will-act causes (formal causality) the moral act to be good or evil; it specifies the will-act morally.

N.B.: Is it possible that two external actions which belong to the same species in the order of nature be of opposite species in the moral order, that is, morally good or morally bad? Yes, answers St. Thomas, this often happens. The action, for example, of killing a man always belongs to the same species in the order of nature; it is always an act of depriving another of his life. In the order of morality, however, such an action may be either

---

tion and as passion. Then he applies his deductions to the specification of the will-act by its end. "Since movements are, somehow, divided into action and passion, each of these receives its species from an act; action, indeed, from the act which is the principle of action, and passion from the act which is the terminus of the movement. Wherefore, heating as an action is nothing else than a certain movement proceeding from heat, while heating as a passion is a certain motion toward heat; it is the definition that shows the specific nature. And either way human acts, whether they be considered as actions or as passions, obtain their species from the end. For human acts can be considered in both ways, either that man moves himself, or that he is moved by himself. Now it has been stated that acts are called human inasmuch as they proceed from a deliberate will. But the object of the will is the good and the end. And hence it is clear that the principle of human acts, in so far as they are human, is the end. In like manner, the end is their terminus, for the human act terminates at that which the will intends as the end; in the same way in natural agents the form of the thing generated is conformed to the form of the generator."

[16] This difficult point will be studied in the question of the objective morality of the will-act. There we shall establish that in the moral order good and evil actions belong to fundamentally distinct species. They belong to distinct species, because they differ by an opposition which is that of contraries. For the good moral act is suitable to the rational nature as ordered to its last end; while the evil moral act is unsuitable to the same rational principle. Moreover, the primary specific determination of moral actions consists in this, that they are good or evil moral acts. The reason is that an act is moral precisely because it is good or evil, that is to say, because it disposes human nature toward or away from its last end. Consequently, any further specification of the act by its object, such as stealing, praying, and the like, is only a more detailed manifestation, a more restricted delineation of its moral goodness or malice.

morally good or morally bad. To kill a man for justice' sake is a good moral act. If, on the contrary, the killing is done for revenge or because of hatred and envy, such an action is unqualifiedly an evil act. Why such a difference? We answer that in the order of nature the specification of the act is had only from the external object. The reason is that the active principle to which the operation is referred is not viewed as rational. In the order of morality, on the other hand, because the action is referred to a rational principle, the end of the will-act is the primary cause of the specification of the act. Consequently, should the object of the external act be in itself morally indifferent, the moral species (goodness or malice) will be determined absolutely by the end of the will-act. To kill for justice' sake is a good moral act; to kill because of hatred or envy or revenge is an evil act.[17]

There are, therefore, three points to our solution:

1. In his human actions man acts for an end, and this end is the object (object-end) of the will-act.

2. In the human act, man acts for an end (object-end of will-act) in a manner which is proper to a rational nature. He freely chooses the end which is the object of the act of the will.

3. This end (object-end), because it is the object of the act of the will, specifies the operation; that is to say, the freely chosen object-end causes (formally) the will-act to be morally good or evil.

We conclude: The human act is specified in the moral order by a freely chosen object-end.

ARTICLE II: Existential Dependence of the Human Act Upon the Last End as Desired

"The principle in the order of intention is the last end."[18]

Problem: The end which is the final cause is the good "as desired." Now the final cause determines an agent to action by

---

[17] *S. Th.*, I–II, 1, 3, ad 3ᵐ.

[18] "Principium intentionis est ultimus finis" (*S. Th.*, I–II, 1, 4, *c*).

moving the appetite, not in the order of exercise but of specification. Obviously, the influx of such a cause upon the action of
the appetite is in the order of intention. Having established in
the preceding article that the human act is specified in the moral
order by a freely chosen end-object, we ask whether this specification is fully intelligible in itself. Does it explain completely the
finality of the human act? The answer to this question is simply,
"No." The reason is that in the order of finality this proximate end-
object is not the first final cause. It must, therefore, depend in
its causation upon the actual influx of a first final cause. Without
such an actual influx, that is, an influx which occurs here and
now, the human act could never be placed. This first final cause
is the last end as desired, that is, the necessary desire for happiness.

Clarification of the Problem: There are various ways of demon-
strating man's relation to his last end.

1. In the philosophy of being and the philosophy of God, from
the necessary finality of any limited nature, that is, of any active
principle which is not its own end, we demonstrated the necessity
of a first active principle which is its own end. The First
Principle communicates this end which is His own Goodness
to all creatures by an impress upon their natures by which each
one is necessarily ordered to a definite end. God, therefore, is,
in some manner, the end of all limited beings; He is their end
in accordance with the capacity of each nature.

2. In the philosophy of man, from an analysis of human nature,
we inferred that a rational nature, because it can know being
as such, is ordered to know Absolute Truth and to love Absolute
Good. Now God alone is Absolute Truth and Absolute Good. The
last end of man, therefore, is, in some manner, to know and
to love God.

3. In the philosophy of morality we begin with an examination
of the human act. The finality of such an act — we observe from
experience and establish by a metaphysical reflection — is freely
determined by man. Now this freely determined finality which
implies a new actuation of the will is not fully intelligible without
an existential dependence upon a supreme final cause. We pro-

pose to prove that a human act cannot be placed without the actual influx of a fundamental and necessary final determination of nature. This necessary final determination which is communicated to the will, and without which the will cannot place a moral act, is the "to be desired" of the last end.[19] It is the appetite of nature to its last end and results from an impress upon nature by its Maker.[20]

Reason for a causal influx from the appetite of nature to the end: Why is it that a human act cannot be placed without the actual final influx from the appetite of nature? The reason is that in the order of final causality, a freely chosen, a freely determined end, because it is a new actuation, a passing from potency to act, cannot be the first final cause.[21] For finality always means, first and foremost, the necessary and unchanging determination of nature to its end. Let us explain: Nature is an active principle which is

---

[19] The necessary determination of human nature in the order of finality (specification) to the absolute good is communicated to the will in this manner. Because man has a rational nature, his intellect is ordered to know being. The knowledge of being which underlies every act of understanding is presented to the will under the formality of good, the possession of which means happiness. Hence, through intellectual knowledge of the good, the necessary determination of human nature to the absolute good is communicated to the will (cf. *S. Th.,* I, 82, 1, ad 3ᵐ). Whatever the will desires, therefore, it must desire under the formality of good. In this way the necessary determination of human nature to the good and of the will to happiness enables the will here and now to love, desire, and choose freely a limited object under the aspect of good. (It would be well for the student to read carefully *S. Th.,* I, 82, 1. Cf. *ibid.,* I, 60, 2, *c.*)

[20] In this article we are not trying to prove God's existence, but only to establish the existential dependence of any moral act upon a first final cause which is the last end as desired.

[21] Although the operation of the will is the act of a perfect being (*actus perfecti*), it cannot take place without a previous actuation of the will both in the order of exercise (efficient causality) and of specification (formal causality). The reason is that the will is a potency which needs to be actuated in order to will. The actuation in the order of exercise is from God who alone can move a being according to its nature (cf. *The Philosophy of Man,* p. 192). The specification is from the object-end known by the intellect and presented to the will. This specification caused by the object-end is a new actuation of the will in the order of final causality. The will-act which follows is not a new actuation in the strict sense; it is the act of a perfect being, of a being in act. It supposes, however, a twofold actuation. We are concerned here with the new actuation caused by the object-end in the order of final causality.

at all times necessarily determined to its last end. It is because of this inclination of a nature to the good of nature, which is the end, that any individual is able to act. Indeed, no being could ever act if it lacked such necessary determination. Consequently, any action placed by a nature must depend upon this fundamental finality. Most of all, the human act being deliberate and free, and implying a new actuation in the order of finality, is unintelligible without the actual influx of the first final cause. Now the radical determination of nature to its ultimate end is the first final cause. The reason is that this determination is not a new actuation in the order of finality. It is the nature itself which by its natural appetite must always tend to its last end.[22]

This necessary finality of nature to its last end is manifested by a basic urge toward the good and results in a natural necessity in the highest appetite of man's rational nature, the will, toward the absolute good. We do not claim that man needs to be aware of the fact that this first determination of nature enters into every act of the will. This knowledge is a discovery; it is the term of our present search. Man, rather, is aware of placing a deliberate, a free act. From this experience the moralist reasons to the necessity of a first final cause which here and now, by being necessarily desired, enables the agent, man, to place an act which is deliberate and free. For a human nature, which is an active principle necessarily determined to a last end, could never place an action independently of the actual influx of the first desired end. Without this influx the human act would be simply unintelligible; it could never exist for it would have no adequate final cause.

The actual influx which results from human nature's determination not only makes the human act possible, but establishes that there must be in the order of execution a last end, a last term of human operations. The reason is that in the practical order, that is to say, in the realm of action, the first principle in the

---

[22] An existing nature is a principle of action (i.e., a perfect unit, a supposit) which by means of its natural appetite must tend necessarily to its end. Nature is necessarily inclined to its end. (Cf. *S. Th.,* I–II, 91, 2.)

order of intention must be the last in the order of execution.[23] In other words, that which first moves the appetite by being desired and without which no action can take place is the end which, being obtained, quiets all appetite.

Preliminary notions for proof: Before proposing a formal demonstration of the dependence of the moral act upon the causal influx of the last end as desired, let us recall some fundamental notions already studied in the philosophy of being and of man.

1. **Some differences between efficient and final causality:** The efficient cause has an influx upon the "to be" of the effect by *exercise of action*. The final cause has its influx upon the action of the agent by *being desired*. From this difference we infer that the efficient cause is *an existing principle of action;* while, on the contrary, the final cause of human action is in the order of intention; that is, it is not a distinctly existing reality, but exists in the intellect of the agent as known and in the appetite as willed. In a more fundamental sense, the final cause of a created nature is the necessary inclination of that nature to its last end as known and willed by its Maker. This inclination is called the natural appetite.

The immediate effect of a final cause is unlike that of the efficient cause. The efficient cause by the exercise of action produces the becoming or the "to be" of the effect which is a distinct reality. On the other hand, the causality of the final cause as regards the appetitive act approaches the nature of a formal cause;

---

[23] Just as the first truth, namely, the knowledge of being, is that without which no other truth can be known, so the first desired good is that upon which depends the goodness of everything else we seek. We may add that this existential dependence of the proximate end of the act of the will upon the first final cause is the reason why the first final cause is also the last end, that is, the term of all actions. Whatever man wills in this life is willed on account of and in relation to the absolute good. For the causal force, the freely chosen specifying element, of the intermediate final causes (particular ends) upon the human act, which is nothing else than their "to be desired," results here and now from their dependence upon the existential influx (i.e., the absolute "to be desired") of the first final cause. Hence, should this first final cause ever be attained, the appetite would be quieted and there would be no need to seek other ends. The first final cause, therefore, is the last end.

it gives direction to the operation of the will; it specifies. There is, however, this difference between the specification caused by a final and that caused by a formal cause: in the first instance the specification is indirect; it is had through the intellectual operation of the agent who wills this because of his knowledge of the end. The formal cause, on the other hand, specifies by being immediately present, by a communication of its own reality, by an actuation of the potency which it informs.

2. **No infinite series of existentially subordinated causes:** In a series of existential causes no intermediate cause is intelligible unless it necessarily depends ultimately upon a first cause. For there can be no infinite series in existentially subordinated causes.[24] In the present question we are considering existential causes in the order of finality. To begin with, some final determination of the will is required here and now in order to place a human action. This determination is caused by the proximate end of the will-act. For a human action must be determined, specified, moved, in the order of intention by the object-end of the act. This proximate end is, therefore, an actuation, a motion in the order of finality. Hence it must depend immediately upon a higher final cause. The reason is that whatever is moved must be moved by another, and this is absolutely true of any motion, or any determination, whether it be in the order of efficient causality or in the order of finality.[25] Consequently, just as we must assert the existence of a first mover in the order of efficient causality, so must we assert the existence of a first final cause (in the order of intention, that is, as desired) which will be the last end (as possessed) of man. "Absolutely speaking, it is not possible to proceed indefinitely in the matter of ends from any point of view. For in whatsoever things there is an existential (*per se*) order of one to another, if the first be removed, those that are ordained to the first must of necessity be removed also. Therefore, the Philosopher proves that we cannot proceed to infinitude in causes of movement, because then there

---

[24] Cf. *The Philosophy of God*, p. 22.

[25] Let us note that motion or determination in the order of finality supposes an intellectual agent (cf. *The Philosophy of God*, Fifth Way, p. 37).

would be no first mover, without which neither can the others move, since they move only through being moved by the first mover."[26]

3. **All actions depend upon determination of the nature to its end:** Finality, first and foremost, signifies the necessary determination of a nature to its end. All actions placed by an individual nature ultimately result from this fundamental determination and must here and now depend upon it. Let us explain the profound significance of this statement. Nature is an active principle determined to a definite end. Consequently, the first determination of action of any nature must necessarily result because of an inclination, a natural appetite to the good which is its end and which each limited nature must seek.[27]

In an individual nature which is not its own "to be," a necessary determination to an end distinct from the nature is impressed by the Creator.[28] The result of this impression caused efficiently by God's action is a "to be desired" of the end. This necessary urge of nature toward its end is called the natural appetite. Hence, any operation of a creature will be, in some manner, a manifestation of this fundamental desire of nature toward its end. Now the end sought will differ in accordance with the perfection of each nature; a rational nature will necessarily tend to the absolute good; an irrational being, toward a particular good.[29] Consequently, if the

---

[26] *S. Th.,* I–II, 1, 4.

[27] If the nature is pure act, it possesses its end; indeed, it is its own end. God, the Pure Act, is His own Goodness. Hence, the essential act of God is knowledge and love of self. This action which looks to the Divine Truth and Goodness is necessary, for in God to act is to be. All other divine operations, which are free, are the manifestations and communication of God's knowledge and love of Himself and must terminate outside Himself.

[28] The natural appetite is an inclination which inheres in a nature from the ordination of the first Mover (cf. 2 Sent. Lib. II, dist. 27, qu. 1, a. 2). A nature has a natural appetite in that it is inclined to its end (cf. *S. Th.,* I, 6, 1, ad 2ᵐ). The natural appetite is not a power of the soul distinct from its other powers (cf. *S. Th.,* I, 80, 1; I–II, 30, 1, ad 3ᵐ; *De Ver.,* XXII, 3); it is the nature itself as necessarily tending to its last end (cf. *The Philosophy of Being,* p. 148).

[29] In a nonrational agent there is no known subordination of end. The reason is that only an intellectual being can understand end and means as such. Consequently, every action of a nonrational nature is in a way the attainment of its

nature is not rational, its operations will be necessary, not free; if, on the contrary, the nature is rational, it will be able, as a result of its necessary inclination to the absolute good, to choose as regards the particular good. All actions, therefore, depend upon the necessary determination of the nature to its end.

4. **A freely chosen end cannot be the first final cause (last end):** This truth can be easily established. Any nature is necessarily ordered to its last end. This first final determination is absolute; it is the nature itself necessarily tending to its end, for nature is nothing but a principle of action necessitated to its end. Consequently, the last end as desired is identical with the natural appetite. It never varies; it is a constant of nature. On the other hand, the object-end of the will-act which we call a proximate end is freely chosen. Such an object-end (as desired) is a new determination in the subject, a new actuation, a passing from potency to act. A freely chosen end cannot, therefore, be the last end as desired which is the first final determination of a nature.

Proof: No human act is intelligible without an actual influx from the last end as desired: When we analyze the human act, we note that it is placed on account of an end-object which is freely chosen. Obviously, this freely chosen end cannot be identical with the last end which must always necessitate nature. A freely chosen end, we note further, is a limited determination; it is a passing from potency to act. Now any transition from potency to act is not intelligible without dependence upon a higher cause in the same order. Consequently, since an infinite series of existentially subordinated causes is a contradiction, we must admit the existence of a first final cause which is not a passing from potency to act, but is the nature itself as tending necessarily to its last end by its natural appetite. No human act, therefore, is intelligible from the point of view of finality without an actual (here and now) causal influx from the last end as desired.

Let us propose this proof in syllogistic form:

last end. For the last end of such a creature is to manifest the perfection of its Creator by its being and operations.

Since an infinite series of existential causes is not possible, a passing from potency to act is not intelligible without an actual influx from a first cause.

But every human act presupposes a passing from potency to act, an actuation in the order of finality.

Hence, no human act is intelligible in the order of finality without an actual influx from a first final cause which is the last end as desired.

N.B.: Because of this actual dependence, every human act necessarily disposes the nature toward or away from the last end. Without such actual dependence, the moral order would be a mere figment of the mind or at best an extrinsic denomination arbitrarily established by the will of God. *The existential dependence of every human act upon the last end as desired, that is, upon the necessary desire of the nature for its last end, is a central truth in Aquinas' metaphysics of the moral act.*

ARTICLE III: Some Properties of the Last End

The causal dependence of the human act upon the desire for the last end which we have just established is, of course, the central question of this chapter. Because of this causal relation, we may easily infer four properties of the last end of man. These properties will help us understand the nature and solution of the moral problem. They are as follows: (1) there is only one last end of man; (2) whatever man wills in this life is willed on account of and in relation to this last end; (3) the last end is the same for all men alike; and (4) the last end viewed subjectively differs in man from that of other creatures.

1. **There Is Only One Last Subjective End of Man:** We have seen that the first final principle is the last end of human nature. It is the last end of man, for the first in the order of intention is necessarily the last in the order of execution. That there is only one last end can be established in a threefold manner, namely, (*a*) from the actuation of nature, (*b*) from the definition of nature, and (*c*) from the generic determination of the human act.

a) Only the last end can entirely satisfy the rational appetite, since it is sought as the perfect good of nature. Hence, if something else were sought after the attainment of the last end, this would indicate that some perfection is lacking and therefore is desired and sought. In such a case this other perfection, not the first, would be the last end. Consequently, there is only one last end of man.

b) Moreover, we know that the first good sought by nature is its last end, for the necessary inclination of a nature to its last end is its dynamic definition. A nature is nothing else than a principle of action, a supposit which tends necessarily by its natural appetite to its end. Hence, the first good which is desired by the natural appetite is the last end. But a nature can tend naturally to only one last end; otherwise the nature would not be one but several, since nature is a principle of action which necessarily tends to its end. The last end of human nature, therefore, is necessarily one.

Argument: That which is *naturally* (necessarily) desired as first principle of all operations can only be one. "Because nature tends only to one" (*S. Th.,* I–II, 1, 5).

But the will naturally desires the last end as principle of all its operations (proved in the preceding article).

Therefore the last end of man is one.[30]

c) Finally, while the specific determination varies for each human act, the generic determination is common to all. Now the fact that there is only one common generic determination indicates that the last end is one. Let us explain. By specific determination we mean the objective moral goodness or malice of the human act. By generic determination we mean that these acts are free and therefore that they are moral acts. Now the will-act receives its specific determination from its proximate end. The reason is that

---

[30] This argument applies primarily to man. It is true, however, that each non-rational nature acts for a definite last end. The end of a nonrational creature is to manifest God's perfection by being what it is and by placing necessary actions. Unlike the last end of man which is the attainment of the absolute good, the last end of a nonrational being is in a manner achieved in every individual necessary operation.

this end is the object of the will and therefore specifies; in other words, the proximate end causes the act to be good or evil. On the other hand, the human act receives its generic determination from the last end of man; that is to say, these acts are free and therefore moral because of the last end, the absolute good, to which the nature of man is necessarily ordered.[31] Now just as the many specific determinations which vary in each moral act suppose distinct proximate ends, so the unique generic determination which results from the first final cause of all moral acts must point to the one constant last end.

We may now state the argument: While the specific determination varies with each act, the generic determination for all human acts is the same. But the distinction of specific determination results from this, that the proximate end which is the specifying cause of the moral action varies and is distinct in each act. Therefore, the cause of the common generic determination which is the last end must be one and the same.

2. **Whatever Man Wills in This Life He Wills on Account of the Last Subjective End:** The possession of the last end is the perfect good of man. Whether the nature of this supreme good is known or not, man has a necessary inclination or appetite to the good of his nature. All particular goods, therefore, which are sought by the free appetite are sought because they share in the last end in some way. The reason is that these particular objects are desired and sought in so far as they appear good, that is, under the formal aspect of the end which is the good. For, since the appetite is necessarily ordered to the good, it cannot be moved except by an object which must, at least, appear good.[32]

This same demonstration can be viewed from the analysis of subordinated final causality. The secondary desirables move the

---

[31] It is because of this necessary determination of the will by the last end that human acts are free and therefore moral. For in man the natural appetite to the good of nature results in a necessary inclination of his highest appetite, the will, to the universal good. Now the will as regards a particular good is able to place a free moral act precisely because of this necessary determination to the supreme universal good of human nature.

[32] Cf. *S. Th.*, I–II, 1, 6, *c.*

agent by reason of the first desirable. Now the first desirable is the last end. Hence, all other things are willed for the sake of the last end.

N.B.: It can be inferred from this argument that one need not understand the true nature of the last end, for the desire of human nature for the last end signifies primarily an inclination of nature which may or may not be known as such. Hence, in the enjoyment of games, in the study of the speculative sciences, and in the practice of the arts, which are ends in themselves,[33] man tends to these particular ends because they appear good (*sub ratione boni*). Yet in choosing these various activities man may not be aware of their connection with his natural appetite for the absolute good.

Difficulty: Against the doctrine that whatever man wills he wills on account of his last end it will be argued that not only do many men fail to seek the last end, which is the absolute perfection of human nature, but that they deliberately go against such an end by placing human acts which are opposed to its attainment.

The answer to this difficulty has already been suggested. Since the object of the act of the will is the good, any human act is willed under the formality of good which is that of the last end. Men, however, may not only ignore the true nature of the last end, but, because they are free, they may deliberately seek a particular good which is not conducive to their true end. Hence, even those who erroneously and even sinfully desire and seek happiness in those things in which the true end of man is not found cannot turn away from the necessity of the appetite willing any object under the aspect of the good which in its absolute perfection is the end of their nature. They cannot do away with the inclination of nature to happiness; they cannot refrain from intending their last end which they at times sinfully seek in the wrong objects.

3. **The Last Subjective End Is the Same for All Men:** A nature

---

[33] "They are ends in themselves"; that is to say, they do not necessarily dispose one toward the attainment of the last end.

can have only one last end, since the necessary determination of
a nature to its end must be according to its specific perfection.
For the last end consists in the attainment of the good of nature,
of a good necessarily proportioned to the "whatness" of the nature,
that is to say, to its specific capacity for perfection. Now all men
possess the same specific nature; they are all rational animals. The
last end, therefore, is common to all men. It consists in the
possession of the absolute good, and this possession is the true
happiness of man. In point of fact, all men seek the fulfillment of
their perfection in the possession of some good which they believe
will bring complete happiness. Unfortunately, many look for this
happiness in things in which they will never find it, whether
it be in riches, in pleasure, in learning, or even in the practice
of virtue. Hence, although all men necessarily seek their end,
happiness, which is the attainment of the supreme good, many
err regarding the object in which they expect to attain this
happiness. We repeat, the last end which signifies complete happiness is the same for all men.

**4. In the Attainment of the Last End Man Differs From Other
Creatures:** The last subjective end is both the first principle, the
first desired, the first final cause, and also the term of all human
actions. The last end, therefore, when desired and sought is a
final cause; it exists only in the order of intention. When attained
it is the effect of action; it exists in the order of execution. It
is the ultimate term of the human act. Our problem is stated
thus: Is the last end, which is the same for all men, also common
to other creatures? In order to solve this problem, we should,
first of all, distinguish between the end viewed objectively, which
is the object in itself, God Himself who is supreme good, and the
end viewed subjectively, which is the object as desired and as
attained, or in the words of St. Thomas, "the use or attainment
of the desired object."[34]

---

[34] St. Thomas has never used the expressions *objective* and *subjective* end. He
speaks of *"finis cuius,"* which signifies the object in which the nature of good is
found, and *"finis quo,"* that is, the use or attainment of the end (cf. *S. Th.,* I–II,
1, 8, *c;* I, 26, 3, ad 2^m).

Same Objective End for All: God is the ultimate objective end of all being: that is to say, He, Absolute Goodness Itself, is the first object in whom the nature of good is found and from whom the goodness of creatures is derived. If, therefore, we speak of the last end of man as regards the thing itself which is the end, we must declare that all creatures are alike in this, that God is their last end.[35]

Subjective End Differs: When, however, we examine the end as desired as well as the attainment of the end sought, or, in other words, the last subjective end of all creatures, it will appear immediately that the end of man differs vastly from that of other creatures. The reason is that the ultimate subjective end must be proportioned to the capacity of the created nature in accordance with its specific perfection. In man, the rational creature, the attainment of the last end which is the possession of the absolute good must be had by actions of intellectual knowledge and love, since these are the supreme acts of man as man. Only in such acts of knowledge and love, as will be explained, can man ever hope to attain the complete perfection of his nature and possess complete happiness.

On the other hand, other creatures not endowed with an intellectual nature, and therefore without freedom in their operations, constantly attain their end by being what they are, and by actions that are in accordance with the determination of the various natures which they received from God. Their end is to manifest God's glory[36] by being what they are here and now.

Coeli Enarrant Gloriam Dei

---

[35] This truth was established at length in *The Philosophy of God*, p. 45 ff.

[36] "God seeks not profit but glory, that is to say, a manifestation of His goodness" (*S. Th.*, I–II, 114, 1, ad 2^m).

SUMMARY

Question I

NECESSITY OF ACTUAL INFLUX OF LAST END AS DESIRED UPON EACH HUMAN ACT

The *human act* is an operation which proceeds from a free, a deliberate will. The human act is either elicited or commanded.

The *end* is that on account of which something is and is done.

> Objective End — The object in which the nature of good is found.
> Subjective End — The good as desired, as attained or possessed.

> As desired, it is a cause (final) and exists only in the order of intention. It formally determines action of agent. As possessed, it is the effect of action and is in the order of execution.

Application:

> The objective end of human nature is the absolute good — God.
> The subjective end of human nature is the desire and the attainment of the absolute good.

> *a*) Happiness consists in the attainment of the absolute good.
> *b*) The natural desire for happiness is the first final cause of the human act (to be demonstrated).

Article I: *The Human Act Is Specified Morally by a Freely Chosen End-Object.*

1. In his human actions man acts for an end which is the object of the will-act.

2. Hence, he chooses *freely* this proximate end (object-end). In this he differs from all other creatures which are necessarily determined to operation.

3. This proximate end specifies the act of the will; it makes the act morally good or bad, because the proximate end is the object of the will-act.

Article II: *The Moral Specification of the Human Act Is not Intelligible Without a First Final Cause.* In other words: *The Human Act Depends Existentially Upon the Last End As Desired.*

The freely chosen object-end (proximate final cause) of the will-act is a new actuation (a passing from potency to act) of the will in the order of specification. No actuation, however, of a potency (the will) is intelligible without actual dependence upon an existential cause. Now an infinite regress in existentially subordinated causes is unthinkable. Hence there must be a first final cause upon whose influx the moral act depends here and now. Obviously, this first final cause cannot be a new actuation. It is human nature itself as tending necessarily and constantly to its end, the absolute good, by its natural appetite. This necessary inclination of nature to its ultimate end is communicated to the will here and now through intellectual knowledge of the good.

Article III: *Properties of the Last Subjective End*

1. There can be only one last end of man because:
   a) The last end actuates nature perfectly.
   b) A nature has only one end.
   c) Generic determination which results from the nature of the last end is the same for all human acts.

2. Moreover, it is on account of the last end that one is able to place a human act, because the object of the will is sought in so far as it appears good.

3. This end is the same for all men, because all men have the same specific nature.

4. If we speak of the last end of all creatures, we must distinguish between:

   a) The last objective end — God, the supreme good.
   b) The last subjective end — *attainment* of the objective end. This attainment differs:

      1) In man — the last subjective end consists in the most perfect knowledge and love of God of which man is capable.
      2) In nonrational beings — it consists in their manifestation of God's perfection by being what they are in their nature and operations.

Question II

ERRORS REGARDING THE OBJECT OF MAN'S DESIRE FOR HAPPINESS

Prologue

Although man tends necessarily to his last end by a necessity of nature, he is free to deviate from it in his human acts. This deviation is sometimes due to a wrong understanding of the nature of his last end; that is to say, man may err as regards the object which if attained should render him happy. From our study of metaphysics and of the philosophy of man, we know, of course, that in general the end of any rational creature consists principally in the intellectual possession of the absolute good which is the infinite God. Consequently, a rational being, ordered as it is to the absolute, cannot remain in the contemplation of a limited truth nor can it rest in the possession of a limited good. Men, however, often act as if they considered such limited and imperfect good to be of supreme value. They have, at times, sought these ephemeral objects with every possible effort. In a word, they have made them the end and purpose of their lives. This is undoubtedly a far-reaching error in the order of action. For, if the object of their endeavors is not the true end, every free act tending toward such an object results in a wider deviation from the true end; every effort is an added impetus, another step toward the frustration of nature.

In this question we shall examine various limited objects which are often sought by men as if they were the last end. It will be shown why these cannot be the term and fulfillment of man's nature. In other words, we shall limit ourselves to a consideration, not of what the true object of man's happiness is, but of what it is not. St. Thomas divides the various goods[37] in which man might erroneously seek his supreme happiness into three classes:

---

[37] *S. Th.*, II–II, 73, 3, *c;* cf. I–II, 2, art. 1–8.

exterior possessions, goods of the body, and perfections of the soul. The first class, exterior possessions or goods of fortune, consists in material riches, be it money or what money can buy, or again such things as honor, position, a good name, and power. The second class of goods is intrinsic to the body. The most important, of course, are the conservation of life and health, the pleasures of sense, and especially carnal pleasures. The third class is the goods of the soul. These embrace the various perfections which the soul may acquire, such as wisdom, learning, and moral virtue. We insist that in none of these do we discover the true and perfect good which is the ultimate end for man.

Division: There will be three articles in which we shall establish successively that the object of man's happiness is not to be found: (1) in the goods of fortune, (2) in the goods of the body, or (3) in the goods of the soul.

ARTICLE I: The End of Man Cannot Be the Possession of the Goods of Fortune.

The principal goods of fortune which men sometimes mistake for their last end are: wealth, honor, glory, a good name, and power. We shall prove individually and collectively that these cannot be the last end.

Wealth: Without doubt, the possession of wealth cannot be the last end of man. The last end of a thing is not for the thing itself; rather, the thing is for its last end. Now it is obvious that riches are for man, not man for riches. For the end and purpose of riches is to better human nature. Clearly, then, wealth cannot be considered the last end of man, for wealth is ordered to man as to its end. Consequently, those who make the acquiring of wealth and hoarding of money the supreme purpose of their existence act unreasonably and therefore go against their rational nature. Such a mode of life is morally evil.

Honor, Glory, a Good Name: Nor can it be affirmed that the supreme happiness of man consists in obtaining honor, glory, or a good name. Glory is usually defined as an approving knowledge accompanied by praise. Now true praise results from a true knowledge of the goodness of an individual to whom we give glory. It is given on account of this goodness. Honor, on the other hand, is the reward of virtue; it is an attestation of the excellence of the man who is being honored. Finally, a good name, a good reputation, which indicates that one is well thought of by others, is undoubtedly the most precious of all external goods. For without it, the life of man, which is that of a social animal, would be very difficult and unpleasant. The reason is that a man whose reputation is totally evil would be shunned by his fellows. He would be an outcast from society. St. Thomas remarks that a good name is that external good which comes closest to a spiritual good.[38] The reason is that a good name which is founded on truth results from and depends upon a virtuous life.

We conclude that, in general, glory, honor, and reputation result from a certain excellence, from unusual attainment, from rare talents which exist in the one who is being honored and acclaimed. Obviously, these external goods presuppose an intrinsic perfection possessed by an individual; they are given on account of a personal attainment. Hence, the excellence of such a perfection is the reason, the end of the proffered glory and honor. A good name, honor, or glory cannot be the end of man.

It follows from this that to bend every effort, and to direct every endeavor, to sacrifice even health, life, and the moral virtues solely to obtain honor, glory, and fame is foolish and vain, since these exterior goods are for man, not man for them.

Power: Power is a thing of great value to men. To be sure, one of the strongest human desires is, in some manner or other, to obtain power and dominion, to acquire control, and to exert influence upon other men. In itself, power is not an evil; indeed, it may prove a great good if used prudently and with justice. To seek power, however, as if it were the supreme end of life is against the moral order. Two obvious reasons may be mentioned:

---

[38] " . . . a good name excels riches, because it is nearer to spiritual goods" (*S. Th.*, II–II, 73, 3, *c*).

1. Power is a principle for doing something else; that is to say, it is a means; hence, the possession of power cannot be the last end. On the contrary, the attainment of the absolute good is in itself complete happiness and, consequently, could never be a mere means, a principle for doing anything else. The possession of the supreme good, not the obtaining of great power, is the term and therefore the last end of man's nature.

2. Power can be used either for good or for evil. The last end, on the other hand, is the good of man. Power, therefore, cannot be the last end.

Against every type of exterior goods, St. Thomas brings four general arguments[39] which we quote:

> Now four general reasons may be given to prove that beatitude (happiness) consists in none of the foregoing external goods. The first reason is that, since beatitude is the supreme good of man, it is incompatible with any evil. Now all the foregoing can be found both in good and evil men. The second reason is that, since it is of the nature of beatitude that it should be sufficient of itself . . . it is necessary that once beatitude has been obtained, no necessary good should be lacking to man; for instance, wisdom, bodily health, and the like. The third reason is that, since beatitude is the perfect good, no evil can come to anyone from beatitude. This is not true of the aforesaid, for it is said (*Eccles.* 5:12) that "riches are sometimes stored up to the evil of their owner"; and the same is clear in the other three. The fourth reason is that man is ordered to beatitude through interior principles, since he is naturally ordered to it. The four goods enumerated above are more from exterior causes, and for the most part from fortune; hence, they are also called the goods of fortune. Therefore, it is evident that beatitude in no way consists in those goods.[40]

---

[39] St. Thomas here argues that the possession of the various external goods cannot be the happiness (beatitude) of man, for true happiness consists in the possession of the absolute good.

[40] *S. Th.*, I–II, 2, 4, c.

ARTICLE II: The End of Man Cannot Be the Possession of Goods of the Body.

The most important, the most ardently cherished and carefully guarded goods of the body are its conservation by reason of its union with a living form, its health, strength, beauty, and, of course, the various sense operations. Two general arguments may be offered to show that the possession of the goods of the body cannot be the last end of man.

1. **Essential Argument:** Obviously, the less perfect must be for the sake of the more perfect; matter, the potency, is for the form, which is its act. Hence, the body is for the sake of the soul, not the soul for the body. The goods of the body, therefore, are for the soul. Now the end of the soul is the end of man, since it is because of the soul, the substantial form, that man is man. Hence, the end of man cannot be the possession of the goods of the body.

2. **Existential Argument:** Moreover, man results from the existential union of soul and body. In this union the existence of the soul does not depend upon the body. This appears from the nature of the soul which is a subsisting form, that is, a form whose "to be" (*esse*) is independent from matter. Such a form, when united to matter, communicates not only its specific perfection but existence as well. Consequently, because of this existential dependence of body upon soul, the goods of the body are necessarily ordered to the good of the soul as to their end.

N.B.: We should note that in themselves the goods of the body are more perfect than the external goods of wealth and the like.[41] The reason is that the latter are immediately ordered to the body,

---

[41] "But because the good of the body excels the good of exterior things, sins by which injury is done to the body are more grievous than those by which injury is done in exterior things. Therefore, among all sins which are committed against one's neighbor, the more grievous is homicide through which the life of the neighbor, now actually existing, is taken away. Following this is adultery which is against the right order of human generation by which man enters life. Following these, then, are the exterior goods. Among them, a good name excels riches, because it is nearer to spiritual goods. . . . And, therefore, slander is a greater sin in its genus than theft, but less than homicide or adultery" (*S. Th.*, II–II, 73, 3, *c*).

while the goods of the body are for the soul. It would be unreasonable, therefore, to sacrifice health and life solely to acquire riches.

Carnal Pleasures: Although carnal pleasure, since it is a good
of the body, cannot be the end of man, nevertheless, because of
the nature of pleasure which in itself is not a means, we shall
devote some reflection to the problem of sense pleasure. Let us
begin with a rather formidable difficulty.

Difficulty: The pleasures of the flesh are such that one often
does not desire them in order to obtain some other perfection;
they are sought for their own sake. Now that which is sought
for itself and not for the sake of anything else is an end, not a
means. Carnal pleasures, therefore, are the end, the supreme
happiness of man.

In order to give a definite solution to this problem, we should
begin with a brief metaphysical analysis of the notions of delight
and of happiness.

Delight:[42] "Delight is the appetite's rest in the good possessed."[43]
It is, therefore, an act of the appetite; it consists in a motion
of the appetite.[44] This motion is wrought by the desired object
which, in some manner, is now known to be possessed and is
therefore intentionally possessed as known.[45] For delight, which
is an act either of sense (concupiscible appetite) or of the intellectual appetite (will), must be determined in the order of specification by an operation of the faculty of knowledge. This knowledge

---

[42] Recall the fundamental division of the good studied in *The Philosophy of
Being,* p. 184: the useful, the virtuous (*honestum*), and the delectable. The delectable
principally results from the virtuous end, but it may and often does flow from the
useful which is the means. (Cf. *S. Th.,* I, 5, 6.) If delight or pleasure accompanies
the means (*bonum utile*), as for example, in the case of a good moral act ordered
to a higher end, such delight gives us strength and courage to continue our
endeavors. The joy of fruition which follows the possession of the end, gives peace
and quiets the appetite. (Cf. *S. Th.,* I–II, 2, 6, ad 1^m.)

[43] *S. Th.,* I–II, 2, 6, ad 1^m.

[44] Love and delight are distinct operations of the appetite. Love is the first action.
Delight is the last of the series. It is the fruition of the possessed good.

[45] There are various types of possession: material, sensual (i.e., by sense knowledge), and intellectual. The last two are in the order of knowledge. The most
perfect type of possession is intellectual. (Cf. *S. Th.,* I–II, 31, 2, ad 1^m.)

may be either of the actual attainment of the object here and now, or it can be the knowledge of a purely intentional possession, as when the object is attained in hope or in memory. Whether the object is known to be actually or only intentionally possessed, this knowledge which is a possession of the object desired causes the specification of the act of appetite which we call delight. Delight, therefore, is not the possession of the good which we call happiness. Rather, it results from such possession as its property.[46]

Joy and Pleasure: Now delight is really a generic term, for there are two types of delight according to the perfection of the appetite. There is a twofold delight: one is the act of the sense appetite, that is to say, the quietude, rest (*quies*) of the concupiscible faculty in the sensible good which has been attained; the other is the fruition of the rational appetite, the will, in the intelligible good.[47] The delight which is the act of the intellectual appetite is often termed joy;[48] that of the sense appetite we call pleasure.

Happiness: From the analysis of delight we infer that, whether it be sense pleasure or intellectual joy, delight can only result from knowledge of the good possessed. Now the attainment of the desired good is called happiness.[49] Consequently, delight, which

---

[46] Property or proper accident is an accidental perfection which necessarily flows from an essence but is distinct from it.

[47] Cf. *S. Th.,* I–II, 31, 3 & 4; cf. also I–II, 30, 1.

[48] When delight terminates a moral act, it is generally called fruition.

[49] "Happiness consists in the possession of the good" (*De Malo,* v. 1). Happiness is either true or false:

True happiness is the possession of the supreme good. True happiness is either perfect or imperfect.

Perfect happiness is the perfect intellectual possession of the supreme good. Such perfect happiness is the last end of man. It is not attainable in this life.

Imperfect happiness is the imperfect possession of the supreme good in this life. It is true but incomplete happiness.

Imperfect happiness consists:

1. Primarily in an imperfect but efficacious knowledge and love of God who is the supreme good.

2. Secondarily in the possession of various created goods as subordinated to the knowledge and love of God. (*S. Th.,* I–II, 3, 2, ad 4^m.)

False happiness consists in the possession of created goods in opposition to the

is the rest of the appetite in the possessed good, cannot be of the essence of happiness but rather flows from it, just as a proper accident flows from a nature from which it is really distinct. Delight is not happiness; rather, it results from happiness and is therefore distinct from it. Hence, delight is the property, not the essence of happiness. It follows from this argumentation that delight in general, and *a fortiori* the pleasure of sense which results from the known possession of a sensible object, cannot be the end of man, for they are certainly distinct from the possession of the supreme good which is the last end.

First Argument: The end of man is the possession of the absolute good. On the contrary, delight (whether joy or pleasure) does not consist in the possession of the good but rather results from such possession as its property. Therefore, delight is not the end of man.

To the difficulty, that we seek a good in order to obtain pleasure, because, absolutely speaking, delight is the last end, we reply that this difficulty results from a failure to distinguish between efficient, formal, and final causes. Delight is the proper accident of the good possessed. Consequently, it exists by reason of the good which is known to be possessed. This good is "in a way" the efficient principle of the delight. Hence, we seek the good, from which results delight, its necessary consequent.[50]

---

possession of the supreme good (i.e., in opposition to knowledge and love of God) (*S. Th.,* I, 26, 4, ad 1ᵐ).

[50] The end when intended is in the order of *final* cause; when possessed (happiness) it is in the order of *formal* cause; when enjoyed it is in the order of *efficient* cause (as causing delight, for a property results from its subject as from its efficient cause by a certain "resultance"). This then is the genesis of delight: First, the end being known and desired moves the will to action (finality). Since, however, the end is viewed and desired as good, it is the object of the will. Hence, it specifies the will-act and is therefore its formal cause. The act being placed and the effect (end as formal cause) being attained, there results, as a natural consequence of the term of the act which is the possession of the desired good, a property of this possession, that is, delight. *The end (final) as possessed (formal) is the efficient cause of delight (property).* "It comes to the same whether we desire good or desire delight, which is nothing else than the appetite's rest in good: thus it is owing to the same natural force that a weighty body is borne downward and that it rests there. Consequently, just as good is desired *for* itself, so is delight desired *for* itself if the preposition *for* denotes the final cause. But if it denotes the formal or rather

If, however, we view delight in so far as it is desired, we must admit that delight is sought because apprehended as good (*sub ratione boni*), for the good, not delight, is the object of the will. The end, therefore, is not delight but the good.

Second Argument: Another reason why the pleasures of the body cannot be the last end of man is that they are *limited, imperfect goods,* since pleasure consists in an operation of the sense appetite which follows sense knowledge. Consequently, the possession of the good which precedes this pleasure is necessarily the possession of a limited good because apprehended by a faculty which is partly material. Now the perfection of man, as man, consists in this, that being an intellectual creature, he is capable of knowing and loving the universal and the absolute. His happiness, therefore, cannot be restricted to mere sense knowledge and to its property which is sense pleasure.

We conclude: Carnal pleasure cannot be the supreme happiness of man: (1) because it results from the known possession of sensible good; it is only a distinct property of such possession; and (2) because sense pleasure is a limited good.

N.B.: Our doctrine stands between two extreme positions: one is that of the Hedonists, and the other, the irrational tenets of the Puritans. The Hedonists claim that pleasure is the end of

---

the motive cause, thus delight is desirable for something else, i.e., because of the good, which is the object of that delight and consequently is its principle and gives it its form: for delight is desired because it is rest in the thing desired" (*S. Th.,* I–II, 2, 6, ad 1ᵐ).

The following parallel text will help us understand this difficult analysis: "When the will is said to delight in a thing for its own sake, this may be understood in two ways. First, so that the expression *for the sake of* be taken to signify the final cause; and in this way, man delights in nothing for its own sake except the last end. Secondly, so that it designates the formal cause; and in this way, a man may delight in anything that is delightful by reason of its form. Thus it is clear that a sick man delights in health for its own sake as an end; in a sweet-tasting medicine, not as in an end, but as in something having a delightful taste; and in a bitter medicine, in no way for its own sake, but only for the sake of something else. Accordingly, we must say that a man must delight in God for his own sake, as being his last end, and in virtuous deeds, not as being his end, but for the sake of their inherent goodness, which is delightful to the virtuous" (*S. Th.,* I–II, 70, 1, ad 2ᵐ).

man; that pleasure is the supreme, the only true motivation. The Puritanical position is just the contrary: pleasure is evil; pleasure is sinful. We have proved conclusively against the teachings of the Hedonists that pleasure is not happiness, not even imperfect happiness. Hence it cannot be the end of man. For the end of man is happiness, that is, the possession of the absolute good, and delight is not that; it is only a consequent, a property of happiness. As regards the unphilosophical doctrines of the Puritans and their numerous followers, it is sufficient to point out that pleasure and joy are the proper accidents of the good done or possessed. Since a proper accident flows necessarily from its subject, in this case the possessed good, it follows that in itself delight is good. Indeed, pleasure properly controlled and subordinated to the virtuous good (*bonum honestum*) can be a great help in the moral life of man. It becomes evil when accepted as an end in itself and not subordinated as a means to the attainment of the last end. For to intend as the end that which is only the property of the possession of a sensible good is to go against the truth of the moral order.

Difficulty — Knowledge of Last End: A difficulty may arise regarding our awareness of the supreme end. The question is sometimes asked, "Is it necessary to realize in the midst of pleasure and joy that these are not the supreme end?" We answer that it is not only unnecessary but often impossible to do so because of the intensity of the pleasure and the dependence of our mind upon the world of material objects. What is necessary is that we do not freely and positively exclude the relation of dependence which the particular good or pleasure has to the supreme end.[51] For to do so would make a human act morally evil.

Difficulty: People often ask why it is then that the pleasures

---

[51] Theologians and spiritual writers distinguish between actual and habitual intention. Actual intention means that we are deliberately aware of our dependence on the supreme end and place our human act accordingly. Habitual intention indicates that the order to the end has been accepted but is not revoked in the present action. Actual intention, as we shall see later, increases the intensity and perfection of the human act.

of the senses are generally the most powerful, the most overwhelming experience of this life. St. Thomas explains that as a result of man's essential composition of soul and body the proper and proportionate object of man's knowledge in this life is the material essence. Because of this composition, man's knowledge begins with sense experience, and by this means he arrives at the "proper" intellectual knowledge of the material essence of the object. Things that are material, that is, sensible objects alone, are known connaturally, that is, as they are in themselves. Consequently, the pleasure which flows from such perfect knowledge is often far more vehement than that which results from the knowledge of spiritual beings and from abstract truths.[52] That is why many men give themselves to the pleasures of sense and are often completely ignorant of the fact that even in this life intellectual and spiritual delight can be far more satisfying.

Let us conclude briefly. Pleasure, like all the other goods of the body, is a limited, a participated good. Hence, it cannot be the ultimate end but must be sought, accepted, and controlled in accordance with the measure of right reason, so that it is always subordinated to the true end of man.

ARTICLE III: The End of Man Cannot Be the Possession of the Goods of the Soul.

Happiness is the last end of a rational nature. It consists in the possession of the absolute good. Throughout this question we are examining the various objects erroneously sought by men as the object of happiness. Directing our search to the goods of the soul, we discover that neither the soul itself, nor any action which perfects the soul can be the true object of man's happiness. For as we have often explained, the only object which can be

---

[52] Because of original sin, man has lost not only the despotic but even the perfect political control of reason over his lower appetites. The passions, therefore, unless constantly disciplined, can overcome the rational nature by their violence. This reason, however, belongs to theological study and cannot be examined in a philosophical discussion.

the last end of man is the absolute good, since only the absolute good by being attained, can actuate all the potencies of a rational nature, and thereby cause man to be truly happy.

On the other hand, if we speak of that operation by which the soul attains the absolute good, then we should state that the end of man is a good of the soul. For — as we shall establish in the next question — man attains his end primarily by an operation of the intellect. In the present article, however, we are limiting ourselves to a consideration of the object of happiness. Consequently, we must declare that such an object cannot be the soul or any good of the soul, be it learning, wisdom, or any virtuous action.

Proof:

1. *As regards the soul itself:* The last end is not in potency to any act since it is the actuation of all potencies.

But the existing soul, because its essence is distinct from "to be," remains in potency to innumerable accidental perfections.

Therefore the soul cannot be the last end.

2. Neither can the various *accidental actuations* of the soul be the end of man, since these actuations are limited and participated perfections. Now the end of man is the perfect good, for it must fill the natural appetite of the human will for the absolute good. Consequently, neither the virtues — whether intellectual, such as wisdom, knowledge, learning, art, and prudence, or moral, such as justice, temperance, and fortitude — nor the actions which result from these virtues can be the end which is the object of the will's desire; none of these participated goods can be the last end of man. The happiness of man can be found only in God, the unparticipated good.

> . . . For beatitude is the perfect good which wholly quiets the appetite; otherwise, it would not be the ultimate end if there yet remained something to be desired. Now the object of the will, which is the human appetite, is the universal good, as the object of the intellect is the universal true. From this it is clear that nothing is able to quiet the will of man except the universal good. This is not found in any created thing but only in God, because every creature

has participated goodness. Wherefore, only God is able to satisfy the will of man. . . . Therefore, in God alone is the perfect happiness of man.[53]

SUMMARY

Question II

ERRORS REGARDING THE OBJECT OF MAN'S DESIRE FOR HAPPINESS

Prologue

The objective last end of man is the absolute good: God Himself.
The subjective last end of man is the possession of the absolute good.
The happiness of man consists in the possession of the absolute good.
Happiness, therefore, is the last subjective end of man.

Every nature has a necessary inclination to its end. Hence, human nature has a natural desire (appetite of nature) for happiness. Although the desire for happiness is man's most fundamental desire (first final cause), men often err as regards the nature of the object which being attained will cause them to be truly happy. The happiness of man which is his last end does not consist in the possession of the following goods:

Article I: *The Goods of Fortune*

Wealth is for man, not man for wealth.
Honor, glory, a good name are given and obtained because of some accomplishment, some intrinsic perfection to which they are directed.
Power is a principle for doing something else; it can be used to do evil.
On the contrary, the last end is not for man; man is for the last end.

Article II: *The Goods of the Body*

Essential argument: The less perfect is for the more perfect; matter is for the form; the body is for the soul.
Existential argument: Body depends upon soul for existence.
Happiness which is the end of man is the intellectual possession of the absolute good.

---

[53] *S. Th.*, I–II, 2, 8, *c.*

Delight is an act of the appetite. It consists in the rest of the appetite in the possessed good known as possessed. It results from the possession of the good as a property of such possession.

Delight is either:

   a) *Joy* which is the delight of the rational appetite (will).

   b) *Pleasure* which is the delight of the sense appetite (concupiscible power).

Pleasure cannot be the last end. Two arguments can be given:

   a) Happiness which is the end consists in the possession of the good. Delight (joy and pleasure) results from such possession.

       Therefore, delight is not the end of man. Delight results from the knowledge of the possession of the good. It is a distinct property of the possessed good.

   b) Pleasure is a limited good. Hence, it is not the last end, which is the absolute good, but it must be subordinated to the last end.

Article III: *The Goods of the Soul*

Not the soul: The soul is in potency; it needs to be actuated in the order of existence and in the order of action. It cannot be the last end which is the actuation of all potencies.

Not a perfection of the soul: These perfections are all limited accidental forms; whereas the last object of man's happiness is the supreme good.

N.B.: The last subjective end of man, his happiness, which is the possession of the supreme good, will be had by a good of the soul, that is, primarily by an operation of the human intellect.

Question III

NATURE OF MAN'S HAPPINESS

Prologue

Problem: The last objective end of man is God, the absolute good. The last subjective end is the attainment, the actual possession of that supreme good. This subjective end of man we call happiness. True happiness, therefore, is the attainment, the possession of God, man's supreme good.[54] Our problem is to determine in what the attainment, the possession of God consists.

Act of Intellect and of Will: The only faculties of man which are potentially infinite are his intellect and will. Consequently, we may state that the possession of the infinite God, which is man's happiness, can be had only by means of an act of intellectual knowledge accompanied by intellectual love. Let us examine: (1) why this happiness consists primarily in an act of the intellect, (2) the requisites for such an intellectual union, and (3) the nature of this union.

ARTICLE I: Why This Happiness Consists Primarily in an Act of the Intellect.

1. Complete Happiness Can Be Had Only in the Next Life:

It is obvious even from casual observation that complete happiness is not had in this life, for the operations of man on this earth lack the perfection necessary for a stable union with the good possessed.[55] Hence, in this life, we can attain only to an incomplete and imperfect happiness[56] in accordance with the degree of understanding and love of God we reach. From this fact, we argue that the last end of man is attained not in this life, but in the next.

---

[54] Cf. *S. Th.,* I–II, 5, 1, *c.*

[55] Perfect happiness "is consummate perfection which excludes every defect from the happy" (*ibid.,* 4, ad 1^m). Hence, perfect happiness cannot be had in this life, "for the present life is subject to many *unavoidable* evils, to ignorance on the part of the intellect, to inordinate affections on the part of the appetite, and to many discomforts and sufferings on the part of the body" (*ibid.,* 3, *c*).

[56] A certain participation of happiness may be had in this life. For man can participate in his last end by knowing and loving God though imperfectly. Hence, man can enjoy happiness, imperfect happiness, in this life. "According to the present state of life, the highest perfection is had by means of an operation which unites man to God; but this operation neither can be continuous, nor, consequently, is it one only. . . . For this reason, in the present state of life, perfect happiness cannot be attained by man. . . . Insofar, therefore, as we fall short of the unity of that operation, so do we fall short of happiness. Nevertheless, it is a participation of happiness; and so much the greater, as the operation can be more continuous and more one" (*S. Th.,* I–II, 3, 2, ad 4^m).

Argument: Man is made for complete happiness, his last end, which consists in the possession of the supreme good. It follows that this happiness must be attainable. For, if the last end were not attainable, such total frustration of nature would imply that human nature is a contradiction, a non-being. For nature is a principle of action to its last end, that is, to an end which is attainable. A nature, therefore, whose end is not attainable is not intelligible; it implies an existential contradiction; it is a non-being. Now we know from observation that complete happiness is never attained in this life. We must conclude, since man's soul is incorruptible, that is, immortal, that complete happiness must be obtained in the life after death.

2. **How is this happiness attained:** What is the nature of the operation necessary for the possession of the supreme end? First, we note that it could not be a sense operation, for the object of such an operation is an object proportioned to the capacity of a sense faculty — a material object, not the infinitely perfect God; a spiritual action, an intellectual operation is required. The reason is that only the intellect, whose capacity for knowledge of truth is infinite, and only the will (the intellectual appetite) which is necessitated to love the absolute good, are capable of operations which could unite man with an object that is Infinite Truth and Infinite Goodness. The possession of God, therefore, the supreme good, is attained by means of a union of intellectual knowledge and love, that is, by intellectual and volitional acts.

3. **Primacy of Intellect:** Primarily and essentially, of course, this operation is of the intellect, for in order to love, we must know; in order to enjoy, we must possess the good desired and sought. Indeed, the act of the will which terminates in the delight, in the fruition of the good possessed, may be considered as necessarily resulting from the intellectual possession of the object obtained in an act of knowledge. This delight is the consequent of the possession of the good which takes place in the act of knowledge; it is, therefore, a proper accident of this intellectual possession. Consequently, we may state with the Angelic Doctor that the

happiness of man consists primarily and essentially in the intellectual possession of the infinite God.

ARTICLE II: Requisites for the Attainment of Happiness

As regards the necessary conditions for the attainment of the last end, St. Thomas insists especially upon two requisites: the rectitude of the will and the necessity of good works.

a) **Rectitude of the Will:** The rectitude of the will is the due order to the end. Indeed, this rectitude is nothing else than the right inclination or disposition of the will of man toward his last end.

That the right inclination of the will is a necessary requisite for the attainment of the last end can be immediately inferred from the already established dependence of the will-act upon the actual (here and now) desire for the last end (first final cause). Because of this actual dependence, it is manifest that the proximate object-end which is freely chosen by the will should be in accord with the last end. For, since the nature of man is directed in its human actions by its highest appetite, which is the will, should the object-end freely chosen by the will-act not be in accord with the relation of human nature to its end as expressed by right reason, the resulting disposition caused by such an act would be an inclination of the will to an end opposed to that of nature. The will no longer would retain its rectitude, its right order to the last end. Clearly, as long as this disordered state obtains, man's true happiness can never be attained. Nature is frustrated.

In order to establish this important inference, St. Thomas proposes an argumentation founded on the nature of the last end, which consists in the possession of the absolute good. This possession is simply a union (primarily of knowledge) analogous to the union which takes place between matter and form. Now the final cause of the will-act is in the order of specification, that is, in the order of formal causality. The reason is that the proximate end of the will-act is its object. Since an object specifies and therefore is in the order of a formal cause, the attainment of an end implies a union somewhat analogous to that of form and matter. A form, however, cannot be united to any matter but only to that material principle which is properly disposed for the reception of such a form. In the moral order, which is the order of the intention of the will to the last end, only by means of a will-act which is proportionate to the rational nature and therefore based on right reason can the disposition necessary for the attainment and possession of that end be obtained. Now this proper intention, this disposition to the end, is nothing other than the rectitude of the will. Consequently, the rectitude of the will is a necessary requisite for the attainment of the end.[57]

b) **Necessity of Good Works:**   Good works are taken to signify good moral actions. The rectitude of the will, which is the right ordering of man to his true end, is necessarily maintained and even perfected by good works. For, if human actions were not good, they would be caused by an evil will and would imply an aversion from the last end. On the other hand, good moral actions maintain, develop, and perfect the true order of the will to man's last end, because they result from a will that is properly ordered. Good works are, therefore, in this way necessary for the attainment of the last end.

ARTICLE III: Nature of Union

The possession of the infinite God is primarily an intellectual union. What the nature of this union is we shall relinquish to theologians. Although as philosophers we are able to know with

---

[57] We hardly need to add that once the end is attained the rectitude of the will cannot but endure. For the end is the supreme good of the will, to which the will is necessitated. Hence, once it is possessed, the will cannot turn away from its fruition. (Cf. *S. Th.,* I–II, 4, 4.) We learn from theology that because of man's elevation to a supernatural end, the rectitude of the will cannot be had without the supernatural gift of grace.

absolute certitude that the end of man is God and that we attain this end by an act of intellect, nevertheless, the manner in which the possession of the supreme good actually takes place transcends our connatural knowledge. The reason is twofold. First, this attaining of the end does not take place in this life. Secondly, because of the elevation of human nature by grace, the nature of this end, we learn from theologians, is a knowledge of God; not, however, an abstract, imperfect knowledge derived from creatures, but an intuitive knowledge of His essence, seen as He is in Himself. Now our natural mode of knowledge depends upon material essences, which are the proper object of man's intellect. Consequently, we have no connatural means of arriving at any knowledge of the nature of this supernatural union. For this we need a revelation from God. Obviously, the consideration of a revelation has no place in a philosophical treatise.

Reason and Revelation: We may, however, point out the fact as a matter of interest and no longer of philosophical deduction that no solution proposed to the problem of the end of man can be completely satisfactory unless we rise to a knowledge of this divine revelation. For in this revelation, which comes to us from God, besides the philosophical truth known from reason that the nature of man is of itself capable of knowing and loving God as his end, we learn that by a merciful dispensation of Divine Providence the nature of man through the gift of sanctifying grace is elevated to an end which transcends all things created, that is, a supernatural end which is the actual, intellectual vision of the Divine Essence. Man, therefore, is made capable of seeing God as He is in Himself. This vision which takes place in the next world is made possible by a supernatural gift called the light of glory which strengthens the human intellect, enabling it to withstand the impact of the Divine Essence. For, according to the Angelic Doctor, the intelligible species which actuates the intellect of man and enables it to break forth into the act of understanding is not a representative species educed from the possible intellect, but the Divine Essence itself. The act of understanding is the operation of man, an immanent action, the act of a perfect being (*actus perfecti*).

Man sees God as He is. This vision is man's supernatural happiness, his beatitude.

We repeat, it is not for us philosophers to discuss these sublime matters, for they are beyond the limits of our natural, reasoned search for truth. But it is good to know that the obscurity which reason experiences in its search for truth can be dissipated by a light superior to that of the created intellect.

We should not infer from this that the findings of reason in its effort to erect a philosophy of morality are erroneous. On the contrary, they are not only true but necessary in enabling us to lay a solid and secure rational foundation for such a philosophy. We merely recognize the limitations of human reason.[58]

Note on the Natural End of Man:[59] When speculating on the nature of a possible natural end, had man's nature not received the elevation of grace to a supernatural vision, philosophers generally admit that the happiness of man would have consisted in a series of intellectual operations by means of which man would have known God discursively, that is, through an abstractive knowledge derived from creatures. This discursive, abstract, and successive knowledge, they explain, would have sufficed for the natural happiness of man. For, if man had been created and placed in the state of pure nature, the vision of the Divine Essence would not have

---

[58] That is why, after a course in the philosophy of morality, it would be wise to introduce the student to the great revealed truths of the elevation of man to a supernatural end, of his fall, and of his redemption.

St. Thomas, the Christian theologian, examines the problem of man's beatitude in accordance with the data obtained from revelation. Because this little work is a philosophical treatise, we have refrained from following Aquinas' development.

[59] Although St. Thomas does not discuss the nature of a natural end, he states the possibility of such an end had man been created in the order of nature. " . . . by a natural inclination man is ordered to an end which is connatural to him . . . it was therefore necessary that something supernatural be added to order man to a supernatural end" (*S. Th.*, I–II, 62, 3; cf. *De Malo*, V, 1, ad 15ᵐ). Moreover, he explains that in a state of pure nature there would be no right (*nullum debitum*) to a vision of the Divine Essence. Hence, the only happiness possible would be a happiness connatural to a rational creature. "There are two kinds of happiness, one proportioned to human nature which man can (could) attain by the principles of his nature. The other happiness exceeds man's nature so that man can reach it only by divine power, according to a participation of the divinity . . . " (*S. Th.*, I–II, 62, 1).

been proportioned to his created intellect. In this state, therefore, the human intellect, in order to attain its natural happiness, could never have required nor obtained a complete rest (*quietatio*), a complete actuation, in any one single object known, in one single act of understanding. Such a knowledge even of God would have been necessarily limited and imperfect. Nor could man have had any reasonable desire for an intuitive vision of the Divine Essence, since in its final state the created intellect would never realize the possibility of seeking an end which is not proportioned to its connatural capacity. When, therefore, St. Thomas, the Christian theologian, speaks of a natural desire for the beatific vision, he speaks as a Christian realist who accepts the revealed truth that the nature of man is now ordered to a supernatural end, and by this *desiderium naturale* he means the desire of an elevated nature for a connatural knowledge of the Divine Essence.

It is true that perfect (supernatural) happiness (beatitude) is a total actuation (*quietatio*) of intellect and appetite; and it is also true that this perfect happiness cannot be had except in the actual possession of the absolute good, God as He is in Himself, and not as represented by a created image. Now such a possession is impossible to a created intellect in its natural state, since the mode of existing of God exceeds infinitely that of the creature. For, while God is "to be," man has only a participated act of existing. Hence, a created intellect in its final natural state would clearly understand that it cannot rationally desire such supernatural possession. Indeed, in this natural state a created intellect could never know of itself and without a divine revelation that the supernatural vision of the Divine Essence is possible. For the truly supernatural, that is to say, that which transcends created nature, can never be rationally thought of as possible by unaided reason. This is true, not only of the possibility of the elevation of a created intellect to the vision of the Divine Essence, but of the Trinity, of the Incarnation, of Transubstantiation as well.[60] That is why when speaking of the state of the souls of unbaptized children who are in limbo, after

---

60 "*Et quamvis nullam repugnantiam apprehendamus in hoc, quod dicimus, videre modo supernaturali Deum per essentiam, non valemus tamen naturaliter ostendere,*

stating that they have the perfect knowledge which is connatural to their rational nature, St. Thomas states definitely that these souls do not grieve in not being able to see God, because they do not see the truth of the possibility of such a vision. *"Non cognoscunt et propter hoc non dolent."*[61]

Natural happiness, therefore, does not mean the actual, absolute satisfaction (complete actuation) of the appetite of intellect and will. Rather it means, in the first place, a continuous succession of highly perfect acts of knowing the truths and loving the goods that are proportioned to the natural capacity of man. But most of all, it consists in a very perfect knowledge and love of God,[62] in accordance with the connatural mode of existing of man, so that in his final state the natural man, if there had been such a man, would have enjoyed the knowledge of divine truth and the love of divine goodness only as participated by and reflected in creation.

We may add that it is opposed to the natural power and virtue of a created intellect which has not received the elevation of grace that its appetite be at any time fully actuated, since of itself such a created appetite cannot be naturally satiated by one object but must pass from one object to another or consider successively various

---

quod revera nulla repugnantia in eo sit. Et nihil naturaliter scire possemus de possibilitate divinae visionis, sicut nec de possibilitate unionis hypostaticae cum Deo, nec de possibilitate Trinitatis, aut transubstantiationis" (Mauri, Giuseppe, S.J., *De Deo Tractatio Metaphysica,* Manuscriptum, Venetiis, 1889, p. 400).

[61] "The souls of the children (in limbo) do not lack any natural knowledge which is due to separated souls according to their natures, but they lack that supernatural knowledge which in this life is planted in us by faith. It belongs, however, to the (perfection of) natural knowledge that a soul know it is created for happiness (beatitude) and also that such a happiness consists in the possession (*in adeptione*) of the perfect good. But that this perfect good, for which man was created be that glory which the saints possess, is above natural knowledge. . . . And, therefore, the souls of these children do not know that they are deprived of such a good (although they have the perfect knowledge which belongs to their natures), and therefore they do not grieve" (*De Malo,* V, 3).

[62] Difficulty: Since the act is successive and limited, God is not required and necessary as the end of man.

Answer: An object of knowledge of infinite perfection would have been required, for the intelligibility of any limited object would be ultimately exhausted by successive acts of knowledge. In point of fact the intellect of man is in potency to know absolute truth.

aspects of the same object. Hence, in a nature which has not been elevated, there can be no natural appetite for the intuitive vision of the Divine Essence.

Obviously, in the state of nature the natural capacity of intellect and will could never be fully actuated in one act, nor could man ever attain the absolute possession of the supreme good in a vision of the Divine Essence which we call perfect happiness. Nevertheless, man's operative potencies can be properly and connaturally actuated according to the condition of his nature by a knowledge and love of God which is connatural to these potencies. This may be called the natural happiness of man. For nothing is lacking, nothing more is reasonably desirable beyond that which is connatural. In the state of pure nature, if man had attained his natural end, he would have been truly happy.

Finally, let us not forget that the abstract knowledge of God in the final state of man would have been the most perfect, connaturally possible. For, most of all, such knowledge would have been obtained through an immediate knowledge of a spiritual form, namely, the soul, now present to the intellect in an intelligible manner. Man would have possessed and enjoyed a natural happiness.

SUMMARY

Question III

NATURE OF MAN'S HAPPINESS

Already established:

The last objective end of man is God, the supreme good. The last subjective end of man is, in some manner, the possession of God, the supreme good. This last subjective end of man is his happiness. Man's happiness is the possession of God, his supreme good.

Article I: *Happiness Consists Primarily in an Act of the Intellect.*

Problem: In what does this possession of God consist?

Solution:

1. *When:* Certainly not in this life. We know from observation that human nature does not attain this end here on earth. Therefore, man's happiness must be attainable after death, in the continued life of the immortal soul. To deny the possibility of the attainment of the end is to imply that human nature is a contradiction, a non-being.

2. *How:* By means of a union of intellectual knowledge and love. The reason is that only the faculties of intellect and will have infinite capacity. Hence, by intellectual and volitional acts.

3. *Primacy of intellect:* Essentially, happiness consists in an act of the intellect by which man attains an intellectual possession of God in a union of knowledge. The act of fruition of the will accompanies this knowledge and results from it as its property.

Article II: *Conditions Necessary for the Attainment of Happiness*

1. *Rectitude of will:* Rectitude of the will is right direction of the will to man's last end. It gives the necessary disposition to the nature of man for possession of God by causing proper direction to true end. An evil will destroys such disposition because it intends an evil end. The reason is that the specification of the human act depends upon a desire for the last end. Because of this actual final dependence, the human act disposes the nature toward or away from the last end. Consequently, the rectitude of the will is destroyed whenever the object-end of the will-act is contrary to the relation of human nature to its last end.

Possession of the absolute good is a union like that of matter and form. For such union rectitude of the will is a necessary disposition in the subject.

2. *Good works:* Good works are good moral actions. When placed, they imply, maintain, and perfect the will's rectitude. Evil works destroy this rectitude.

Article III: *Nature of Union*

Reason and Revelation:

Reason tells us that in the state of pure nature the natural happiness of man would consist in a succession of highly perfect acts of intellectual knowledge and love of God. These acts would be in accordance with the connatural mode of existing of man. Such knowledge would be abstract, discursive, and analogous because it would be obtained from our knowledge of creatures.

Revelation tells us that man's elevated nature is ordered to a supernatural end, the vision of the Divine Essence. To attain such an end, we need the grace of God. Grace, however, does not destroy nature; it supposes and perfects it. Hence, our philosophical inferences regarding the nature and end of man are true and of extreme importance but necessarily incomplete.

CHAPTER II

THE MORAL ACT

Prologue

Man's elevation to a supernatural end which is a connatural vision of the Divine Essence is a revealed truth. Knowledge of this revealed truth is unattainable by the unaided intellect of man. Consequently, a philosophy of morality cannot pretend to give us a complete answer to the problem of the moral act in all its existential implications. The reason is that the aim and conclusions of philosophy are limited to the findings of unaided reason. Consequently, as regards the human act, a science of morals is limited to inferences drawn from the consideration of man in the state of pure nature and ordered to a natural end. On the other hand, in the present order — so we learn from theologians — the moral act has an existential status all its own. In the present order of existence, the moral act is caused by a nature which through an original actuation of its obediential potency, although wounded by sin, is now ordered to a supernatural end which consists in an intuitive vision of the Divine Essence. Hence, any moral act placed by this active principle in such existential conditions will be existentially different from that placed by a nature which supposedly has not received an obediential actuation and which, therefore, being in a natural state is necessarily ordered to a natural end.[1]

---

[1] A science of the existential moral act demands a study of man as he is actually, that is, either in the state of sin or of sanctifying grace which latter implies the infused virtues and the gifts of the Holy Spirit. In either situation man is ordered to a supernatural end. Hence, the law which should govern his human actions is necessarily more extensive than the natural law. For law results from the

The existential status of a moral act is understood by referring the operation to its rational active principle as ordered to its last end. Now if we accept the revealed truth of the elevation of man's nature to a supernatural end, it becomes obvious that the moral act in its present existential constitution cannot be studied adequately in a course of philosophy which limits itself to the findings of reason. In its fullness, therefore, the study of the existential moral act must be left to a philosophy of Christian conduct.

It appears then that our discussion in a course of philosophy cannot examine the full existential significance of the moral act. We shall consider the moral act as referred to a rational nature without recognizing and examining the fact that this existing rational nature is ordered to a supernatural end. Consequently, our consideration of the human act will be largely in the order of its essential constitution. This philosophical study, although neither complete nor final, is nevertheless true and necessary. It is true, because grace does not destroy nature; on the contrary, it presupposes it and perfects it. It is a necessary study because without a thorough and profound understanding from reason of the essential nature of the moral act, no true *science* of Christian conduct, no true *science* of moral theology could be developed. For, having accepted the data of revelation, it is by means of the findings of reason that we can institute a scientific approach to an understanding of the existential moral act. The philosophical study of the moral act is therefore true and necessary although neither complete nor final. It is based upon an essential, rather than an existential, consideration.

Division: There will be five questions: (1) The structure of the moral act. (2) Subjective morality or voluntariness, that is, the reason for the imputability of a moral act. (3) Objective morality, that is, the goodness or malice of the act. (4) The passions and morality. (5) The habits and the moral act.

---

finality of nature to its last end. Consequently, there must be a divine law, the law of faith which works through love. (Cf. *S. Th.*, I–II, 108, 1, *c*.) For "since man is ordained to an end of eternal happiness which exceeds man's natural ability, it was necessary that in addition to the natural law, man should be directed to his end by a law given by God" (*S. Th.*, I–II, 91, 4).

Question I

STRUCTURE OF THE MORAL ACT

In the philosophy of man,[2] we proposed a lengthy analysis of the human act. The approach, however, was rather psychological, not moral. It will be recalled that the central question in this discussion was the nature of freedom in man, and the psychological analysis proposed led to an understanding of the liberty of judgment and choice (*liberum arbitrium*).

In a treatise on moral philosophy, an analysis of the moral sequence of the human act will aim rather at a solution of moral problems. Such an analysis will point, first of all, to the relation of the act of the will to its proximate end.[3] For the proximate end (object-end) gives to the will-act its moral specification. From this relation, the moral unity of the process of the human act will be established as resulting primarily from the dynamism of the intention of the will. For the act of the will which is called intention is the moving factor whose efficient determination to the end pervades the long correlated series of intellectual and volitional operations and terminates in the fulfillment of fruition. The moral unity resulting from such dynamism will be the basis for enumerating distinct moral acts.

Moreover, the classification of the various operations by their immediate relation to the order of the end and to the order of means[4] will enable us to distinguish between various types of moral acts, as for example, thought, desire, and action. Finally, in an effort to understand the function of practical reason upon action in the order of the means, we shall be able to discover the place for the prudential judgment together with the true foundation of law. These

---

[2] *The Philosophy of Man*, p. 183 ff.

[3] There are three operations of the will which look directly to the end: volition, intention, and fruition.

[4] We should distinguish between the proximate end or object-end and the order of the end and of means. The end-object is the specifying element of the will-act. The order of end and of means establish distinct psychological moments which are integrated in the unity of the moral act of intention.

will be important deductions in the moral order inferred from the psychological analysis of the moral act. Most of all, from an understanding of the structure of the human act, much light will be thrown upon the difficult problems of subjective and objective morality.

Division: The structure of the human act may be viewed according to its chronological and psychological sequence. It may also be examined according to the moral sequence. First, we shall recall the essential facts derived from the psychological analysis of freedom already studied in the philosophy of man. Secondly, we shall propose the moral sequence of the human act. Thirdly, we shall briefly outline various moral problems whose solutions depend upon this analysis.

ARTICLE I: The Psychological Structure of the Human Act

Unity of Moral Act: We should never lose sight of the existential unit, the rational supposit, we call man. "Actions belong to supposits." Not the intellect, not the will, but *man* acts; he acts by means of intellect and will. Likewise, the cutting-up, the dissecting of the psychological process into distinct parts should never make us forget the unity of the moral act. I see a certain object; I love it; I want it; I choose what appears to be the most apt means; I proceed to get the object. I reach it; I enjoy its possession. The operations of intellect and will in such a process are obviously successive and distinct. The morality of the act, however, is one, for this unity of the moral act is due to the intention of the will which directs and unifies all the resulting operations of intellect and will by its efficient dynamism.[5] The moral act which embraces such a complicated psychological sequence has real unity. It is the unity of intention of the will to its proximate end.

Dual Causality, Specification and Exercise: Because the moral order is the order of the will to the end, it presupposes the order

---

[5] "The intention is related to either (internal and external act) somewhat as the form" (*S. Th.,* I–II, 19, 8). "The intention looks to the end in this manner, that the end is considered as the term toward which something else is ordered . . . we intend (to attain the end) by means of something else" (*S. Th.,* I–II, 12, 1, ad 4ᵐ).

of knowledge. For the end cannot be desired unless it be known. The freedom of man is a freedom of judgment and choice. The reason is that the specification of the act of the will, its *formal* determination, is from the intellect. The will, of course, is the *efficient* principle of the free act, since not only does it elicit the act of choice, but it directs as well the operation of the intellect in forming the judgment necessary for the specification of choice. We should, therefore, speak of mutual, simultaneous causality, comparable only to that of form and matter. The resulting inference from this is that man enjoys a freedom of judgment and choice which he exercises through the interrelated operations of intellect and will, the intellect causing formally (order of specification) and the will causing efficiently (order of exercise) the free act of choice.

N.B.: When we speak of judgment, and especially of moral judgment, and of judgment of truth, we do not mean a logical composing or dividing, but an estimation, a judging of values whether ontological or moral. In this wise does St. Thomas use the terms *judgment* ("iudicium") and *to judge* ("iudicare"); never, to my knowledge, does he refer such words exclusively to a logical composition and division. Rather, he speaks of enunciations, of proportions, of subject and predicate. Likewise, the words *to apprehend* and *apprehension* are not to be taken according to their more modern logical content of simple apprehension. In the writings of the Angelic Doctor, these terms, *"apprehendere"* and *"apprehensio,"* as well as *"iudicium"* and *"iudicare,"* usually signify a moral or ontological or an epistemological estimation, a judging of objective values whether ontological or moral. It is in this manner that the sense faculty of knowledge in man, and in an irrational animal, judges in some manner of the nature and existence of an object in a judgment of experience. It is in this way that the very first moral apprehension by the intellect of a good which is the end implies a judging of its moral value, that is, of its objective morality.[6] Following St. Thomas' mode of

---

[6] We shall learn later that this first moral apprehension of a good, which is the proximate end of the will-act, presupposes a judgment of the norm and a judgment of conscience.

expression, we shall limit our usage of the terms *judgment, judging, apprehend* to an estimation of ontological and especially of moral value. As regards the logical composition and division of subject and predicate, we think it better, in order to avoid unnecessary confusion, to speak of "enunciation," and of the intellect logically "composing and dividing."[7]

Analysis of Psychological Sequence: In the interrelated series of intellectual and volitional operations, which we term the moral act, we discover three psychological stages during which the will is concerned (1) with the end, (2) with the means, and (3) with the execution. In each of these moments we find various operations of the will and intellect moving each other efficiently and formally. The intellect moves the will in the order of specification by presenting the good to be loved; the will moves the intellect in the order of exercise by directing it to focus upon this or that object, or on this or that aspect of the same object. The free act resulting from this mutual causality of interaction is "materially the act of the will and formally the act of the intellect."[8] It is, therefore, in the will as in a subject, but the formal specification is from the intellect as efficiently directed by a previous or by an accompanying act of the will.

1. Order of the End: The first operation is always one of the

---

[7] We grant that a moral and an ontological judgment will be expressed by a composition or a division. This mode of expressing a moral and an ontological judgment is necessary for organizing our knowledge and communicating ideas. The actual judging, however, by the intellect of a moral or ontological value is not a formal and explicit relation of predicate to subject; it is not a logical composition or division; it is an apprehension of reality and is psychologically a simple act of knowledge. By *simple* we do not mean to exclude the distinct elements necessary for such an operation. Ontologically, the act of understanding ("intelligere," the "to understand") presupposes a distinct intelligible species and terminates in a distinct "word" (*verbum*). Morally, such an act must be preceded by a judgment of the norm and accompanied by a judgment of conscience. It is regrettable that the now common use of the terms *judgment* and *apprehension* in the logical sense has confused many issues and not only made it extremely difficult to interpret St. Thomas properly, but has led some to believe that a moral, as well as an ontological, judgment could not be had without a logical composition and division.

[8] *S. Th.,* I–II, 13, 1, *c.*

intellect. We must know before we are able to love.[9] The intellect first apprehends[10] the good and presents it to the will. This particular good is the object of the will-act, its proximate end. The act of the will, volition, which follows the apprehension of the good and is specified by it, is a free act. The reason is that the apprehension of the intellect is really a judging of values, an estimation of the morality of the object. Now the will can never be necessitated to a particular good whenever this object is an end and not a means.[11] Consequently, the will-act is not necessarily determined, that is to say, specified by this end which has been examined and judged in the intellectual apprehension. This free act is the first moment of the moral process. It is the act of volition (*velle*), the "to will."[12]

Following this act of volition, the intellect, now under the efficacious influence of the will, considers this good as attainable or not

---

[9] There is no question here of speculative knowledge, which is concerned with the true, but of the practical knowledge of the good. Only under the formality of good can the intellect move the will to action. "The knowledge of the true does not move the appetite unless viewed as good and desirable" (*S. Th.*, I–II, 9, 1, ad 2[m]). Recall the distinction between the speculative and practical intellect. (Cf. *The Philosophy of Man,* p. 131 ff.)

[10] The terms *apprehend* and *apprehension* do not signify a logical simple apprehension which has no direct connection with a real object; they mean a judging of moral and ontological values. Hence, when the intellect apprehends the moral good, it understands and judges, at least in a general manner, its objective morality. This process generally implies some reflection and deliberation.

[11] According to St. Thomas the will can sometimes be necessitated to a particular good by what he calls the necessity of the end. This merely signifies that when an end has been freely willed, if there is only one possible means by which we can attain the end, then the means is willed necessarily (*ex necessitate finis*). (Cf. *S. Th.,* I, 82, 1.)

[12] Scholastic writers speak of certain necessary motions of the appetite (*actus primo primi*) which sometimes precede the moral free act and may even influence its morality. These are the spontaneous acts of the sense appetites; they are called passions and emotions. These passions, in the ordinary process of knowledge, are caused directly by sense knowledge and generally precede the intellectual apprehension. Such spontaneous reactions are not free, since the necessitating object of the sense appetite is the particular good. Hence, they are not moral acts, but they often affect the morality of the will-act by coloring the phantasm from which the intellectual apprehension, the judgment of reason is obtained.

attainable.[13] The intellect then forms a judgment in which it proposes to the will the end as attainable.[14] Thereupon follows the act of the will called *intention*. "Intention is an act of the will in relation to the end."[15] This operation which is specified by the knowledge of the end as attainable is a free act. Should there be only one possible means, the process of the elicited moral act is terminated. The reason is that in willing the end this means is necessarily willed (*ex necessitate finis*). The intention in such a case is identical with the act of choice, and the order of execution immediately follows.

2. **Order of the Means:** Let us suppose that there are various means by which this good may be attained. In this case a consideration or deliberation as to what may be the most apt means must follow. Moved by the *intention,* the intellect in an operation called *counsel* envisages the various means. To this operation, which may require a number of distinct correlated acts of intellect and will, the will consents in a general way and urges the intellect to reflect, to consider, and to deliberate. This the will does by directing (efficient causality) the intellect to consider the good discovered in this or that particular means. This act is called *consent*. The intellect, then, under the efficient direction of the will forms a *practical judgment,* that is, a judgment which looks to action and resolves itself into a sort of precept[16] (*ratio praeceptiva*). This is the judgment which,

---

13 The will may also direct the intellect (order of exercise) to remain in the contemplation of this particular object. This, we shall see, is called a moral act of thought.

14 Should the end be proposed as not attainable, the will does not intend such a good. The moral act is thus terminated.

15 *S. Th.,* I–II, 12, 1, ad 4[m]. In the intention, in willing the end as attainable we implicitly will the means. "The intention of the end, and the willing the means are one and the same motion" (*ibid.,* article 4, *sed contra*).

16 We should note that the various operations of the intellect considered thus far lie in the practical order, the order of action, of practical reason. They become more so (that is, operations of the practical, not of the speculative intellect) as they approach choice. This explains why the virtue of prudence, which is a habit of the practical intellect, is formed and developed by the operations called counsel, practical judgment, and most of all, by the act of precept, whenever these operations are proportioned to right reason. It should be added that the third operation, that of precept (*ratio praeceptiva*), is the proper act of prudence.

being freely evolved under the influence of the will (order of exercise), determines, that is, specifies the free act of *choice* which follows immediately. Choice, then, is the free act *par excellence;*[17] it completes the *elicited* human act.

3. **Order of Execution:** We have now reached the order of the *commanded* human acts, that is, the placing of action by other faculties which are under the control of reason. Moved efficiently by the act of choice, the intellect issues a command to the will to direct to action the various faculties and members whose operations are needed for the attainment of the end. This is the *imperium* or command. The command by the intellect determines (order of specification) the will, which is the supreme cause in the order of exercise, to move the various members to action. This act of the will which moves other faculties and members to operation is called *use.*[18]

Finally, once we have attained the good desired, the intellect understands this fact and presents to the will the knowledge of the possession of the good. This knowledge is an intellectual possession of the end which we call happiness.[19] This judgment of possession determines the will specifically to the act of *fruition* which is the delight resulting from happiness. The last act of the will, therefore, is concerned with the end, nor with the means. For the delight, which is fruition, is the property of the possessed good.[20]

---

[17] We do not mean to deny that volition, intention, as well as consent, are free. The point we wish to make is that the act of choice manifests more completely to us the nature of freedom.

[18] The *imperium* or command is by no means identical with the precept (*ratio praeceptiva*). They are two distinct acts. The precept occurs just before the act of choice and specifies it. Precept follows immediately the practical judgment, and, although a distinct act, it is, as it were, a sort of resolution from the "this ought to be done" to the "do it." On the other hand, the command or *imperium* generally takes place after choice since it specifies the act of the will called *use*.

[19] The possession of a created good when subordinated to the last end is true happiness but only imperfect and incomplete. When such possession is not properly related to the last end, it is a false happiness.

[20] Fruition of the will is the property of the intellectual knowledge of the possession of the end. Hence, fruition *necessarily* results from this knowledge. It should be noted also that some delight, some imperfect fruition, may be had at every stage of a good moral act even when the act is immediately concerned

The following diagram may help us to visualize the psychological process of the moral act.

ORDER OF THE END

Intellect: Specification, formal causality.

Will: Exercise, efficient causality.

1. *Knowledge* of the good; a judging of objective morality.

2. *Volition* of the good. Either man
   1) wills to remain in contemplation of the good, or the will
   2) moves the intellect to form a judgment of the good as "attainable."

3. *Judgment* of the good as attainable.

4. *Intention:* I will the end. (Motion of will to end as term of means.)

ORDER OF MEANS

5. *Counsel:* a consideration of the various means.

6. A general *consent* to the means *in globo*. This act influences the following practical judgment.

7. *Practical Judgment:* One definite means is proposed as more suitable. This practical judgment resolves into a distinct act, the precept (*ratio praeceptiva*), "do this."

8. *Choice:* I freely will this means to the end. This is the completion of the elicited act.

---

with the means, and not with the end. For any action of life, because it is a reality, is a good. Moreover, because it is immanent, a vital action is an ontological perfection of the agent, and therefore it is possessed by the agent. Hence, some delight, some imperfect fruition, may accompany the knowledge of the possession of the good even when imperfect.

Order of Execution

Commanded Acts

9. *Command or Imperium:* The intellect issues a command (specification) to the will to move to action the proper faculties.

10. *Use:* The will moves the other powers of man to action.

11. *Judgment* of actual possession of the good.

12. *Fruition:*[21] Delight floods the soul as a result of this intellectual knowledge of the possession of the good.

N.B.: This order need not be adhered to rigidly in all human acts. The intention, as we have already indicated, is sometimes identical with the act of choice when there is only one possible means. It may also happen that the moral act does not go beyond the consideration and acceptance of a thought. In such a case, consent and fruition may take place after the first volition; in such a moral act there is no intention. Again, Aquinas explains[22] that a certain kind of use may precede choice, as, for example, when the will moves the intellect to consider one means rather than another.

Moreover, the interrelated operations of intellect and will which occur in the various orders of end, means, and execution may be indefinitely multiplied according to person, place, and object.[23] In spite of these various complications, the unity of the human act remains undisturbed because of the virtue of the intention which, in its reaching out to the end, unites all the successive psychological moments into the oneness of a moral act. Should this process be interrupted so that the intention is withdrawn or changed to an-

---

[21] Note that the act called fruition is not a commanded act, but results from knowledge of the possession of the good, for it is the property of intellectual possession. Not only may it occur after and as resulting from a commanded act, but even after an elicited act of thought and desire, for some possession of the good can be had in hope and in memory.

[22] *S. Th.,* I–II, 17, 3, *c.*

[23] This is especially true of counsel and consent.

other end, the renewal of the process either by a different intention or by reactuating the first would constitute a new moral act.

ARTICLE II: The Moral Sequence of the Human Act

In his analysis of the process of the moral act, an analysis which occurs in the *Prima Secundae,* questions VIII through XVII, St. Thomas follows a sequence which at first may seem puzzling. Instead of the psychological process just explained in the preceding article, instead of the chronological sequence of end, means, and execution, St. Thomas, first of all, groups together the acts of the will which look directly to the end. The reason, no doubt, for such grouping is that the Angelic Doctor is endeavoring to propose a solution to the problem of morality, not to the psychological problem of freedom. Hence, because the specification of the will-act is from the proximate end, St. Thomas is primarily concerned with those acts of the will which result from the direct knowledge of the end. Now the end is presented directly to the will by the intellect, either as *desirable,* as *attainable,* or as *possessed.* From these three types of knowledge of the end result three acts of the will: *volition, intention,* and *fruition.* Psychologically, the act of fruition is the last moment,[24] the terminus of the process. St. Thomas accords it second place in his arrangement. The first operation which he studies is volition; the second, fruition. Why such disregard for the natural sequence of the psychological process? The reason, no doubt, is that we are not dealing with a psychological, but with a moral problem. Now the moral act begins with volition, ends with fruition, and is formally made a unit by the intention. In this manner, by bracketing, as it were, the moral order between the two extreme acts of the will and by emphasizing the dynamism of the intention, St. Thomas approaches the moral problem from a purely moral point of view. He indicates that all the other operations occurring in this process belong to the moral act because they are found between volition and fruition and are

---

[24] Perfect fruition results from the possession of the last end. Hence, it is chronologically the last act. Imperfect fruition may occur after any act of the psychological process, even after volition.

subject to the unifying dynamism of the intention. Another reason for considering fruition immediately after volition is that in a moral act of thought, in which the contemplation of an object by the intellect is voluntary, the act of fruition accompanies and follows volition.

Division: There are two parts to the analysis of the moral sequence of the human act found in questions VIII to XVIII in the *Prima Secundae:* first, the elicited acts; then, the commanded acts.

I. Elicited Acts

First, we consider the elicited acts which are ordered directly to the end; secondly, the elicited acts which look primarily to the means. There are three acts of the will in the first class: volition, fruition, and intention; and there are three in the second: choice, consent, and use.

A. *Regarding the End*

1. Volition: St. Thomas here unfolds a general treatise of the will as willing, indicating the various reasons for motivation, determination, or the lack of it. Much of this has been presented in the treatise on the will.[25] Let us add one remark regarding the relation of this act of volition to the good. The first motion of any appetite is to the good, since the good is the object of the appetite. Hence, the first act of volition is to the good as known and presented by the intellect. It follows that the turning away from an evil, which is also an act of the will, can never be the first "to will," but a "to will not." Such a "to will not" supposes a previous act of volition to the good.

2. Fruition: Fruition pertains to the moral act; it terminates it. Hence, in a strict sense, perfect fruition is not found in brute animals.[26] No complete fruition is had in the accomplishment of the

---

[25] Cf. *The Philosophy of Man,* p. 186 ff.

[26] Fruition in itself is not a free act, since it is a property of the possession of the good. That is why St. Thomas explains that imperfect fruition is found in irrational animals. In man, however, fruition belongs to the moral act; it is voluntary in its cause (*in causa*), for the intellectual knowledge of the possession of the end, which is its specifying element, is under the control of a previous free act of the will.

means; and, of course, in the order of intention, fruition which results from hope is not absolute, but incomplete.[27] Absolute fruition is only had as a result of the possession of the last end.

3. **Intention:** Intention looks to the end, not absolutely as volition, nor in so far as we rest in its possession as in fruition, but "it looks to the end according as the end is the term of something which is ordered to it."[28] The end here is not the last end, but the end of the will-act. The intention, therefore, establishes the unity of the moral act; it orders the means to the proximate end. Hence, in a complete moral act which comprises not only the internal acts of the will, but the external execution as well, the intention is the most important element in the moral process, for it is the directive (efficient causality) of all the operations which follow. The intention is the reason for the unity of the moral act and for its vital dynamism.

B. *Regarding the Means*

1. **Choice:** In this second stage of the moral act, St. Thomas studies not only the operations of the will, but because of their importance in the process of deliberation, he analyzes those of the intellect as well. The sequence, however, which he proposes is not at all psychological, but moral. He begins with a lengthy treatise on choice which, chronologically, is the last operation in the series of acts ordered to the means. The reason is that choice is the most important operation in the order of the means, but not absolutely. For choice belongs to the moral order primarily because of the virtue of the intention.

2. **Counsel:** Counsel is an act of the intellect; it is an inquiry into the various means. Its moral constitutive element is formed under the influence of the intention. It should be noted that when counsel is directed in accordance with right reason, it becomes the first act of the virtue of prudence. This virtue, we know, is the regulator of all the moral virtues and of their actions. Its first operation, which is counsel, is a deliberation regarding the means. It

---

[27] *S. Th.*, I–II, 11, 4, ad 1[m].
[28] *S. Th.*, I–II, 12, 2, ad 4[m].

is an imperfect act and seeks to perfect itself by resolving itself in a judgment of that which is directed to the fulfillment of the intention to the end. St. Thomas remarks that counsel proceeds by way of resolution, indicating, thereby, that under the impetus of consent, the intellect will form a practical judgment looking to action, a judgment which will finally terminate in the act called precept.[29]

3. **Consent:** Simultaneous with and specified by counsel is the consent of the will, directing the intellect to form a practical judgment of what is better for the attainment of the end. This judgment is, of course, the act of the intellect, and if formed in accordance with right reason, it may be considered as the second act of the virtue of prudence, that is, judging what should be done because better for the attainment of the last end. From this judgment of what should be done and under the influence of the will, the intellect now forms a sort of precept: "Do this." This precept, when issued according to reason, is the third and most perfect act of prudence. The precept, therefore, is not an act of the will, but of the practical intellect, for it looks immediately to the specification of the will-act. Precept is the specifying cause of choice; it is followed, or rather accompanied, by choice.

4. **Use:** Curiously enough, St. Thomas places use as the last of the elicited acts. Use is the act of the will efficiently moving the other faculties of man to action. Hence, it is generally thought to be a commanded act. The truth of the matter is that use is found at every stage, at every psychological moment of the process, except at the initial act of knowledge of the end. For as regards all the other acts of the intellect, the will must move the intellect efficiently throughout the entire process. This efficient directing of the intellect by the will is the operation called *use*. Hence, use is found in every stage of the psychological process. It is, therefore, of vital importance in the moral act. For should the will cease to move the intellect at any point, the moral act would come to a stop at that very moment.

---

[29] The act called precept (*ratio praeceptiva*) is an act of the intellect distinct from the practical judgment. Its function is to specify the will-act called choice.

Choice precedes use if they are referred to the same thing. But nothing prohibits that the use of one should precede the choice of another. And because the acts of the will react on one another, *in any act of the will* can be found *consent, choice,* and *use;* so that it may be said that the will consents to choose and consents to consent and uses itself for consenting and choosing. And always those acts ordered to that which is prior are prior.[30]

II. COMMANDED ACTS

Command (*Imperium*): St. Thomas mentions two operations: one directly, command, and the other only indirectly, use. Command is an act of the intellect which follows choice. It presupposes, therefore, an act of the will and takes place only in virtue of that act. It is an intellectual operation, because an order has to be expressed intellectually before it can be promulgated and executed. The command of the intellect is primarily to the will (order of specification) which is the first moving power (order of exercise) of all the members and faculties of man.

It should be noted that a form of command occurs both before and after choice. The act of command which takes place before choice is called precept (*ratio praeceptiva*), and when in accord with reason such a precept belongs to prudence. Here, however, we are considering rather the command which follows choice and depends upon it. St. Thomas calls it the command or *"imperium"* to distinguish it from the precept. The *"imperium"* results from the elicited act. This act of command is really the formal aspect, the specification of the act called *use* which moves the members to operation. For there is a use of that which is to the end. Such an act is a commanded act of use.[31]

Such then is the moral structure of the human act. In this sequence the operations of the will to the end are supreme in their importance. For the human act is established by this, that the will

---

[30] *S. Th.,* I–II, 16, 4, ad 3^m. This text is extremely important. It indicates why and how a completed moral act may be had at any moment of the psychological process.

[31] ". . . the use of that which is for the end, in so far as it is subject to the executive power, follows command . . . " (*S. Th.,* I–II, 17, 3, *c*).

freely places itself in the order of morality by a deliberate volition, controls the entire process by the act of intention, and terminates and fulfills the cycle of this order by fruition, which is the rest of the will in the end possessed. The human act, although it is a series of elicited and commanded operations which are distinct psychological moments, possesses a real unity in the moral order.[32]

ARTICLE III: Inferences From the Analysis of the Moral Act

Let us, by way of summary, restate some inferences which can be obtained from the analysis of the moral act.

1. **Numerical Distinction Between Moral Acts:** From this analysis we learn, in the first place, the supreme importance of the intention. It is, we remember, the unifying bond of the various stages of the human act. Consequently, in determining the number of moral actions, whether good or evil, we depend upon the singleness of intention. If the intention actually remains unchanged, the moral act is one, no matter how long and complicated be the series of interrelated operations of intellect and will. If, on the contrary, the intention is broken either because of an interruption which breaks the continuity of its influence or because of a change of direction to another end, the moral act is complete, and a new and distinct human act begins. An example will clarify this point. Should one begin to distribute alms to the poor in order to display his liberality out of vanity and in the midst of this distribution change the direction of his intention so that he now continues to give alms for the love of God and neighbor, he is responsible for two distinct moral acts, one evil and one good. Moreover, should

---

[32] "However, just as in the genus of natural things some whole is composed of matter and form (as man, who is one natural being, although he has many parts, is composed of body and soul), so also in human acts the act of a lower power is related as matter to the act of a higher power, in so far as the lower power acts in virtue of the higher power moving it; and so also the act of the first mover is related as form to the act of the instrument. Hence, it is clear that command and the commanded act are one human act, as any whole is one, but is many according to its parts" (S. Th., I–II, 17, 4, c).

he renew his first evil intention, not the same identical moral action, but a new and distinct human act begins. Clearly, the intention is of supreme importance in the moral act.

2. **Where Do the Various Types of Moral Actions Belong in the Psychological Process?** From our analysis we can also gather the reason for the distinction between moral acts of thought, of desire, and of external action. The third type, external action, presents no difficulty. They are commanded actions and are in the order of execution. Concerning moral acts of thought, we ask to what moment in the series of operations do they belong? Moral acts of thought take place immediately with volition. For volition can freely move the intellect to a continued contemplation of the object viewed as good. It is clear that any human act supposes free consent. St. Thomas explains that there could be a consent with volition, that is, an acceptance of the goodness or malice found in the contemplation of the thought without the will intending the good as attainable.[33] The imperfect fruition which may accompany and follow this consent terminates the series necessary for a human act. This act then is complete. There is no intention in the will, since no means is intended. Finally, acts of desire are either perfect or imperfect. An act of imperfect desire presupposes an intention which is inefficacious as regards placing the external act. A perfect act of desire is had when the external action is not placed solely because of impeding extrinsic causes and not because of the weakness of intention.

3. **The Place of Prudence in the Moral Act:** From the first deliberate act of volition to the final fruition, the entire process of the moral act belongs to practical, not to speculative, reason. This important fact results from the formal causality of intellect upon will, which causality is found at every moment of the process. There is no speculative contemplation of truth in the process of the moral act;[34] it is strictly an order of action which evolves and resolves

---

[33] "In any act of the *will* can be found consent, choice, use" (*S. Th.*, I–II, 16, 4, ad 3^m).

[34] Even in the moral act of thought, the acts of the will called volition and consent are in the order of action; they are related directly to the last end.

itself into a real command and terminates in fruition. The realm of morality is the order of doing, the order of action of a deliberate will which seeks the good. It is, therefore, the order of practical reason to the good, not in mere making, but in freely doing. That is why the intellectual habit, which develops when the various operations of the psychological process are proportioned to the nature of man as rational, is not the speculative virtue of wisdom nor the habit of science, but the practical virtue of prudence. The acts of that virtue, the regulator of all moral virtues, will be elicited if we intend, consent, and choose in accordance with right reason. For prudence is the true knowledge of things to be done. The first act of prudence, then, as we have noted, will be counsel, that is, a deliberation in accordance with right reason; the second, the practical judgment, "This is the best means to the end; it should be done"; the third, the most perfect, is, we might say, a continuation, an evolution, a resolution of this practical judgment into a precept: "Do it." Then follows the act of choice, the term of the elicited act.

4. **Framing a Human Law:**[35] From the above we may infer a basis, not for the natural law, but for the correct framing of human law. In no way does the natural law depend upon the analysis of the moral act, for "the natural law is the participation of the eternal law in the rational creature."[36] The following, however, is true. Having discovered the natural law, whose fundamental expression is right reason, the civil legislator is able, by means of a process analogous to that of a good human act, to establish good and useful laws for the commonwealth. Law is the rule of action and is defined by Aquinas as an *ordinance, a command of reason;* for law is a reasonable command and not a blind arbitrary whim of the lawmaker. Consequently, a law which is opposed to right reason is no true law. No one should observe it, since it is unreasonable.

Correct framing of human law can be shown to be analogously similar to the psychological sequence of the good human act in this

---

[35] Cf. Lottin, Dom Odon, *Principes de Morale* (Louvain), Vol. I, p. 72.

[36] *"Participatio legis aeternae in rationali creatura lex naturalis dicitur"* (*S. Th.,* I–II, 91, 2).

wise: Law, first of all, is founded on the knowledge and love of the common good. Hence, it should be specified by reason, for the common good is the good of human nature. Such an eminently reasonable good, because attainable, is sought as the end by the intention. In order to attain it, the means will be considered, deliberated upon. Now, in order that these means may be apt to an end which is the common good, they should be specified in accord with right reason. Following our analysis of the human act, the reasonable means which are deliberated upon in the act of counsel will be determined in the practical judgment, willed by choice, and promulgated by the operation of the intellect called command. A law, therefore, framed in this fashion cannot be an arbitrary directive of the will. It is a command of reason for the common good, promulgated by the law maker.

5. **Morality of the Act:** Finally, this analysis lays a foundation for the solution of the problem of the morality of the human act in this manner: (1) It establishes clearly the distinction between internal and external acts. (2) It indicates that the object which specifies the internal act of the will is the good as known, not necessarily as it exists. (3) This fact will help us understand why internal acts are always voluntary and therefore imputable to their authors. (4) This discussion, then, will pave the way for a solution to the problem of voluntariness.

These are a few of the immediate inferences resulting from the analysis of the moral act.

SUMMARY

Our discussion of the moral act in THE PHILOSOPHY OF MORALITY is largely on the essential plane. The inferences as regards the objective and subjective morality of the act will be drawn from an essential reflection upon human nature as such. Hence our conclusions although true are not complete because man's present existential state is not examined.

Question I

STRUCTURE OF THE MORAL ACT

Article I: *Psychological Structure*

Unity of the moral act. The intention unifies the various psychological moments.

A twofold causality enters into the formation of a moral act: specification by intellect, efficiency of will. Man acts morally by means of intellect and will.

Moral judgment must precede and accompany the act of will. The words judgment and apprehension signify moral estimation; they do not mean logical composition or division of subject and predicate.

Analysis of psychological structure: see diagram on pages 69–70.

Article II: *Moral Sequence*

Extreme importance of acts of will which are directly connected with the end: volition, intention, fruition.

Analysis:
1. Elicited acts
   Looking directly to end — volition, intention, fruition
   Looking to means — choice (counsel), consent, use
2. Commanded act — command

Article III: *Inferences from Analysis*

1. Numerical distinction between acts depends on intention
2. Various types of moral acts:
   Thought — depends on volition
   Desire — intention is necessary
   External act — order of execution
3. Place of prudence — the acts of prudence occur before choice. The third act, precept, specifies choice.
4. Framing of human law should be effected by a process similar (analogously) to that of the good moral act.
5. A foundation for solution of problems of objective and subjective morality.

Question II

SUBJECTIVE[37] MORALITY OF THE HUMAN ACT OR VOLUNTARINESS

Prologue

The Problem: The morality of the human act may be examined from two points of view: the subjective aspect and the objective. Objective morality consists in the goodness or malice of a moral act in itself. This objective morality depends principally and primarily upon the object of the act, for the object is like a formal cause and therefore specifies the operation. The second aspect of morality may be called subjective. It looks not to the morality of the act in its objective determination, but to its imputability; that is to say, it inquires into the reason why the objective morality of the act may or may not be ascribed to its author. To impute, that is, to charge or credit someone with the responsibility, the guilt or merit of such an action, is an extrinsic denomination, an attribution from without. Such attribution of guilt or merit to be true must be based on an intrinsic reality in the subject. The philosopher wants to know what this reality is. The answer is *voluntariness*.

We shall devote this question to a search after a clear understanding of this psychological reality, voluntariness, which is the true reason why merit or guilt is incurred in placing a human act. There will be two articles: (1) What is voluntariness? (2) What are the factors which may impede voluntariness?

---

[37] St. Thomas does not use this term. His point is that human acts are human, that is, moral, because voluntary. (Cf. *S. Th.,* I–II, 6, *Proemium.*) Then he inquires into the meaning of voluntariness. The words *objective* and *subjective* are used throughout this treatise in their ordinary English meaning: *objective* morality, that is, the goodness or evil of the act in itself; *subjective* morality, that is, the intrinsic reason in the subject for the imputation of the goodness or malice of the act to the individual subject who placed the act.

ARTICLE I: What Is Voluntariness?

Before attacking the problem of voluntariness directly, it is necessary to propose some fundamental notions regarding the objective morality, that is, the goodness or malice, of the human act. Ordinarily, the human act is composed of internal and external act. Moral union results from the singleness of the act of the will, the intention, which controls, directs, and unites the external operation with the internal act. We distinguish sharply, therefore, the two components: the internal act of the will and the external act.

Objective Morality: The objective morality of an act is the goodness or the malice of the act in itself. In general the determining factors of this objective morality of the human act are three: object, end, and circumstances as referred to a rational active principle. The object, namely, that which terminates the operation, e.g., killing an innocent man, specifies the action; that is to say, the object makes it be that kind of an action, to wit, a murder. The end is the reason for seeking the external object, e.g., killing a man in order to rob him. The circumstances are the particular conditions of the object, e.g., the man I killed is my father. A circumstance, therefore, is a further determination of the object; it supposes the object and individuates it. Object, end, and circumstances are the causes of the goodness or malice of the human act. They determine its objective morality.

Internal and External Act: We should note, however, that the way in which these three factors determine the goodness and malice of the internal and of the external act varies profoundly. The object of the external act is the reality produced by the act: the killing, the giving of alms. It is distinct in its determination from end and from circumstances. On the other hand, the object of the internal act is the good as known and desired. Hence, it is the end and includes the external object and circumstances as known. These distinctions will be very helpful in solving our problem of voluntariness.

What Is Voluntariness? Moralists generally insist that the objective morality of an action, its goodness or its malice, is attributed, or imputed, to the subject of the operation because the act is voluntary.[38] Voluntariness is an intrinsic reality in the subject of the act because of which the objective morality of the act is imputed to its author. Because of voluntariness man becomes worthy of praise or of blame. A voluntary act, therefore, is meritorious or demeritorious. We ask what is the most fundamental reason for this imputation, for this merit or guilt?

Not Identical With Freedom: At first one might be inclined to identify voluntariness with freedom and to think that because an act is free it must be voluntary. This is not always the case, for I could kill a man freely, thinking in good faith but erroneously that he wants to kill me. Such an objectively evil act is free but certainly not imputable and therefore not voluntary. It is true that a voluntary act in this life is always free.[39] But not every free act is imputable as we know from experience and observation. A concrete example will not only manifest this distinction, but it will help us visualize the problem of voluntariness and formulate its true definition.

Problem Exemplified: The boy Peter picks someone's pocket. In the first instance, he does it because he wants to steal. In the second instance, he steals because he has been ordered to do so by his father whose punishment he fears should he fail to obey. In the

---

[38] The term *voluntary* is derived from the Latin *voluntas,* which signifies the will. Actions which are called voluntary must proceed from the will. We shall see, however, that every action which proceeds from the will is not necessarily voluntary. For a voluntary act is not only one which proceeds from an intrinsic principle, the will, but one which presupposes a perfect knowledge of the end.

[39] A voluntary act is always a free act in this life, because the will-act can never be necessitated to a particular good which on this earth is always its proximate end-object. There can be no necessary acts of the will in this life because the object-end of the will-act must always be presented as a particular good. The natural inclination to the supreme good, however, is nature itself tending to the end. Consequently, in the next life the act by which man loves the supreme good as intellectually possessed in the attainment of the last end is a voluntary and necessary act; it is not free. It is voluntary because it flows from the will with perfect knowledge. It is a necessary act because the will is necessitated to the absolute good. Voluntariness is not freedom.

third case, Peter, *erroneously* thinking that he recognizes his pocket-book, wants to recover his lost or stolen property.

Obviously, the imputability of the objective morality of the external act of theft will vary in each of the examples given. In the first case, the boy is simply guilty of stealing. In the second instance, there is some doubt as to his culpability because of the fear which may impede the voluntariness of his action. In the third occurrence, Peter is clearly not guilty; the objective morality of the effect cannot be ascribed to him.

Reason for Imputability: Although the effect is objectively the same, namely, taking something which does not belong to him, the objective morality of the action cannot be attributed uniformly to Peter. Now evidently the reason for such difference in the imputability of the act results from the disposition, the inclination, of the will to the external effect. To the question, then, as to what is the most profound reason for ascribing the objective morality of an external effect to its author, we answer that the *will's proper inclination* toward the external effect is the true foundation for such imputability. This proper inclination of the will to the object willed is what we call voluntariness. In order, therefore, that "the human acts be meritorious or demeritorious, it is necessary that they be voluntary."[40] They are voluntary because of the will's proper inclination to the effect placed.

Definition: *Voluntariness is the proper inclination of the will to the act.* "Voluntariness," explains the Angelic Doctor, "implies that the motion and act are from the proper inclination (of the will)." "A voluntary (action) is that which is in accordance with the inclination of the will." "Something is voluntary because the will is borne toward it."[41]

Conditions Necessary for Voluntariness: If voluntariness is the proper inclination of the will to the effect, we ask what are the

---

[40] *S. Th.,* I–II, 7, 2, *c.*

[41] ". . . *hoc autem importat nomen voluntarii quod motus et actus sit a propria inclinatione*" (*S. Th.,* I–II, 6, 1, *c*). ". . . *voluntarium dicitur quod est secundum inclinationem voluntatis*" (I–II, 6, 5, ad 2ᵐ). "*Dicitur enim aliquid voluntarium ex eo quod voluntas in id fertur*" (I–II, 6, 7, *c*).

conditions required for such an inclination?[42] St. Thomas mentions two essential conditions: first, the act must flow from an intrinsic principle, the will; secondly, a true and perfect knowledge of the end is necessary.[43]

The first requisite needs no explanation. A voluntary act proceeds from the intrinsic principle called the will which is the rational appetite of man.[44] The second necessary condition is a perfect knowledge of the end. This end is, of course, the proximate end of the act of the will. It is, therefore, the object chosen freely by the will. The perfect knowledge of this end which is necessary for

---

[42] Every action or motion flows from an efficient principle. Sometimes this principle or efficient cause is wholly distinct from, wholly outside of, the thing moved, as when I throw a stone. Sometimes the motion flows from an *intrinsic* principle, as in the case of living beings.

We note, moreover, that since every motion or action is directed or determined to an end, a thing is moved *perfectly* by an *intrinsic* principle when, because of a perfect knowledge of the end, the intrinsic principle moves itself, determines itself to the end. When this takes place, we discover that both the motion and the determination to the end are from an intrinsic principle. Such actions or motions which flow from an intrinsic principle and presuppose this perfect knowledge of the end are called *voluntary actions*. That is why St. Thomas explains that the name voluntariness signifies that the motion, the action, results from the will's proper inclination.

[43] *"Ad rationem voluntarii requiritur quod principium actus sit intra cum cognitione finis"* (S. Th., I–II, 6, 2, c). *"Voluntarium sequitur cognitionem finis"* (*ibid.*).

[44] There can be no voluntariness without some act of the will. Indeed, voluntariness is had even when there is no external effect placed, as for example, I will not-to-do what I should do; in such a case the effect is the foreseen result of the failure to place an external act. There exists an inclination of the will toward such an effect, as for example, "the sinking of the ship because the helmsman refrains from steering." St. Thomas (S. Th., I–II, 6, 3), however, goes farther and states that even when we do not place the interior act of the will, as for example, neither forming a decision to do or not to do, but deliberately remaining undecided when it is clearly our duty to make up our mind, a certain voluntariness exists, and consequently a certain degree of guilt is incurred. The reason is that, in this case, to withhold deliberately our decision is an act of the will, and therefore there is an inclination of the will not to make such a decision. There can be no voluntariness, no merit, no guilt without at least some implicit act of the will, as for example, in a sin of omission. ". . . the cause (even of a sinful omission) in so far as it is voluntary must always include some action, at least the internal act of the will" (S. Th., I–II, 71, 5, c).

voluntariness includes a true knowledge not only of the object, but also of the circumstances, at least of those which have an influx on the objective morality of the act, since these last give the complete determination to the morality of the object. St. Thomas remarks that to possess such a perfect knowledge of the end, we should understand not only the thing itself which is the end, that is, the term of our action, but also its very nature as end, that is, its objective morality. Finally, we should know the moral nature of the means.[45] In other words, perfect knowledge of the end signifies that we must have a knowledge of the *complete objective morality* of the effect produced.

Voluntariness, therefore, supposes two factors: (1) an intrinsic principle from which the voluntary act flows, and (2) a knowledge of the effect that is so perfect as to include circumstances. Hence, something voluntary (*voluntarium*) could also be defined as "that whose principle is in the agent with knowledge of circumstances."[46]

Problem of Voluntariness Regards Only External Act: We note that perfect knowledge is always had as regards the internal act. The reason is that the object or end of the internal act which is the good as known includes the circumstances as known. Hence, *an internal act is always voluntary, always imputable to its author;* the will by its proper inclination is borne toward such an object *as known.* Therefore, the problem of voluntariness, that is to say, whether or not an action is imputable to its author, is raised only as regards the external act. For it may happen that the effect of the external act as placed is not the effect as known and desired. This, however, can never be the case in an internal act, since the object of the act is in the order of knowledge.

Knowledge of Circumstances Necessary: Since the circumstances are the last determining factor of the objective morality, it follows

---

[45] *"Perfecta quidem finis cognitio est quando non solum apprehenditur res quae est finis, sed etiam cognoscitur ratio finis et proportio eius quae ordinatur in finem ad ipsum"* (*S. Th.*, I–II, 6, 2).

[46] *"Voluntarium definitur illud cuius principium est in ipso operante cum scientia circumstantium"* (*In II Phys.*, lect. 1). It is evident that knowledge of circumstances supposes knowledge of end and object.

that whenever a human action flows from an intrinsic principle, the will, and is preceded by knowledge of the circumstances, such an action is voluntary and therefore imputable. This is the meaning of Aquinas' lapidary phrase, "The human act is judged to be voluntary or involuntary according to knowledge or ignorance of circumstances." Again, "Voluntary acts have certain circumstances according to which they are judged to be voluntary."[47] Consequently, complete ignorance of certain circumstances may at times cause involuntariness.[48] This is the case whenever the unknown circumstance is a distinct specifying principle. An example of this is had in the act of playing when one should work. This act, although morally good in its object, becomes an evil act because of the circumstance *when*. In this case ignorance of the circumstance *when* would prevent voluntariness. For, although the act is objectively evil, the inclination of the will because of ignorance of the evil circumstance is not to an evil act. The act as morally evil is not imputable; it is not a voluntary action. Let us examine what these circumstances are, and why the knowledge of extrinsic circumstances should have such a direct effect in determining the degree of guilt or merit of the elicited act.

Enumeration of Circumstances: Following Aristotle's division, St. Thomas enumerates eight distinct circumstances: who, what, where, by what aid, why, how, when, and about what.[49] The most important of all these circumstances is the one which reaches the act from the point of view of the end, the "why." The second in importance is the "what," for it is that which affects directly the effect: What did he do?[50]

Circumstances Considered Moral Accidents: These circumstances as viewed in the moral order should be considered as the individuat-

---

[47] *"Actus humanus iudicatur voluntarius vel involuntarius secundum cognitionem vel ignorantiam circumstantiarum"* (S. Th., I–II, 7, 2, c). *"Actus voluntarii habent quasdam circumstantias secundum quas diiudicantur"* (S. Th., I–II, 6, Proemium).

[48] *"Ignorantia circumstantiarum causat involuntarium"* (S. Th., I–II, 7, 2, sed contra).

[49] Cf. S. Th., I–II, 7, 3, c.

[50] The circumstance "what" gives the last accidental determination to the nature of the object.

ing accidents of the effect. For just as the function of material accidents is to determine, that is, to manifest, the individuation of the
subject as this existing corporeal nature, so do the circumstances in
the realm of morality establish the last determination of the objective morality of the act. The particular conditions of any singular
thing are called its individuating accidents. But the particular conditions of a moral act are the circumstances of that act. Therefore,
the circumstances of a moral objective act are to be considered its
individuating accidents.[51] Consequently, although in the order of
nature these circumstances are often realities distinct from and
existing outside the moral act, nevertheless, in the moral order
they may affect the goodness or malice of the object. According
as they are known or not known by the subject, they affect the
imputability of the moral act.

Necessity of Knowledge of Circumstances for Voluntariness:
Consequently, any factor which impedes the perfect knowledge of
these circumstances may affect voluntariness, that is, the volitional
inclination of the will to the effect, and with it the merit or
guilt imputable to the subject. That is why St. Thomas insists
that voluntariness depends upon the knowledge or the ignorance
of these circumstances. For the circumstances are the last determinant of the objective morality of the object and cannot be known
unless the object is properly known. Hence, if we understand
the circumstances, we possess the perfect knowledge required
for voluntariness.

Voluntariness and Involuntariness: Voluntariness, which is the
proper inclination of the will to the effect, depends (1) on an
intrinsic principle (will) of the action, and (2) on the perfect
knowledge of the effect, that is, the knowledge of the objective
morality of the act. Hence, there can be no voluntariness (1) when
the principle of the action is extrinsic, or (2) when there is a lack
of sufficient knowledge of the objective morality of the act. In
either case the action which results is not a voluntary act, but is
involuntary and therefore not imputable. We may state then that

---

[51] Cf. *S. Th.*, I–II, 7, 1, *sed contra*.

involuntariness is caused by violence (physical coercion) and by invincible ignorance. *Voluntariness,* therefore, signifies volitional inclination toward the effect. *Involuntariness* implies that the effect produced is contrary (repugnant) to the inclination of the will.

Under these two headings — violence, as resulting from an extrinsic principle, and *ignorance,* which is a lack of sufficient knowledge — we may place the various impediments which diminish the voluntariness of the act and even cause it to be involuntary. St. Thomas enumerates four of these: physical coercion, fear, desire (*concupiscentia*), and ignorance. Physical coercion (violence) and fear he places under the heading of extrinsic principles. These two affect voluntariness because the act, instead of flowing from an intrinsic principle, the will, is influenced by an extrinsic principle. On the other hand, the passion of desire and ignorance may imply a lack of sufficient knowledge. It will be noted that fear presents both aspects of involuntariness. It is from an extrinsic principle, but like all passions, it may also cause ignorance, at least indirectly, that is, in so far as it affects the judgment of reason. For this reason we prefer to group all impediments to voluntariness under three headings: (1) physical coercion, (2) passions, and (3) ignorance.

ARTICLE II: Factors Which Affect Voluntariness

1. PHYSICAL COERCION OR VIOLENCE

The first of the factors which may impede voluntariness is violence, that is, physical coercion. Violence is an extrinsic physical force applied to a nature by an extrinsic agent. Violence causes in the subject a change which is opposed to its natural inclination. Consequently, the subject concurs not at all in the change caused by violence. The classical example is that of a stone thrown upward. The motion is caused by an extrinsic principle and is against the natural inclination of the stone.

Violence is directly opposed to voluntariness. (1) It is from an extrinsic principle, while voluntariness flows from an intrinsic principle, the will. (2) Nature in no way co-operates with violence; it is directly against nature and therefore against the will which belongs to the rational nature of man.

Violence does not affect the freedom of the will as regards the elicited act. For, as was shown in the philosophy of man, the will is a natural and intrinsic inclination and therefore cannot be affected by an extrinsic force. Nevertheless, violence can and does affect the external act;[52] it destroys its status of commanded act. Clearly, there can be no voluntariness, no volitional inclination toward an effect caused by violence, since the effect placed is contrary to the will-act. Consequently, the goodness or malice of the effect produced cannot be attributed to the subject, for there is no inclination of the will toward the effect and hence no voluntariness. On the contrary, there is involuntariness, that is to say, the inclination of the will is directly opposed to the effect placed.[53]

2. Passions

In General: Voluntariness may also be affected by the passions. Because of its intensity a passion may, at least indirectly, interfere with the perfect knowledge of end, object, and circumstances, which knowledge is necessary for a voluntary act. Let us explain this statement. Passions are the operations of the sense appetites and are caused by sense knowledge. All passions, when they occur before the consent of the will, are apt to darken the judgment of reason which precedes the free act of the will.[54] In that way, they interfere with the perfect knowledge required for perfect voluntariness. Consequently, passions may diminish the guilt of the act

---

[52] *S. Th.*, I–II, 6, 4, *c.*

[53] It should be noted that whenever an external cause goes against the will's own inclination, should the will reject such an extrinsic influence and produce the effect according to its first voluntariness, the merit or guilt of the act will be greater. This increase results from the greater intensity of the will's inclination which is now necessary to overcome or at least to resist this external influence.

[54] *"Passiones . . . cum obnubilent iudicium rationis, ex quo dependet bonitas moralis actus, diminuunt actus bonitatem . . . "* (*S. Th.*, I–II, 24, 3, ad 1^m). Cf. I–II, 10, 3.

which follows according to the remaining degree of knowledge.[55]
It may even happen at times that the violence of spontaneous
passion completely overwhelms the judgment of reason, so that
a man is at that moment reduced to the state of a brute animal
without reason. In such a case — which, according to St. Thomas,
rarely occurs — there is no act of the will, no freedom, no
human act.

All this is quite obvious. On the other hand, the opposite holds
true as regards a passion which is willed and accepted previous to
the placing of the external act. There is no question here of losing
one's reason or of diminishing the clarity of knowledge, since
the passion is freely willed and is therefore, at least at first, under
the control of reason. Such a passion, explains St. Thomas, increases
the perfection of the moral act.[56] Consequently, it increases the
merit or guilt of the subject.

In order fully to apply these principles, St. Thomas proposes an
analysis of two distinct and opposed types of passions: desire[57]
of good and fear of evil. The reason he chooses these two is that
they exemplify two fundamental attitudes of the sense appetite,
namely, motion toward a good and away from an evil.

Passion of Desire: Now in the analysis of the passion of desire
for a sensible good, the principles discussed are perfectly applicable:
antecedent desire, proportionately to its violence, will diminish
voluntariness because of the darkening of the judgment of reason
which it causes. Consequently, the imputability of the goodness
or evil of the act will be affected by such an antecedent desire
of the good. On the contrary, a *consequent* desire, because accepted,
not only will manifest the perfection of the act of the will by
which it is accepted, but it will cause through the judgment of
reason an increase of the morality of the will-act which follows.
The objective morality of the internal act will thereby be made more

---

[55] Spontaneous passions diminish the *objective* morality of the internal act. They
also diminish the voluntariness (subjective morality) of the external act.

[56] ". . . et sic passio animae addit ad bonitatem actionis" (loc. cit.).

[57] The word used by St. Thomas is *concupiscentia* which should be translated
as desire, not concupiscence. Concupiscence is only one kind of desire.

perfect, and consequently the merit or demerit resulting from the action will be greater.[58]

Fear of an Evil: On the other hand, because an evil as such is feared, never loved by an appetite, it can never be willed, desired, and accepted in the manner of the good. Consequently, although absolutely speaking the act of the will is voluntary, fear does not perfect voluntariness. This may be explained thus: The passion of fear differs from that of desire in this way, that fear refers to an evil, while sense desire refers to a good. But evil in itself is opposed to the natural inclination of the will to the good. Hence, the fear of evil is more apt to go against voluntariness than the sense desire of a good.[59] For that reason, he who acts from fear retains a certain repugnance of the will to that which he does. Indeed, were it not for the fear of an evil, he would not act thus.[60] On the contrary, "one who has accepted the passion of carnal desire does not retain his repugnance to the act. The lustful man acts counter to what he may have first proposed to do, but

---

[58] "Therefore, if passion is considered according as it precedes the act of sin, so it must diminish the sin; for an act is a sin in so far as it is voluntary and is existing in us. Something is said to be in us through reason and will; wherefore, in the degree that reason and will act of themselves and not through the impulse of passion, the greater is voluntariness and the more it is in us (*et in nobis existens*). Accordingly, *passion diminishes sin in so far as it diminishes voluntariness.* Consequent passion, however, does not diminish sin but rather increases it; or better, it is a sign of its greatness in so far as it shows the intensity of the will toward the act of sin. And so it is true that the greater the lust or desire with which anyone sins, the greater the sin" (*S. Th.,* I–II, 77, 6, *c*).

[59] Fear of its very nature diminishes voluntariness. The reason is that the object of fear is an evil and is therefore opposed to the inclination of the will to the good. Desire, on the other hand, diminishes voluntariness only accidentally (*per accidens*). It does this when a spontaneous desire because of its violence impedes true knowledge of the objective morality of an act. (Cf. *S. Th.,* I–II, 77, 7, *c*, et ad 2^m.)

[60] An action which results from the fear of an evil has a certain similarity to an action caused by violence. It is true that strictly (*simpliciter*) speaking an action done through fear is voluntary, because the will is the intrinsic principle of the act. Nevertheless, it resembles an action caused by violence because in like manner the will retains a certain repugnance to the act. "But, if we consider what is done through fear, as outside this particular case, and inasmuch as it is repugnant to the will, this exists only according to our consideration of things; and consequently it is involuntary, considered in that respect (*secundum quid*), that is to say, outside the actual circumstances of this or that particular case" (*S. Th.,* I–II, 6, 6, *c*).

certainly not counter to what he now desires. On the other hand, the fearful man acts presently against that which even now he still desires."[61]

We conclude: Although a man acting under the influence of fear may remain free, and consequently, although the will-act possesses true voluntariness; nevertheless, the perfection of this inclination to the effect is somewhat affected.

3. IGNORANCE

Principle: Ignorance of the determining factors of the act, that is, ignorance of the objective morality of the effect produced, causes the elicited act of the will to be involuntary regarding this effect.

The truth of this statement is evident from the fact already established that voluntariness is the inclination of the will toward a desired effect. Now there can be no desired effect and therefore no inclination, no voluntariness, when sufficient knowledge of the morality of the effect is not had.

Moralists distinguish between two types of ignorance: *vincible* and *invincible*. The second is blameless; that is, in a state of invincible ignorance one cannot help being ignorant. The first, vincible ignorance, could and should have been dispelled. There is, as a result, a certain guilt incurred in placing an act, since the subject is responsible for such vincible ignorance. The degree of guilt depends upon the degree of responsibility toward obtaining the required knowledge.

St. Thomas presents a more detailed psychological study of ignorance in order to establish the relation between the various types of ignorance and the perfection of voluntariness or lack of it. He proposes three types of ignorance: concomitant, antecedent, and consequent.

a) *Concomitant* ignorance accompanies the act but has no direct influence upon it, so that although there is ignorance of what is being done, nevertheless, even if the effect were known, the act

---

[61] *S. Th.*, I–II, 6, 7, ad 2[m].

would be done just the same. This type of ignorance has no direct or indirect influence upon the act. Hence, there is neither voluntariness nor involuntariness regarding that action but simply non-voluntariness,[62] since there can be no actual inclination of the will toward that which is unknown. The classical example is that of a man who kills his foe thinking to kill a stag, but who would have willed to kill his foe had he been aware of the fact of his enemy's presence.

b) *Consequent* ignorance follows the act of the will, and is therefore voluntary. There are two classes of consequent ignorance. The first is called *affected* ignorance, such as "when a man wills not to know that he may have an excuse for sin."[63] The second is the ignorance of one who should know and could know, as, for example, when one did not obtain the knowledge he should have. This ignorance, therefore, was due to his own *culpable negligence*. The act which follows such ignorance is voluntary in its cause.

Since in either of these ways ignorance is voluntary, it cannot cause unqualified involuntariness. The second type, however, may cause a limited involuntariness, that is, in so far as the act would not have taken place had there been knowledge of the effect.

c) *Antecedent* ignorance precedes the act of the will. It is not voluntary and is had as regards some circumstances of the act which one was not bound to know. This ignorance causes unqualified involuntariness. The effect is not imputable to its author.

Inasmuch as these various types affect voluntariness, which is the inclination of the will toward the effect, we are able to infer greater or less guilt or none whatever.[64]

---

[62] *Voluntariness* means volitional inclination toward the effect. *Involuntariness* means that the effect produced is repugnant (or would be repugnant if it were known) to the will (as when coercion is exerted by an extrinsic agent). *Non-voluntariness* means simply no actual volitional inclination toward or against the effect although there would have been had the effect been known adequately.

[63] *S. Th.*, I–II, 6, 8, *c*.

[64] Cf. *S. Th.*, I–II, 76, especially art. 4.

SUMMARY

Question II

VOLUNTARINESS

Problem:

Why is a moral act imputable to its author?

Solution:

Because it is voluntary.

Article I: *What Is Voluntariness?*

1. Voluntariness is the intrinsic reality because of which the objective morality of the human act is imputed to the subject.

2. This reality is the proper inclination of the will to the effect placed.

3. Voluntariness (i.e., the proper inclination of the will to the moral effect) requires:

   a) An intrinsic principle, the will, from which the act flows.

   b) Knowledge of the objective morality of the act. This knowledge should include the morality of object, end, and circumstances. Hence, any obstacle to these two conditions will affect voluntariness.

Article II: *Factors Which Affect Voluntariness*

1. Physical coercion causes involuntariness, because the effect is contrary to the inclination of the will.

2. Passions:

   a) Antecedent passions diminish voluntariness, because they diminish true knowledge of the objective morality of the action.

   b) Consequent passions, by increasing the intensity[65] of the consequent will-act, increase the objective morality of the consequent will-act, and manifest the perfection of voluntariness as regards the external act.

N.B.: Fear diminishes voluntariness, because the will is never inclined naturally to the action which is conditioned by fear.

3. Ignorance:

   a) Vincible (consequent) — the act is more or less voluntary.

   b) Invincible (antecedent) — causes involuntariness.

---

[65] This point will be studied in the next question.

Question III

THE OBJECTIVE MORALITY OF THE HUMAN ACT

Prologue

Problem: We come now to the central problem of this chapter, namely, the problem of the objective morality of the human act. We should note that there is no question here of discovering which human acts are good and which are bad, but rather of finding *why* a human act is good or evil. In order to discover the objective morality of the human act, we shall have to examine its various specifying elements. We shall consider not only the proximate end, which is the object of the internal act of the will, but we must examine also the external act, its form or object, the individuating accidents which are its circumstances, and the various relations to the rational principle which result from these specifying elements.

Division: This treatise is divided into three parts. In the first we shall examine the goodness or malice of the human act in general. The principles inferred will then be applied to the second and third parts which study respectively the goodness or malice of the internal and external acts. In the course of this exposition, several difficult questions, such as the norm of morality and the problems of erroneous and doubtful conscience, will be discussed.

The first part contains four articles. The first article is an analysis of the good in general and its application to human acts; the second examines successively each determinant of the morality of the human act; the third studies the specific distinction between good and evil moral acts; the fourth proposes the true measure or norm of morality.

PART I. THE GOODNESS OR MALICE OF THE MORAL ACT IN GENERAL

ARTICLE I: The Good in General

Mode of Procedure: Ethics is a philosophical study. It is, therefore, necessarily based upon metaphysics. We shall begin by recalling certain metaphysical principles which were studied in the philosophy of being. These principles we shall then apply to the moral act.

The Good in General: We describe being as "that whose act is 'to be,' " and we explained in metaphysics that being and the good are convertible because being is good inasmuch as it exists.[66] The reason is that the good is the formal aspect of the perfect. Now perfection is act, and the highest act of any being is its "to be."[67] Hence, a being is more or less good in so far as its mode of existing is more or less perfect. Consequently, "every creature partakes of goodness in so far as it partakes of the act of existing."[68] The good, therefore, is sought in the existential order. Hence, *the good* viewed absolutely or *unqualifiedly (simpliciter) imports the plenitude of existing.* Let us enlarge upon this statement. We speak of goodness in the order of a created nature in this manner: A limited existing being we understand to be more or less good according to the fullness of its existence. The most profound reason for such a statement is, of course, that the act of existing is the highest perfection of a limited being, since this act is a participation in the perfection of God who is Pure Existence. We should observe, however, that unqualified goodness in a creature does not result solely from the fact that it exists substantially. The goodness which is predicated of a creature because it is a substance must

---

[66] Cf. *The Philosophy of Being*, p. 183.

[67] " 'To be' is the actuality of all acts, and for this reason it is the perfection of all perfections" (*De Potentia*, VII, 2, ad 9^m).

[68] *"In rebus autem unumquodque tantum habet de bono quantum habet de esse"* (*S. Th.*, I–II, 18, 1, *c*).

be limited, must be qualified. A tree, for example, is not necessarily a good tree because it is a substantial being. Goodness can be attributed to it only in so far as it is a being, hence, qualifiedly. For the unqualified (absolute) goodness of a creature results in the last analysis from the accidents which perfect the individual substance.[69] A tree, therefore, is unqualifiedly or absolutely good, not merely because it is an existing tree, but because its accidental perfections, its properties of size, health, fruit-bearing capacity, are such as make it a good, a perfect tree. If, then, any of the accidental actuations necessary for the perfection of a given tree should be lacking, we would speak of the tree as being not a good, but a faulty, an imperfect tree; it lacks the fullness of existence. It is not absolutely good, and, if we speak absolutely, we must declare that such a tree is bad, although in a qualified, limited way, that is, in so far as it is a being, a substance, it is good.

In short, a created nature, a limited being, is absolutely good, unqualifiedly perfect, when it possesses the various accidental actuations necessary for the perfection of its existing substance. It lacks goodness, it is bad, when it is deficient as regards some of these proper accidental actuations. "Hence, as much as it has of existence, so much has it of goodness, while in so far as it is deficient in the fullness of existing (which is proper to its nature), so far does it fail in being good and is said to be evil. If, however, it does not exist (has no being) and possesses no goodness, it could not be called good or evil."[70]

The Common Notion of the Good Applied to the Human Act: The human act viewed as a moral entity has a mode of existing all its own. Although it is composed of distinct psychological operations which depend for their distinct existence upon the first efficient cause, nevertheless, viewed in the moral order, the human act, depending as it does upon the vital dynamism of a single intention, has a true unity. Consequently, as regards its objective morality, the human act, precisely because of the unifying intention,

---

[69] In a creature the absolute or unqualified good, that is, the plenitude of existence, is convertible with qualified being (accidents), while unqualified being (substance) is the qualified good (Cf. *S. Th.*, I, 5, 1, ad 1[m]).

[70] *S. Th.*, I–II, 18, 1, *c*.

possesses in an analogous manner an existential unity in the moral order. Now the unit which comprises the fullness of the moral "to be," that is to say, the goodness of the moral act, is composed of parts. These parts are the specifying elements of the human act: end, object, and circumstances.

The good imports the plenitude of existence. Hence, the plenitude of moral existence will depend on this, that nothing due to the perfection of the constitutive specifying elements of the human act is lacking. If each element is proper, that is to say, if it lacks nothing of its due perfection, the human act will possess the fullness of its moral existence. It will be unqualifiedly good. On the contrary, if any or all of these constitutive parts are deficient in the perfection due them, the act itself will be lacking in the fullness of its moral "to be"; it will be unqualifiedly evil.

What are these elements and when are they deficient in their due perfection? We shall see in the following article that these determinants of morality are three: the object, end, and circumstances. These determine the moral specification of the human act, because they are necessarily related to an active principle in so far as it is rational. Consequently, in order to possess the due or proper perfection, that is to say, the perfection required for a good moral specification of the act, they must be suitable to the rational principle as rational; they must be reasonable or, as St. Thomas often puts it, they must be in accordance with right reason. If, on the other hand, these constitutive elements are lacking in their due perfection, that is, if they are against right reason, the specification caused by them will be evil.[71]

We conclude: Since goodness demands the fullness of perfection due to a being, and since the plenitude of the moral "to be" of a human act requires that all its constitutive or specifying elements be suitable to the rational nature, it follows that a human act is good morally when all these constitutives, namely, the object,

---

[71] Although unqualifiedly evil in the moral order, the same act in the order of nature may be a good act. "An evil action can have a proper effect, according to the goodness and being that it has. Thus adultery is the cause of human generation in as much as it implies union of male and female, but not in as much as it lacks the order of reason" (*S. Th.*, I–II, 18, 1, ad 3^m).

end, and circumstances of the act are suitable to human nature in so far as rational. Such an act is unqualifiedly good, and, therefore, it will perfect man and dispose him toward his end. On the other hand, the human act is morally evil when one or all of these determinants of morality are not in accord with right reason. "The human act is said to be evil if it lacks the measure determined by reason, or its due place, or something of the kind" (*S. Th.*, I–II, 18, 1). Such an act is unqualifiedly evil; it causes man's will to be turned away from the last end.[72]

Principle: From the fact that the good viewed absolutely (unqualifiedly) imports the fullness of existence, this extremely important principle must be inferred: *"Evil results from a single defect whereas good results only from a complete cause."*[73]

---

[72] Modern moralists when speaking of good and evil moral acts are wont to use the terms right and wrong, e.g., this is right, this is wrong. It seems to us that the terms "right" and "wrong" are wider in extension than "moral good" and "moral evil." "Right" in the English tongue is applicable to any order. We say that this word is the right word, that it is the exact word, *"le mot juste"*; we affirm that this opinion is wrong, that is to say, it is not correct. Hence to apply the word "right" to the human act by saying this act is right, meaning that it is morally good, may be misleading.

Moreover, when these same moralists use the expression, "this is right, that is wrong," one may wonder whether the true signification of "right" and "wrong" in the moral order refers to the objective morality of the act, or to the subjective morality of the act, or to both.

Finally, we are sometimes left with the impression, because the word "right" is generally used with reference to an extrinsic norm, that even in its moral application "right" implies a relative, not an absolute reality.

For these reasons we believe it more satisfactory to follow the ordinary terminology of Aquinas. He speaks of the "goodness and malice" of the human act, that is to say, of its objective morality. He explains, moreover, that imputability of the (objective) goodness or (objective) malice of the act is had only when the act is voluntary, and therefore that such imputability is not extrinsic. It is the inclination of the will itself.

It is true that St. Thomas has sparingly applied the term "rectus" to the human act, but only as a consequent of its moral objective goodness. He does this in order to indicate the necessary "rectitude" of the will to its last end. The fact that the act is right (*actus est rectus*) is therefore a *consequent* of the human act because of its objective moral goodness. "The human act," St. Thomas explains, "is right (*rectus*) whenever it tends (*procedit*) to the end according to the order of reason and of the eternal law" (*S. Th.*, I–II, 21, 1).

[73] *S. Th.*, I–II, 18, 4, ad 3[m].

ARTICLE II: The Determinants of the Goodness or Malice of the Human Act: The Object, the Circumstances, and the End

We must now examine the three determinants of the objective morality of the human act, namely, the object, end, and circumstances. We would like to show in what manner these constitutive elements of the moral "to be" actually determine its moral specification. In other words, what is the nature of their influx in causing the act to be morally good or evil. Now the causal element which is most closely connected with fullness of existing is the formal, for the form communicates specific perfection, that is to say, it gives to a being its "whatness." In other words, the formal cause is that which makes a thing be what it is. Now just as in natural things the species is caused by the substantial form, so an action gets its specific determination from its object.[74] For the object stands in relation to an action somewhat as form to a natural being. Consequently, the primary goodness of a human act is that which it derives from a suitable object.

1. **Object:** The object of an action is the first specifying factor of that action. An example will clarify this statement: When we analyze the operation called sight or vision, we explain that the object of such an operation is color, for it is the object as colored which causes the actuation of the faculty, and therefore determines the nature, the quiddity, of an operation. Color, then, is the formal aspect of the actuation of the faculty and enables it to act. Color determines the nature of the act; it specifies the operation; it gives the operation its specific form.

Let us apply the principle, "the object specifies the act," to the human action. Because the specifying factor of any operation is its object, we should infer that the object of a moral act, that is, the object as referred to a rational nature, gives that act its primary

---

[74] In like manner, "motion (receives its species) from its term." *Ibid.,* 2, *c.*

specific determination.[75] Hence, if the object is suitably proportioned to the rational nature of man as related to his supreme end, the specific determination caused by such an object is good; if, on the other hand, the object is not in accordance with right reason but opposed to it, as for example, the killing of an innocent man, this evil object indicates that the act is evil. We conclude: The object is the first specifying factor of the moral act. Because it causes the "whatness," the object is the first, the most fundamental determination of the goodness or malice of the human act.

2. **Circumstances:** The complete fullness of perfection which is due a being of nature is not from the substantial form alone. The properties, for example, which are only accidents are necessary for such plenitude of existence. In like manner, in the human act the complete fullness of perfection does not result from the formal cause, that is, from the object alone. Much is added to the perfection of the act by the circumstances which stand in relation to the act as do proper accidents to a being of nature. Thus the act receives perfection from suitable circumstances. On the other hand, if some perfection proper to the human act is lacking, the act will be unreasonable, and therefore evil.

> For the fullness of its goodness does not wholly consist in its species, but something is added from those things which come to it *like* certain accidents. And of this sort are the due circumstances. Therefore, if something is lacking which is required for due circumstances, the action will be bad.[76]

Distinct Specification: Besides the fact that the circumstances need to be suitable to the rational nature lest they vitiate the human act, it happens sometimes that certain circumstances add a distinct specification from that given by the object, as for example, stealing in a holy place. In such a case, the circumstance known as *place* causes the theft to be also a sacrilegious act. This added

---

[75] The object of the internal act is the end. The object of the external act is "that about which the external action is concerned (*circa quod est actio exterior*)" (*S. Th.*, I–II, 18, 6, *c*). This object is distinct from the end of the agent.

[76] *S. Th.*, I–II, 18, 3, *c*.

specification by a circumstance occurs whenever the circumstance is a principal condition of the object.[77]

3. **The End:** The perfection, the fullness of existing in a creature depends upon its causes. The reason is that a cause is a principle which has a direct influx on the "to be" of another. We discovered the fundamental goodness of an action by examining the nature of its formal cause, which is the object. Besides this dependence of the "to be" and therefore of the fundamental goodness of a thing upon its formal cause, we find in a creature another type of dependence, this time upon an extrinsic cause, the agent.

St. Thomas points out that "as the 'to be' of a thing depends upon the agent and upon the form, so the goodness of a thing depends upon its end." The reason is that the end determines the agent to produce the form. Consequently, "human actions, and all other things which depend upon another, have the aspect (*ratio*) of goodness from the end upon which they depend, besides the absolute goodness which is in them (because of their form or object)."[78]

To understand this text we should recall: (1) that the specific determination of the internal act is from the *end* (object-end) which is the object of the will; (2) that the specific determination of the external act is from the external *object;* (3) that the human act is a unit in this way, that the external act to be moral must depend efficiently (order of exercise) upon the internal act of the

---

[77] *S. Th.,* I–II, 18, 10, *c.* How does one determine that the circumstances are morally relevant? What is the principle which enables us to determine whether a circumstance is a "principal condition of the object," that is to say, whether it is a distinct specifying element? The answer is that we discover such a specifying element by comparing the various circumstances with the norm, right reason. We are thereby able to gauge the moral value of these circumstances, and to discover whether any of these manifests a distinct specifying element. "A circumstance is sometimes taken as the essential difference of the object, according as it is related to the reason; and then it can specify a moral act. And it must needs be so whenever a circumstance transforms an action from good to evil, for a circumstance would not make an action evil, except through being repugnant to reason" (*S. Th.,* I–II, 15, ad 4[m]).

[78] *S. Th.,* I–II, 18, 4, *c.*

will as willing the end as well as willing the freely determined means.

The end[79] has various functions as regards the parts and as
regards the whole of the human act:

1. As related to the internal act, the end is the *object*. It specifies
the act of the will and includes object and circumstances.

2. As related to the object of the external act, the end is the
circumstance "why."[80] Consequently, sometimes it adds a further
specific determination to the object.

---

[79] The use of the word "end" in the course of morality may prove confusing.
First we spoke of the end-object which determines the will-act; then in the structure
of the moral act, the order-of-end was shown as preceding the order-of-means. Now
we are considering the moral specification of the human act caused by three distinct
elements: end, object, circumstances. Certainly the term "end" has a different
signification in these various uses.

Let us dispose first of the order-of-end as preceding the order-of-means. The
point in question here is the sequence of psychological moments. In the same
human act there are distinct chronological moments; these moments are classified
under three headings: order of end, of means, and of execution. Now in the analysis
of the psychological structure of the act we discover that the order-of-end must
precede that of means. There is no problem here of the specification of the act.
If, however, we look at this psychological sequence from the point of view of
the specification of the will-act, then the end-object is one. For the various psychological moments are united by the dynamism of the intention which in willing
the object-end in the order-of-the-end implicitly wills the necessary means.

Hence, when we speak of the object-end, we are considering the specifying element
of the internal act of the will. Now the will-act is one morally, and its object-end
which gives the act its moral specification is viewed as one. This object-end includes
the specifying elements of end, object, and circumstances which are viewed not
as existing but as known, and therefore are united in the act of knowledge and of
appetite. The will-act, therefore, is specified by one element, the object-end, which
contains object-end and circumstances as known.

Finally, the external act can receive a threefold specification from three distinct
elements: object, end, and circumstances. That these are distinct elements is easily
shown. The object of the external act is that about which (*circa quod*) the act is. It
exists in the order of execution, e.g., killing a man. The end is communicated by
the will-act. As final cause, it exists in the intentional order, e.g., I kill for revenge.
Finally the circumstances are further determinations of the object of the external
act which are in the order of existence, as for example, time, place, etc. It is
possible, therefore, to discover in the external act a threefold specification caused
by three distinct elements.

[80] This point has not always been accepted by moralists. It is, however, undoubtedly
the thought of St. Thomas, as is evidenced by many texts. Cf. *In II Sent.*, dist. 36,

3. As related to the *whole* human act, the end is like its *form,* so that the whole human act is "viewed formally with regard to the end, but materially with regard to the object of the external act."[81]

4. As related to the external act, it is "like" an *efficient* cause in this, that it causes the external act to be part of the whole human act. This it does by determining the agent (the will) to move the other faculties and members.

Difficulty: Here an obvious difficulty arises. If the end of the will-act specifies, how can the object, which in the external act is distinct from the end, also specify? There are various possibilities to be examined. The first possibility is that one of the two species is evil and one good; as for example, I steal in order to give alms. In such a case, the action is evil, since the good can be had only from a complete cause, while evil results from any defect. Hence, the primary specific determination of the whole human act is from the evil determinant.

Whenever end and object are both good or both evil, then we may further distinguish according to the relation of the object to the end. If we find that the object is *of itself* related to the end, we conclude that there is only one type of malice or goodness: for in this case, the species given by the object is related to that given by the end as species to genus. If, on the contrary, the object is not naturally related to the end, but just happens to be ordered to this end because of the will of the agent, we shall find two distinct goodnesses, or two distinct malices, as for example, killing for the sake of stealing. The first specific determination, however, will be from the end so that in the example given the moral act is more the act of theft than of murder.[82]

In short, in placing an external act, whenever the object is of itself related to the end, this object is as a species under its genus. If the object is not related to the end, the act is of two distinct

a. 5; *De Malo,* II, 6, *c.,* et ad 1^m; *S. Th.,* I–II, 7, 3, ad 3^m; *ibid.,* 4, ad 2^m; I–II, 18, 9, *c;* I–II, 18, 6, *c.*

[81] *S. Th.,* I–II, 18, 6, *c.*
[82] Cf. *S. Th.,* I–II, 18, 6, *c.*

species, but the specification from the end is taken as the formal element of the moral act. In such a case, however, there are two distinct species, two distinct elements of goodness or of malice.

It may be objected that no act, no operation, can be of two species. This is really not a difficulty, for even in the order of nature we often find that the same substance, when viewed differently, belongs to two distinct species; for example, the same thing may be white and sweet. (Cf. S. Th., I–II, 18, 7.)

Indifferent Moral Act:[83] Moralists generally teach that no individual concrete act is indifferent, but that such an act is either morally good or morally evil. We note, however, that certain external human actions, when considered only from the aspect of the specific determination given by their objects, are neither good nor bad morally, but indifferent. Walking and standing, for example, do not of themselves indicate a moral good; their objects do not of themselves manifest a relation of suitability or unsuitability to the rational nature of man as do other actions, such as the morally good act of praying, or a morally evil act of murder. In the abstract, therefore, these actions are indifferent, since the object which is their form gives no moral specification. As soon, however, as we consider an action in the concrete, that is, with all its individuating circumstances, and most of all with its end, the act is no longer indifferent: it is a moral act. The reason is that such an act in the concrete results from a deliberate will. It supposes an intention which wills an end that is either in accord with right reason or not, that is either reasonable or not, and consequently good or evil. Hence, the commanded human act which results from the free intention to an end is in the moral order and is good or evil, not necessarily by reason of the object, but because the intention of the will is morally good or evil, that is, reasonable or not.

Let us note in passing that when moralists speak of an action that is intrinsically evil, they wish to indicate primarily that the object which is the specifying factor or form of the act — in so far

---

[83] Cf. ibid., 8 and 9.

as referred to an active principle which is rational — is against right reason, as for example, killing an innocent man, and the like.

To conclude: The determinants of objective morality of any act are the end, the object, and the circumstances. Since the good is had "from a complete cause, and evil results from any defect," should any one of these factors be evil, the act is unqualifiedly evil; if all are morally good, that is, in accordance with right reason, the act is good morally.

The function of these factors is clearly stated by the Angelic Doctor:

> . . . In a human action, a four-fold goodness may be considered: one according to its genus, in that it is an action, because as much as it has of action and of being (*entitate*), so much has it of goodness. . . . Another according to its species, which goodness is derived according as the object is suitable. A third according to its circumstances, as if according to certain accidents. Fourthly, a goodness according to its end, as if according to a relation to the cause of its goodness.[84]

ARTICLE III: In Moral Actions Good and Evil Establish Fundamental Specific Differences.

Division: There are three points to be studied: (1) a theory[85] of the specification of an operation by its object; (2) the application of this theory to the moral act which will establish the truth that good and evil moral acts belong to distinct and opposed moral species; (3) the positive element in an evil moral act.

Problem: We have now reached the most profound, the most difficult question in the philosophy of morality. It is this: Why do we speak of good and evil human actions as if implying that the

---

84 *S. Th.*, I–II, 18, 4, *c.* Note that the first goodness mentioned is ontological, which is attributed to any being precisely because it is being.

85 The word "theory" is not taken here to signify a working hypothesis according to common scientific usage. In the same manner as we speak of the theory of act and potency, the term "theory" here really means a philosophical law which is objectively true.

goodness or evil of these actions is their first, their most fundamental specific determination? St. Thomas states the problem thus:
In moral actions are evil and good opposed as distinct species;
do good and evil moral actions belong to distinct species *precisely
because good or evil?*[86]

The momentous significance of this metaphysical problem, which
to the uninitiated might seem a question of logic, appears in the
consideration of the consequences. If evil in a human action is of
distinct species from good, and if this contrariness lies in its direct
opposition to human nature as ordered to its last end, then an
objectively evil act is never permissible but is always to be avoided
since it is opposed to *the last end of man*. On the other hand, if
the distinction between good and evil actions lies in their respective degree of perfection, then moral evil is only a lesser good and
consequently is not necessarily to be avoided.[87]

This problem assumes greater significance in our day when
morality is generally accepted as something personal and relative,
to be gauged according to customs, to the state of civilization, to
pragmatic results, and the like. In this article we propose to show
that the opposition between good and evil moral acts is due to
a fundamental specific distinction which is absolute, because it is
founded upon a comparison with, a referring to, a specifying
measure which is absolute. We propose to show that the distinction between moral good and evil is absolute because it is specific.
Moreover, this specific distinction is between contraries, because it
results from the suitability or non-suitability of the act to its rational
active principle.[88] For it is because of the nature of this active
principle, because it is rational, that the human act is morally
good or morally evil.

---

[86] *"Bonum et malum diversificant speciem in actibus moralibus"* (S. Th., I–II,
18, 5).

[87] A lesser good does not cause a nature to deviate from its end. Hence, no one
is obliged to do the more perfect.

[88] This suitability or unsuitability of the act to its active principle, which is a
rational supposit, simply means that the good moral act disposes the subject toward
its end while the evil act causes a contrary disposition. The end in this case is absolute; it is the possession of unlimited good.

Let us restate our problem: The question is about the good and evil in the moral act. We speak of a moral act, first of all, as being a good or an evil act, implying that the most profound and distinct determination of this act, its first specific determination in the moral order, is that the act is good or that it is evil. Good and evil are the first specific determinations of morality. They establish two supreme species in the various human acts. Why?

I

Theory of Specification: A facile, but only partly true, answer to this query is that, since specification is caused by the object, it follows that the nature of the object accounts for this first specific determination of the act, for the fact that it is good or evil. This answer is not sufficient. The various objects which terminate the operations of life, if viewed solely in their ontological reality, do not suffice to indicate whether the actions which they terminate belong to distinct species. The reason is that the object which specifies an operation is not the "material object," but the "formal object," that is, the object as referred to the active principle of the operation. Perhaps an example will best bring out our meaning. Color and sound as objects of the act of knowledge must specify that operation. The operation then is either "knowing color," or "knowing sound." Do these two operations belong to distinct species? It is impossible to tell just from the object. To do so we must refer these two actions to their active or efficient principle and compare them, as already determined by their formal object (i.e., sound, color), with the nature of that principle. Now, we know[89] that when referred to a sentient principle these two acts, of knowing sound and of knowing color, as specified by their object, are discovered to be of distinct species. Why? Because of the nature of the sentient principle whose object is the particular sensible. Hence, distinct proper sensibles will necessitate operations of distinct species and therefore of distinct faculties.

Quite the contrary occurs if the active principle of the act of knowing color and of the act of knowing sound should be of a

---

[89] Cf. *The Philosophy of Man,* p. 57 ff.

purely immaterial nature. For in this instance, although the operations of knowing sound and knowing color are formally constituted such by their respective objects, nevertheless, the actions do not belong to distinct species and therefore do not require distinct faculties. The reason is that the nature of their active efficient cause, being purely immaterial, embraces all beings in its object of knowledge. Consequently, the specification by the objects, here color and sound, does not diversify the species of the act of intellectual knowledge. We conclude: The complete specification of an operation by its object is discovered by referring the object to the active principle of the operation.

II

Application of Theory to the Moral Act: The specific determination of any operation, and therefore of a moral action, is established not merely by the object which terminates it, but by the object as referred to the active principle of operation. Now good and evil in any action signify suitability and unsuitability to the nature of the active principle. It follows that the action as specified by its object causes in the subject a disposition to or away from the last end. Consequently, when the object as referred to a rational principle of action is found suitable to the rational nature, the operation which is specified by such an object is a good moral action; it perfects the subject by disposing it to its end. On the other hand, if the operation is unsuitable because it frustrates nature by causing a disposition which is opposed to the attainment of the end, the action is evil morally. It is obvious, from this analysis, that something suitable and something unsuitable which belong to the same subject are opposed as contraries, since one disposes toward, the other away from the end of nature. Now contraries in the same subject certainly indicate distinct species. Indeed, they manifest the greatest possible opposition between species which are under the same genus. In the moral order, good and evil actions, though under the same genus as moral acts, must evidently belong to contrary species.

To exemplify our demonstration, we shall examine two definite operations: the first is to-take-what-belongs-to-another; the other to-take-what-does-not-belong-to-another. Now, if the objects which terminate these actions: "what-belongs or does-not-belong-to-another" are referred to a sentient principle, for example, to a dog, or to a man who is out of his mind, and therefore to a principle not viewed as rational, the two distinct actions of taking the object are certainly not opposed as contraries; they do not belong to distinct species since neither is unsuitable to a sentient nature, one which is not viewed as rational; neither causes such a nature to deviate from its determined end.[90] On the other hand, when the objects of these two actions are referred to a rational supposit, it is immediately evident that one of these is suitable because reasonable and the other unsuitable because unreasonable. One action disposes man toward his last end; the other causes him to deviate from that end. One action is morally good, the other morally evil.

Now such opposition is, as we have explained, the opposition of contraries which constitute not only distinct species, but species that are most radically opposed. In the moral order, therefore, good and evil constitute distinct species that are absolutely opposed

---

[90] It will be asked why the distinction between good and evil actions in a non-rational living being is not sufficient for a distinction of species. The answer is that an evil action which flows from such a principle is not wholly unsuitable to the nature. Let us explain this statement. The specific distinction between morally good and morally evil acts is founded on a radical opposition as regards the end. The good action, because it is suitable, disposes the rational nature to its last end; the evil act disposes away from the last end. The opposition is absolute. Not so in a sentient or vegetative act of a nonrational principle. The evil act — as in the growth of a stunted tree — may not fulfill the perfection demanded for a perfect tree. But even such a growth is a perfection. It is simply suitable. Moreover, and this is really the point in question, neither a vegetative nor a sentient act as such, that is, as related to a nonrational principle, can cause a nature to deviate from its end. The end of an irrational creature is to be just what it is — to act, to live, and to die in accordance with the necessary determinations of nature as established by its Maker. There can be no turning away from the end, and therefore there is no foundation for a distinction of species between good and evil operations in a nonrational creature. At best we could speak of a lesser good as regards the individual nature which is made less perfect ontologically. There is no frustration of nature as regards the end. In short, except in the order of morality, good and evil actions do not establish distinct species.

because they are contraries. We conclude: Good and evil in moral actions establish the most profound, the most fundamental specific distinction between moral actions.[91]

III

Positive Element in the Evil Moral Act: Against this demonstration it will be argued that good and evil cannot constitute distinct species, for the simple reason that specific distinction is founded upon a distinct perfection, not on a mere lack of perfection. For even in irrational animals, explains the Angelic Doctor, the substantial form possesses a perfection not found in the soul of man. Irrationality is not a mere lack of rationality. It is a positive perfection. Moreover, we have established conclusively in metaphysics that evil is only a lack of good; it is privative, not positive. Hence, it cannot be the foundation for a distinct species. Good and evil actions in the rational nature, therefore, seem to belong to the same species.

In the order of nature, that is, in the order of an active principle which is not viewed as rational, we grant that there can be no positive element in the evil act to warrant a specific distinction between good and evil operations. The evil act is merely deficient; it is a lesser good; the act is evil because of a lack of perfection,

---

[91] Many modern thinkers deny that morality can be objective and absolute. They do not seem to understand why moral good and moral evil are necessarily distinct species, since such is not the case in the order of (nonrational) nature. They forget that while in the order of nature an evil action is not necessarily opposed to its principle, the contrary holds true for an evil moral act, precisely because it is an unreasonable action and therefore contrary to the nature of man, which is formally rational. It is, therefore, absurd to state that a moral action is good or bad according to time, custom, or effects. A moral act is good or evil because it is suitable or not suitable to human nature viewed formally.

Indeed, it may even happen that an action specified by the same object which is good in the order of nature — that is, an action which is done by a being which lacks intellect and will — is certainly evil in the moral order. The example proposed by St. Thomas is that of the begetting of an offspring outside of wedlock. The action is specified by the object which is good when referred to a sentient principle, man the *animal;* it is evil when referred to the *rational* nature of man. The point we make is that since a human act is from a rational, free principle, it must be referred to a free, rational principle in order that we may know whether it be good or evil. (Cf. *S. Th.*, I–II, 18, 5.)

not because of something positive. That is why an evil act in the order of nature does not designate a distinct species from the good act merely because it is evil. The retarded growth of a stunted tree, for example, may result from a deficient action which is evil only because of a privation of good, because of a lack of perfection. This operation in no way causes the tree to deviate from its true and necessary end which is to be just what it is. Accordingly, St. Thomas insists that in such operations the evil is entirely privative. In the evil of nature, there is no positive element because there is no choosing of an end.

On the other hand, in the moral order, St. Thomas states definitely that the specific distinction found in an evil moral action depends upon a positive element. This positive element, he asserts, is caused in this way, that in the evil moral act, man chooses an end which is not the true end. Now this evil end has an element of good; it is a reality, something positive. The evil act does not merely cause man to turn away from his last end; it directs him to a false end. This false end is something positive which he wills. The evil which is a constitutive difference, a foundation for the distinctive species, is not merely the privation of a good, but a certain good (end) which is known, accepted, and enjoyed.

> Good and evil are *not* constitutive differences *except in moral actions* (in moralibus) which receive their species from the end, which is the object of the will, the source of all morality. And because good has the nature of an end, therefore, good and evil are specific differences in moral things; good in itself, but evil as the absence of the due end. Yet neither does the absence of the due end by itself constitute a moral species, except as it is joined to the undue end; just as we do not find the privation of the substantial form in natural things unless it is joined to another form. The evil therefore which is a constitutive difference in morals is a *certain good joined to the privation of another good;* as the end proposed by the intemperate man is not the privation of the good of reason, but the delight of sense without the order of reason. Hence, evil is not a constitutive difference as such, but by reason of the good that is annexed.[92]

[92] *S. Th.,* I, 48, 1, ad 2^m; cf. I–II, 79, 2, ad 3^m; I–II, 18, 5, ad 2^m. We conclude that only in the moral order can we speak of a specific distinction between good

This is undoubtedly the constant teaching of the Angelic Doctor as attested by definite statements found in his various works.[93] Some interpreters,[94] however, believe that St. Thomas, in his mature years, modified his view of the matter. To prove this contention they propose this one text: "Even in natural things good and evil, which are in accord with nature or opposed to nature, diversify the species of nature; for a dead body and a living body are not of the same species."[95]

It seems that this statement in no way formulates a change of opinion; indeed, there is absolutely no indication of modification of doctrine. St. Thomas merely states what everyone admits, that a change of substantial form implies that the two beings (natures, units) which exist before and after the change are of distinct species. In the things of nature, "good," that is, the more perfect form, and "evil," the less perfect, diversify the species of nature (*diversificant speciem naturae*). He does not claim that in the *actions* of the things of nature good and evil diversify the species of the operations. There is no question of predicating of the same nonrational unit two actions which are specifically distinct, because one action is good and the other evil. True, in the things of nature, the "good" unit (living body) and the "bad" unit may belong to distinct species, but good and evil are not constitutive differences of *actions* except in the moral order.

Conclusion: Only in the moral order do good and evil actions belong to distinct contrary species. For this reason no evil act is ever justifiable, since such an act tends to frustrate the rational nature in the attainment of its last end.

---

and evil actions. For only in moral actions do we find a positive element which is the good in the evil end. In the order of nature an evil act is not specifically distinct from a good action. It implies only a lesser good.

[93] *In II Sent.*, Q. 1, art. 1, ad 5^m; *S. Th.*, I, 48, 1, ad 2^m; *De Malo*, II, 4, ad 10^m.

[94] Cf. Lottin, *Principes de Morale*, II, p. 133.

[95] *S. Th.*, I–II, 18, 5, ad 1^m.

ARTICLE IV: The Norm of Morality

The human act is good in the moral order when its specifying elements (object-end-circumstances) are reasonable, that is, in accordance with the proper relation of the rational nature to its last end. If any of these specifying elements is unreasonable, that is, not proportioned to a rational nature, the moral act is evil. The question arises: How can we know whether these specifying elements are in accordance with the rational nature, whether they are reasonable or not? The answer is that we are able to judge the objective value of these specifying elements by comparing them to the norm of morality.

Problem: A norm is a rule, a measure. It is neither an efficient, nor an exemplary, nor a final cause of action. It belongs rather to knowledge, to the intellect, for a norm enables us to judge properly of an objective value. The norm of morality, therefore, is the rule, the measure, with which we are able to judge absolutely the objective morality of the human act; it enables us to know whether the act is morally good or morally evil. Our problem is to discover this norm.

St. Thomas states that the true proximate rule or norm by which we judge the objective morality of the human act is *right reason (recta ratio)*.[96]

The term *reason* is ambiguous. Reason sometimes signifies the intellect; sometimes it indicates the formal aspect of human nature viewed as rational. In this question we take it to mean a rule or norm of the human act. Let us explain these various significations.

1. The most important function of reason — meaning the strictly immaterial faculty of knowledge called intellect — as a cause of the moral act is to specify the will-act. In our analysis of the structure of the moral act, we discovered that by presenting a good to the

---

[96] The eternal law which is the knowledge of the Divine Wisdom is the supreme norm, the supreme rule. Right reason is the proximate norm. Between eternal law and right reason stands the natural law. On the one hand, the natural law is a participation of the eternal law in man; on the other, it is the foundation for the proximate norm which we call right reason.

will in a moral judgment (judgment of reason), the intellect specifies the will-act; the intellect, therefore, gives the will-act its formal determination from the object as known and judged. If this specifying judgment of reason is in accord with the rule (right reason), we know that the act is good; if opposed to the norm, the act is morally evil. This specification of the will-act by a judgment of reason is not our present problem.

2. Reason may be considered as the formal aspect of human nature, that is, of human nature viewed as rational. In this sense, the word *reason* means the rational active principle to which the object is necessarily referred.[97] The most fundamental specification of the moral act, that is, the fact that it is good or evil, depends upon this relation of the object to a rational active principle which is sometimes called reason. We have studied and solved this problem in the preceding pages.

3. The word *reason* (*ratio*) in St. Thomas when modified by *right* (*recta*) has a technical meaning. It signifies true intellectual knowledge which is habitually (as a habit) in the faculty and can therefore be brought to focus by the memory when needed. This appears from the definitions of the habits of science, prudence, and art. Science is the true knowledge of the "knowable" (*recta ratio scibilium*); prudence, the true knowledge of the "do-able," i.e., of the things which can be done (*recta ratio agibilium*); and art, the true knowledge of the "make-able," i.e., of the things which can be made (*recta ratio factibilium*). In every one of these definitions we note that this true knowledge of the intellect (*recta ratio*) does not merely signify the act of understanding by which we attain such knowledge, the actual "to know" (*intelligere*), but rather the habit itself which is retained in the intellectual memory and can be actuated when needed. Right reason (*recta ratio*) then means a definite habit of the intellect which can easily come to act.

Now just as the true knowledge of the things which can be done (*recta ratio agibilium*), a habit of the intellect, is the immediate directive of the moral act by a prudential judgment; just as

---

[97] "The moral act receives its species from the object according to its relation to reason (*rationem*)" (*De Malo*, II, 5).

the true knowledge of the things to be made (*recta ratio facti-bilium*), an intellectual habit, is the directive in making the artifact, so the simple expression right reason (*"recta ratio"*) without any modifier signifies an intellectual habit, a directive, a norm for judging the morality of the human act. *Right reason, therefore, is the true knowledge of the fundamental, universal, moral principles by which we judge the objective value of human actions.* It is the rule (*regula*) of all moral actions.

Not Prudence: How does such a habit, "right reason," differ from prudence which is the true knowledge of things to be done?

Prudence is a practical habit. Being in the practical intellect, it disposes man to good moral action. Prudence, therefore, is not concerned with a universal, impersonal principle, but with a personal, concrete action. It does not merely judge the value of the act, but it tends to specify the will-act in accordance with right reason. It is a moral virtue. On the other hand, right reason does not look directly to action, for it forms universal, impersonal, objective judgments. Hence, such judgments cannot in themselves be the specifying elements of the moral act. Indeed, the knowledge of the norm does not necessarily incline men to good moral acts. In itself, therefore, right reason is not in the order of action although it is applicable to action.

Right reason, therefore, is not the personal judgment of reason (prudential judgment) which gives the will-act its form, its direction by specification. Nor is it the formal aspect of the active principle, human nature, to which the act is related for its fundamental goodness and malice. It is a habit of the intellect, *the true knowledge* of what universally and impersonally must be done and what must be avoided, a knowledge of what will dispose man toward his last end and what will cause him to deviate from that end.

Not Synderesis: Right reason is not to be identified with synderesis. Synderesis is the natural inclination of the intellect to form moral principles; it is not a distinct disposition of the intellect, but a natural inclination of the intellect. Synderesis is a part of, an aspect of, a function of the habit of principles which looks to the formation of moral principles. Hence, synderesis contains these moral judgments only remotely, that is, as a natural disposition to form them. Right reason, on the other hand, is the true knowledge of these principles either as habitual or actual. Let us add that these moral judgments are called, sometimes, judgments of the natural law (because they express the law); sometimes, judgments of the norm (because they belong to right reason).

Why Not Human Nature: One last clarification. Many moralists generally designate the norm of morality to be human-nature-adequately-taken (*natura humana adequate sumpta*), that is, the rational nature of man as related to its end and to all other beings. How does this norm differ from right reason? Fundamentally, they are identical, since right reason requires a consideration of the finality of nature and all that it entails in order to attain the true knowledge of the principles necessary for judging the morality of human actions. Fundamentally, therefore, right reason and human-nature-adequately-taken really mean the same thing.

Actually, however, right reason is the actual, or at least habitual, *true knowledge* of the principles by which we may *immediately* judge the objective morality of man's action. On the other hand, while from the knowledge of human-nature-adequately-taken I should arrive at the same general universal judgments of the natural law, nevertheless, the mere knowledge of human nature will not give me these immediately, but only after lengthy reflection. It seems, therefore, that in practice in order to judge the moral value of an action we generally turn to right reason, that is, to the true knowledge of the fundamental principles of the natural law which has already been obtained, rather than proceed to reflect upon what human-nature-adequately-taken means as regards this particular action.

Definition: Right reason is the true knowledge of the first principles of the natural law by which we know and judge the objective value of the human act. It is a habit of the intellect; it is the complexus of the fundamental and *universal* principles of right doing, right living, to which we compare the human act in order to know definitely whether it is good or evil morally. It is not the habit of prudence which tends to specify a *particular* personal action. Although looking toward action as such, right reason is rather in the order of universal knowledge than of individual action, since it does not specify a moral act.

Formation of Habit of Right Reason: How is this habit formed? Unlike synderesis, right reason is not an innate disposition. We grant, however, that the innate inclination of the intellect called synderesis is necessary to enable us to form the moral principles which belong to right reason. Moreover, while it is true that right reason immediately depends upon the natural law, we believe that, strictly speaking, right reason is not the natural law. For the natural law is a participation in the divine law; it is the impression of the Creator which necessarily inclines the free nature to its last end. Right reason, on the other hand, is an acquired habit, the acquired knowledge of the principles of right action which are inferred from this radical finality of nature. Right reason, therefore, supposes this participation in the eternal law, this finality. Consequently, the intellect, reflecting upon the inclination of nature to the good proportionated to it, is able to form these first moral principles. These make up the habit called right reason.

The unfolding of the thought of Aquinas regarding the forming of this habit seems to be as follows:

The eternal law is the absolute norm and rule of all actions, for it is the knowledge of the wisdom of God. The eternal law is communicated to us in a limited manner by means of the natural law. The natural law, therefore, is a direct participation of the eternal law in our rational nature. This law consists primarily in the radical finality of human nature to the absolute good. Because of this radical appetite to the absolute good, there are discovered in man tendencies to the good actions which are true dispositions to the last end. Inferentially, contrary actions are judged to be morally evil.

Now the intellect of man, because of its natural inclination (habit of principles) to know the true and to form fundamental principles of thought (habit of understanding) as well as of action (synderesis), is able to infer from the knowledge of the radical appetite of a rational nature to the absolute good, the first principle of the moral law: "Good should be done; evil avoided." "Good," of course, is understood to be that which is suitable to the nature of man as rational, that which disposes him to his last end. Evil, on the contrary, is understood to be unsuitable to the nature of man as rational, because it causes him to deviate from the true end.[98]

After establishing this fundamental principle of the moral law, the intellect, by a consideration of the radical tendencies of nature to those goods that are essential to the attainment of the end, and their contraries, forms the three primary precepts regarding life, sex, God, and neighbor. From these it is able to infer the various judgments of law which establish the moral value of human actions and should govern man in his quest for happiness.[99]

---

[98] *S. Th.,* I–II, 94, 2, *c.* "Now as being is the first thing that falls under the apprehension absolutely, so good is the first thing that falls under the apprehension of the practical reason, which is directed to action; for every agent acts for an end, which has the nature of good. Consequently, the first principle in the practical reason is one founded on the nature of good, viz., that good is that which all things seek after. Hence this is the first precept of law, that good is to be done and promoted, and evil is to be avoided. All other precepts of the natural law are founded upon this; so that all the things which the practical reason naturally apprehends as man's good belong to the precept of the natural law under the form of things to be done or avoided."

[99] *Ibid.* This analysis is proposed by St. Thomas in the following words: "Because good has the nature of an end, and evil, the nature of the contrary, hence it is that all those things to which man has a natural inclination are naturally apprehended by reason as being good, and consequently to be sought by action, and their contraries as evil, and objects of avoidance. Consequently, the order of the precepts of the natural law is according to the order of natural inclinations. For there is in man, first of all, an inclination to good in accordance with the nature which he has in common with all substances, inasmuch, namely, as every substance seeks the preservation of its own 'to be' (esse), according to its nature; and by reason of this inclination, whatever is a means of preserving human life, and of warding off its obstacles, belongs to the natural law. Secondly, there is in man an inclination to things that pertain to him more properly, according to that nature which he has in common with other animals; and in virtue of this inclination, those things are said to belong to the natural law which nature has taught to all animals, such as sexual intercourse, the education of offspring and the like. Thirdly, there is in man an inclination to good according to the nature of his reason, which nature is proper to him. Thus man has a natural inclination to know the truth about God, and to live in society; and in this respect, whatever pertains to this inclination belongs to the natural law, e.g., to shun ignorance, to avoid offending those among whom one has to live, and other such things regarding the above inclination." This text will be carefully analyzed in the chapter on law.

The complexus of these fundamental, universal, and impersonal judgments as known by the intellect and retained by the memory is right reason. Right reason is, therefore, the true knowledge of the moral principles by which we are able to judge the objective goodness or evil of the human act. *Right reason is the norm of morality.*

N.B.: Right reason is not innate in man. There is, however, an innate, a natural rectitude of the intellect, that is, a tendency of the intellect to seek and attain its end which is to know truth and avoid error. An aspect of this natural rectitude of the intellect is the ability to form moral judgments in accordance with the natural law. "There is," explains St. Thomas, "in every nature a natural inclination to the end. Hence, in reason there is a natural rectitude by which the intellect is inclined to its end. Consequently, that which diverts from this end is not in accordance with reason; . . . because the natural law is that in accordance with which knowledge of reason is true."[1]

Supreme Norm: We should add that the most fundamental norm, that is, the absolute norm, is the eternal law. Indeed, right reason as well as the natural law are participations, limited expressions, of the eternal law. Should, therefore, the eternal law be made manifest to us by revelation, we would be bound to follow it, although to feeble human reason such a law might erroneously seem against nature. For the eternal law is the wisdom of God, which is absolute.[2]

> Now in those things that are done by the will, the proximate rule is the human reason, while the supreme rule is the eternal law. Whenever, therefore, a human act tends to the end according to the order of reason and of the eternal law, then that act is right; but when it turns aside from that rectitude, then it is a sin. Now it is evident that a voluntary act that turns aside from the order of reason and of the eternal law is evil and that an act is good because it is in accord with reason and the eternal law.[3]

---

[1] *"Unicuique naturae indita est naturalis quaedam inclinatio in suum finem; et ideo in ratione est quaedam naturalis rectitudo per quam in finem inclinatur; et ideo illud quod abducit a fine illo est discordans a ratione; et quia lex naturalis est secundum quam ratio recta est"* (*In II Sent.*, dist. 42, a. 2, a. 5).

[2] *S. Th.*, I–II, 19, 4, *c.*

[3] *S. Th.*, I–II, 21, 1, *c.*

Conclusion: The proximate norm of morality is right reason, which is a habit of the intellect; it is the true knowledge of the principles of the natural law. This knowledge enables us to judge correctly the objective morality of human actions. Right reason is:

1. The expression (by universal judgments) of the participation of human nature in the eternal law;
2. Based immediately upon the finality of human nature to the absolute good;
3. Formed by a consideration of the radical tendency of human nature to the last end and to the necessary means;
4. Not identical with the natural law, synderesis, prudence, conscience, nor intellect itself;
5. Not an efficient, instinctive force, but a formal rule discovered by the intellect;
6. Not, like conscience,[4] a concrete conclusion based upon a subjective, personal, individual obligation, since such an obligation supposes a previous application of the norm. It is an objective inference from an objective knowledge of man.

INFERENCES

In our analysis of the human act, we have noted that there are two distinct aspects of morality: the subjective and objective aspects.[5] From a consideration of these we draw some important inferences. First of all, we infer two fundamental moral truths and the opposite fundamental errors. Secondly, we propose a practical application of these truths in a brief study of the principle of double effect.

1. *Two Fundamental Truths and Two Fundamental Errors*

Objective Aspect of Morality: In judging the objective morality of the human act, we consider the object of the external act as

---

[4] "Conscience is a certain application of the natural law by way of conclusion to the personal act to be done" (*In II Sent.,* dist. 24, a. 2, a. 4). Some moralists call conscience a *subjective* norm.

[5] These words have a tendentious meaning in modern philosophical language. We use them here in their obvious English meaning: (1) objective, that is, morality of the object of the act, and (2) subjective, that is, imputability to the individual subject who places the act.

referred to a rational principle — e.g., killing an innocent person by one's own authority, blaspheming, giving alms — and conclude that some external acts are good or evil intrinsically, that is, objectively, because, without considering any will or end, the specifying object of the act is suitable or not suitable to the rational nature as ordered to the last end. Consequently, we state this truth absolutely: *There are external actions which in themselves, intrinsically, that is, by reason of their objects[6] which specify them, are of their very nature good or evil independently of the end of the agent.*

Subjective Aspect of Morality: On the other hand, we have seen that a moral act in the concrete, a human act, begins with the internal act of the will which is a voluntary act. We have shown that voluntariness consists in the proper inclination of the will to the effect. Now the morality of an external act is imputable to the subject placing this act only because of voluntariness. There is, therefore, no external moral act in the concrete and no imputability without the subjective element which we call voluntariness. Consequently, we may state this truth absolutely: *No external act is a concrete moral act, that is, no external act is imputable to the person placing the act, unless it is a voluntary act.*

Most of the errors regarding morality are due to a failure to understand properly either the subjective or objective element. Indeed, we might sum up all false notions of morality under two headings:

1. *Materialism,* which denies the subjective aspect, because it denies immateriality and with it the true notion of voluntariness. Hence, in a philosophy that is basically materialistic, morality is viewed necessarily from a utilitarian, pragmatic, and relativistic consideration of what is acceptable or is useful and of what will work here and now. There can be no imputability in the strict sense, no sin and no guilt.

2. *Kantianism* (moral rationalism), which, because it cannot reach the objectivity of the real, is compelled to base morality entirely on an act of the will (categorical imperative) and on the law estab-

---

[6] We mean of course "their formal objects," that is to say, the objects as referred to an active principle which is rational.

lished by the will.[7] Morality, therefore, is not objective and absolute but subjective and relative.

2. *Principle of Double Effect*

The consideration of the two fundamental elements of morality, subjective and objective, enables us to solve a problem that has been a source of anxiety to moralists throughout the years. The problem may be stated in this manner:

It is a fact of experience that sometimes from the same external action two effects may result, one good and one evil; e.g., by defending my life, I must destroy someone else's life. The problem is: When am I justified in placing an action from which two effects flow, one of which is objectively good, the other objectively evil?

St. Thomas throws light upon the problem and suggests a solution in the following text:

> Nothing prohibits one act from having two effects, of which one alone is in the intention, and the other beyond the intention. Now moral acts receive their species according to that which is intended, not however from that which is beyond the intention, since it is accidental. . . . Nevertheless, some act proceeding from a good intention can be rendered illicit if it is not proportionate to the end.[8]

Modern moralists enlarge upon this solution by stating that an action from which two effects will flow, one good, one evil, may be placed when these four essential conditions are fulfilled:

1. *The external act itself* (from which flow two effects) *must be objectively good or at least indifferent*. In other words, the object which specifies the act cannot be intrinsically opposed to rational nature. The reason is clear. We are *never* justified in placing an evil act. Now the external act is specified by its object. Hence, no matter what good effect may follow, we cannot place an action whose specifying object is evil.

2. *The causing of the good effect by the external act must be at least as direct and immediate as the bad*. By this is meant that the

---

[7] We shall show in the chapter on law that law worthy of the name primarily depends upon reason, not upon the will.

[8] *S. Th.*, II–II, 64, 7, *c.*

causal influx of the act into the good effect, and the causal dependence of the good effect upon the act, must not be subsequent to
and dependent upon the causing of the evil effect. (Note that this
is a matter of causal influx, not necessarily of sequence in time.)
The reason, of course, for this second condition is that a good end
does not justify an evil means; it is never permissible to place an
evil action, no matter how perfect the purpose may be.

3. *There should be a proportionately grave reason for placing an
act* from which an evil effect flows. In other words, if the evil is
much greater than the good, we must not place the act; to do so
would clearly be against right reason.

4. *We must never intend the evil effect,* that is, we must not will
an evil effect by the internal act of the will called intention. For if
we willed an evil, the end of the moral act would be evil and
therefore the whole human act would be vitiated.

N.B.: It is possible to know that an evil will follow a good action
and still not to will such an evil. Let us recall the psychological
fact that knowing is not identical with willing. Hence, while we
know that evil may follow, we need not desire it nor intend it.

SUMMARY

Question III

OBJECTIVE MORALITY OF THE HUMAN ACT

PART I. Goodness or Malice of the Moral Act in General

Article I: *The Good*

The unqualified good imports the plenitude of existence in any being.
If any due perfection is lacking, the being is not unqualifiedly good,
but evil.

Principle: Evil results from a single defect, good only from the
complete cause.

The human act to be good must have the plenitude of moral existence.

This plenitude supposes that the constitutive elements of the act—
object, end, and circumstance—are suitable to the rational principle
as rational.

Article II: *The Determinants of the Goodness or Malice of the Human Act*

Object — as referred to the rational principle is the first specifying factor — is like a formal cause.

Circumstances — as referred to the rational principle are the individuating accidents of the act — are like a material cause.

End:

a) As related to internal act — is a formal cause; it specifies the will-act.

b) As related to object of the external act — is the circumstance "why."

c) As related to whole act — is like its form.

d) As related to external act — is like an efficient cause and makes the act moral.

Article III: *Specific Distinction Between Good and Evil Moral Actions*

1. *Theory of specification:* Complete specification of an action is caused by its formal object, that is, by the object as related to the active principle of the operation.

2. *Application to moral act:* The object must be referred to the active principle viewed as rational. If suitable to the rational nature, the moral act is good; it disposes man to his last end. If unsuitable, the action is evil; it causes man to deviate from his last end. Consequently, good and evil moral acts are opposed as contrary species. In moral actions, good and evil establish distinct, fundamental, specific differences.

3. *Positive element in moral evil:* A specific determination is had only because of some positive perfection. Although evil is a lack of good, the evil end which is freely willed by an evil act is something positive. This something positive is the necessary requisite for the specific determination of the evil moral act. Hence only in the moral order do good and evil actions belong to distinct contrary species. For this reason no evil moral act is justifiable since such an act tends to frustrate the rational nature in the attainment of the last end.

Article IV: *The Norm of Morality*

Right reason is the norm.

Right reason is:

a) Neither the intellect which by its operation specifies the will-act;

b) Nor the rational nature to which the formal object of the act is related.

c) It is the true knowledge of the fundamental, universal, moral principles by which we judge the objective morality of the human act.

Right reason is not the virtue of prudence, because it is a true knowledge of universal, impersonal, moral judgments and does not specify the will-act.

Right reason is not synderesis, because it is a distinct acquired habit, not a mere innate inclination to know.

Right reason differs from *human-nature-adequately-taken* in this, that it is the actual acquired knowledge of the moral law which is discovered by a consideration of *human-nature-adequately-taken*.

Right reason is obtained:

1. By a reflection upon the finality, that is, the necessary tendency of human nature to the good. From this reflection the first principle of the moral law is established: "good should be done and evil avoided."

2. By a consideration of the radical tendencies of nature to the goods that are essential to the attainment of the last end, and of their contraries which are unsuitable to the rational nature. From such considerations the three primary precepts of the law are formed. All other more particularized judgments of law can be inferred from these fundamental precepts.

The complexus of all these fundamental, universal, impersonal judgments, as known by the intellect and retained in the memory, is called right reason. It is the true norm of morality.

PART II. THE MORALITY OF THE INTERNAL ACT OF THE WILL

Division: There will be four articles: (1) Is the object the sole determinant of the morality of the internal act? (2) Does an erroneous conscience affect the morality of the internal act? (3) May we act with a doubtful conscience? (4) What are the factors which affect the degree of the objective morality of an internal act; and finally, how can the internal act be conformed to God's will?

ARTICLE I: Is the Object the Sole Determinant of the Morality of the Internal Act?

In the preceding article we established the general principles which enable us to judge the goodness and malice of human acts. We are now in a position to apply these rules to the internal act of the will. For, as everyone knows, there are two types of human actions: the elicited or internal operations of the will, and the commanded acts which, although placed through the instrumentality of the sense faculties and the members of the body, remain under the direction and control of the will. These latter operations are called external acts. The internal act, obviously, is by far the more important of the two types of operations, since it flows immediately from a deliberate will.

Problem: The problem of the internal act of the will may be stated thus: What are the determinants of the morality of this act, or more exactly, what is the formal, specifying cause of its goodness or malice?

Formal Cause of the Morality of the Internal Act: Moral good and moral evil are essentially different; that is, they differ in their specific nature. The reason is that, while the good of man is that which is suitable to his nature, moral evil is directly opposed to that nature viewed under its most formal aspect, its rationality, and as ordered to its last end. Hence, good and evil when predicated of the act of the will manifest two distinct species of human act. What is the formal intrinsic cause of such specification? The answer is, of course, that the object as related to the active principle specifies the act. Consequently, the object of the internal act of the will causes the goodness or malice of the will-act. When the object is good, that is, in accordance with right reason, the act is good; when bad, the internal action is morally evil.

Object: The real point at issue, however, is to determine what we understand by "the object of the internal act of the will." We may say in general that this object is that which the will loves and freely seeks. Now love supposes knowledge of the good. Hence, the *understood good,* as presented by the intellect, is that which the will loves and seeks.[9] In other words, the *understood good* is the object of the will-act.[10] Now the understood good is the end of the will. For the good is the end of any appetite, and the good of the rational appetite is that which is presented by the faculty of knowledge, the intellect. Consequently, the *understood good,* which is the end, is really the object of the will. This brief argumentation indicates that, although the end as regards the external act is really distinct from the object,[11] nevertheless, in the internal act this is not the case, for the end here is not distinct from, but identical with the object. In point of fact, the end of the internal act *is* the object.

[9] St. Thomas devotes an entire article to showing why the goodness of the act of the will depends upon the intellect. For it is the intellect which must present the object to the will as good and properly suited to the will (cf. *S. Th.,* I–II, 19, 3, *c. et* ad 2^m). Finally, the highest measure and rule of the goodness of the act of the will is, as we mentioned in the preceding question, the eternal law (cf. *ibid.,* 4, *c*).

How does the eternal law rule human actions? The eternal law, which is identical with the wisdom of God, is communicated to man by an impression upon nature. This impression establishes the necessary finality of human nature to its last end. The natural law, therefore, is a created participation in the eternal law. It consists radically in the natural appetite of man to the absolute good. This law is discovered by the intellect of man and is actually expressed and habitually retained in the habit of right reason. Now it is obvious that the law, as expressed by right reason, is in the order of specification with regard to the will-act. Hence, the rule of law, that is to say, the causal influx of law upon the judgment of reason which specifies the will-act, will be applied through a judgment of conscience, and should terminate in a prudential judgment. For conscience, by manifesting a personal obligation, tends to resolve itself into a prudential judgment whose function is to determine formally the human act. In this way, therefore, is the eternal law the highest rule of the moral act, and a rule "from which the human act derives its goodness" (*ibid.*).

St. Thomas, the Christian theologian, adds that the eternal law in so far as it looks to the order of grace, that is, to the present existential order of human nature elevated to an intuitive vision of the Divine Essence, is communicated to man by revelation (Divine Law). "Hence in this existential order the goodness of the human will depends on the eternal law much more than upon human reason (i.e., more than upon the natural law as expressed by right reason). Consequently, when human reason fails, we must have recourse to eternal reason." (*Ibid.*)

[10] The object on which the goodness and malice of the act of the will depends . . . (is) not, indeed, the object according to its own nature, but according as it is . . . apprehended by reason . . . The object of the will is that which is proposed by reason . . . (*S. Th.,* I–II, 19, 5, *c*).

[11] The end is in the *intentional* order, that is, in the will-act, while the object is the existing term of the external act.

An example will clarify this statement: I will to kill a man in order to rob him. The object of my internal act, that which I will, is not merely to kill, but *to-rob-by-killing*. The *object-end* is one in my willing. On the other hand, as regards the external action, the actual killing is the object, the formal cause, the "whatness," of the act. Clearly, the intention of robbing is not identical with the actual murder. For while the killing, which is the means, takes place and is a physical reality, the end which I entertain and hope to accomplish is as yet in the intentional order. The end, therefore, which gives a distinct moral determination to the external act, is, as regards the internal act, one with the object.

Circumstances: Circumstances, we saw, sometimes add a distinct specification to the external act. Not so as regards the internal act. Why? Because when known, they are contained in the *understood good*. For circumstances, which as individuating accidents manifest the last determinations of the external object, are either known or not known. When not known, obviously they do not enter into the moral determination of the internal human act. When known, they are included in the understood good which is the object. Consequently, circumstances which are known and willed are one with the object-end of the internal act. They can never, therefore, add a new, distinct moral determination to this act.

Let us conclude. The three constituents of the objective morality of the human act — object, end, and circumstances — are, as regards the external acts, distinct determinants of the objective morality of the act. On the other hand, the *object* of the *internal act* of the will, which is the end and *includes* known circumstances, is the *sole moral determinant*. This important conclusion will enable us to formulate a true and definite solution to the following problem of an erroneous conscience.

ARTICLE II: Does an Erroneous Conscience Affect the Morality of the Internal Act?

Problem: The object which specifies the morality of the human act is the understood good. It is a fact of experience that at times this understood good does not correspond with reality. Such discrepancy is, of course, due to the weakness of the human intellect. This possibility of error brings up the problem of an erroneous conscience. Let us propose this problem. The goodness or malice of the internal act depends upon the object which is the understood good. The intellect by a judgment of conscience judges this understood object to be morally good or morally evil. Now it may happen that the individual subjective judgment of conscience is not in accord with truth. In such a case, conscience would err in directing the will to place an action which is objectively evil. This situation gives rise to two problems: (1) Is the will evil when at variance with erring conscience? (2) Is the will right and good if it abides by erring conscience? In other words, does an erring conscience bind? Does it excuse from guilt?

Conscience: Before presenting our solution, we should first of all propose the true notion of conscience. Conscience, remarks St. Thomas, is neither a distinct faculty nor a habit, but an act. It is an act of the intellect, a dictate of reason, a personal, individual, subjective judgment. *Conscience is the judgment by which we apply our knowledge of the moral law to a personal action done or to be done.*

True Judgment of Conscience Must Be Based on Right Reason: Let us consider how the judgment of conscience is formed. To begin with, every man is endowed with a natural inclination of the intellect to form first principles. This natural inclination is called the *habit of principles,* and it is the most fundamental habit of the intellect. Now just as the first principles[12] are formed by this natural inclination of the intellect[13] seeking to know truth; so in like manner as regards the first practical or moral principles which should direct human acts as their norm and rule, the intellect has a natural inclination to form first principles of the moral law. This natural inclination to form moral principles is called by scholastic

---

[12] Such are the principles of contradiction, of identity, of sufficient reason, of intelligibility, and the like.

[13] This natural inclination of the faculty to form speculative judgments is called *habit of understanding (intellectus).* It is a function of the habit of principles and is not distinct from it.

philosophers "synderesis." It is, if we may use such a phrase, an intellectual sense of right and wrong, an intellectual "taste" for morality. "Synderesis," declares Aquinas, "is a habit which contains the precepts of the natural law. These precepts are the first principles of human works."[14] Synderesis contains these principles only remotely, that is, as an innate inclination of the faculty to formulate such principles. Right reason is the formed, the acquired habit of these moral principles.

Judgments of the Norm: Obviously, the first principles of morality formed by this intellectual habit are not the judgments of conscience. They are universal, objective, and impersonal judgments which propose the true objective norm of morality. First of all, the intellect of man perceives that good is in accordance with nature, evil contrary to it; and hence that good should be done and that evil must be shunned. From this first principle man is able to enunciate the general precepts of the law. These fundamental precepts belong to what St. Thomas designates as right reason, that is, the true knowledge of the universal, fundamental judgments of the natural law.

Three Types of Judgments: Conscience is the application of a universal and objective moral principle to a personal human act. It is, therefore, an appraisal by which we judge the morality of our own actions. In placing an internal act of the will, we distinguish three types of judgments: (1) The judgments of the norm of morality, which belong to right reason and are formed by the intellect. These judgments are objective, universal, and impersonal. (2) The judgment of conscience, which applies the objective knowledge found in the norm to our personal individual actions. It is, therefore, a subjective judgment. (3) The various judgments which occur during the psychological process of the moral act. The function of these last-mentioned judgments is to specify the accompanying act of the will. Such are, for example, the judgments of the end-as-desirable and of the end-as-attainable which specify *volition* and *intention,* and the last practical judgment terminating in the precept (*ratio praeceptiva*) which specifies *choice.* Obviously, since the will

---

[14] *S. Th.,* I–II, 94, 1, ad 2ᵐ.

is free, these judgments of specification may not necessarily be in accord with the judgment of conscience and with that of the norm.[15] An example may prove helpful.

1. *Judgment of the norm:* Stealing is a moral evil because it is opposed to right reason.
2. *Judgment of conscience:* It is evil for me to steal my neighbor's watch.
3. *Judgment of specification:* It is better to steal; or it is better not to steal this watch. (Whichever judgment is freely formed, the will freely follows.) I will or will not to steal the watch.

Obligation: From this discussion we note that not only does the appraisal of conscience suppose a fundamental judgment of the norm, *viz.,* a judgment of the moral law as applied to a personal action, but it contains the resulting knowledge of a personal obligation to observe that law. This obligation is a *moral necessity,* that is, we are not physically coerced, although we understand that a failure to fulfill this obligation means a disposition which causes nature to deviate from its last end.

How does this obligation arise? Obligation, fundamentally, is the moral necessity which results from the finality of a rational nature to its last end. For from the understanding of such finality we infer that a moral act is good, because it disposes us to our happiness; while the evil act frustrates nature. It is a self-evident principle that the good of nature must be sought and that its contrary, evil, must be shunned. Hence, our obligation is to place good acts and to avoid evil. This obligation is moral; yet we can choose to fulfill it or not. We may say, therefore, that our awareness of such an obligation is founded upon the knowledge of the essential suitability of moral good and the opposition of moral evil to the nature of man as ordered to its end. "Since the good," explains Aquinas, "has the nature of an end, and evil is its contrary, those things which reason apprehends as good *must be sought;* their contrary, which reason apprehends as evil, *must be avoided.*"[16] This "must," this universal

---

[15] Whenever the judgment of specification is in accord with right reason, it is a prudential judgment.

[16] *S. Th.,* I–II, 94, 2, *c.*

and impersonal obligation of the first principle of the moral law, is discovered in and expressed by the more restricted precepts of the natural law which are contained in right reason. Consequently, in the application of the law to his own moral actions, man becomes aware of a personal obligation, a moral necessity to do this good and avoid this evil.[17] For these free human operations are the means which can either perfect or frustrate nature in the attainment of its end, the absolute good.[18] We repeat: moral obligation is expressed, first of all, by the first principle of law. This obligation, which is universal and impersonal, is perceived in a more restrictive manner in the knowledge of these various precepts of the moral law. We come to realize a personal and particular obligation by the application of these principles to our own individual human actions.

This personal and particular obligation is expressed by a judgment of conscience. The judgment of conscience, therefore, is the conclusion of a syllogism in which the universal *"must"* of the law, that is to say, the moral necessity which obligates all men, is applied to a personal action. The major of this syllogism is a universal precept of law which is a limited expression of the norm of morality. This premise implies a general obligation. The minor presents a personal action done or to be done. The concluding judgment is what we call conscience; it states an individual, personal obligation. An example will help visualize this process: Because stealing is evil, it must not be done (precept of the law — general obligation). But for me to take this watch is to steal (individual action done or to be done). Therefore, for me to take this watch is an action that must not be done because evil (judgment of conscience; expresses personal obligation).

Problem of an Erroneous Conscience: Let us restate the problem

---

[17] The obligation is moral, not physical. The reason is that man, because of the natural inclination of his rational nature to the absolute good, is endowed with freedom of judgment and of choice as regards the particular good.

[18] Because of the actual dependence of the will-act upon the desire for the last end, a moral action which is not suitable to the rational nature destroys the rectitude of the will. Now the rectitude of the will is a necessary condition to the attainment of the last end. Hence, an evil moral act causes the rational nature to be frustrated as regards the attainment of the end.

of an erring conscience proposed in the beginning of this article; it is twofold: (1) Is the will evil when at variance with an erroneous judgment of conscience? (2) Is the will morally right and good if it abides by such an erring conscience?

Erroneous Conscience: By an erroneous conscience we do not mean one that errs through its own fault, that is, a conscience which culpably errs. It is, of course, true that all errors are founded upon some sort of ignorance. If, however, the ignorance is vincible and therefore somehow culpable, there remains some degree of voluntariness toward the evil effect and therefore some guilt. This is not the problem. The ignorance supposed here regarding the true nature of the effect is invincible, not culpable. Consequently, there can be no voluntariness toward an evil effect which is not known and therefore not willed.

Solution: 1. *Will at variance with erroneous conscience.* Regarding the first query as to whether the internal act of the will which refuses to follow the dictate of an erring conscience is an evil act, the answer is: yes, of course, such an act is morally evil. For, as we have ascertained, the goodness or malice of an act depends upon its specifying object. Now the object of the internal act is not the object as it exists in its own nature, but it is the object *as understood.* This object, therefore, is morally good if it is *understood* as good, that is, in accordance with the judgment of conscience. Hence, should the will not abide by an erroneous conscience by embracing an object which is understood as evil, the internal act will be morally evil. Likewise, in refraining from willing what is proposed as a moral duty by conscience, the will becomes evil. Hence, any internal act of the will which is at variance with erring conscience is an evil act. "The will is evil because it wills evil, not indeed that which is evil in itself (*per se*), but that which is evil accidentally (*per accidens*), through being apprehended as such by reason."[19]

2. *Will abides by erring conscience.* The second problem is thus stated: Is the will which abides by an erring conscience good? We infer immediately that the internal act of the will is good, since it

---

[19] *S. Th.,* I–II, 19, 5.

is specified by the understood good as presented by the erroneous judgment of conscience.[20]

External Act: Whether the will abides by or is at variance with erroneous conscience, in either case, a further difficulty may be proposed regarding the external act, that is, regarding placing the effect. For this effect, contrary to the erroneous judgment of conscience is, in its nature, objectively good or evil according to the specification of its own *existing* object. St. Thomas remarks that neither the moral good nor the moral evil of an external act can be imputed to the one placing the effect with an erroneous conscience. The reason is that the external act is not voluntary because of the lack of true knowledge of the objective morality of the effect. For an erroneous conscience judges the act to be good when it is evil, and evil when good. Hence, the external object is not really known in its moral reality and, consequently, it is not willed. In a word, the external act as specified by its existing object is not voluntary. There is, therefore, no imputable goodness or malice in such an external action. The effect is not willed; it is not voluntary; it simply does not belong to the human act.[21]

This solution hinges upon the doctrine of voluntariness and involuntariness which was proposed earlier in this work. Voluntariness always supposes a true knowledge of the external effect, since it is an inclination of the will toward the effect. Accordingly, when there is no true knowledge of the external effect in so far as it is morally evil, because of blameless ignorance, there can be no voluntariness, and therefore no morality can be imputed for placing the external act. "Ignorance," states Aquinas, "sometimes causes involuntariness. . . . Now moral good and moral evil is found (*consistit*) in an act in so far as it is voluntary. . . . Consequently, the ignorance which causes involuntariness takes away the nature of moral good and moral evil. . . . If, therefore, the error of conscience arises from (invincible) ignorance . . . then that error excuses the

---

[20] When the will abides by conscience, the judgment of conscience is identical with the judgment of specification.

[21] "*Manifestum est quod illa ignorantia quae causat involuntarium, tollit rationem boni et mali moralis*" (S. Th., I–II, 19, 6, c).

will from being evil . . . (since) this ignorance causes the act to be involuntary."[22]

ARTICLE III: May We Act With a Doubtful Conscience?

Problem: Another problem related to conscience and, therefore, somewhat connected with the preceding question, considers the morality of placing a human act when the judgment of conscience brings no certitude regarding the objective moral goodness of such an operation. This problem may be stated in the form of a query: How must we act when in doubt as to the true objective morality of the action we are about to place? Are we justified in placing an action when conscience offers no certain judgment regarding its morality?

Before attempting a formal solution of this difficult problem, we should, first of all, obtain a clear understanding of what is meant by a doubt. Doubt is not the same as ignorance; it supposes some knowledge, such meager knowledge, however, as does not suffice to obtain certitude. It implies, therefore, a lack of certitude. Hence, to realize what doubt is, we must first analyze the notion of certitude.

Certitude: Certitude is not a judgment, but like formal truth, it is found in a judgment.[23] "Certitude," explains the Angelic Doctor, "is the determination of the intellect to one."[24] It consists in the "firmness of adherence of the cognoscitive power to that which it knows."[25] In its formal aspect, this definition indicates the absolute determination of the intellect to one object, excluding thereby other determinations of the faculty to objects opposed to the first. In the same manner, we may say that the firmness of adherence excludes the possibility of adhering to opposed objects of

---

22 *S. Th.*, I–II, 19, 6, *c*.

23 Recall the true signification of the term *judgment.* We do not mean merely a logical composition and division, but an estimation, a judgment of objective truth because of evidence.

24 *"Determinatio intellectus ad unum"* (*In III Sent.*, 23, 2, 2, *c*).

25 *"Firmitas adhaesionis virtutis cognitivae in suum cognoscibile"* (*In III Sent.*, 26, 2, 4, *c*).

knowledge. In this absolute determination of the intellect and in the firmness of its adherence to the object of knowledge, we place the true nature of certitude. It is true, however, that this firmness, although absolute on each level, is susceptible of various degrees according as the nature of the knowledge adhered to belongs to metaphysical, physical, or moral laws.

Another definition proposed by some other philosophers is that certitude is the firm assent of the mind as regards truth, which assent is so secure as to exclude fear of error. This definition in its formal aspect indicates that the security or firmness of the assent is such as to be incompatible with fear of error. Fear, however, is an act of the appetite; whereas certitude belongs to the intellect. A fear of error results in the appetite from a knowledge that is doubtful. For if the mind lacks sufficient evidence for a firm adhesion in the object of knowledge, it perceives the possibility of error. The act of the appetite called fear results from the knowledge of such a possibility. The reason is that "the true" is the good of the intellect, while error is an intellectual evil. Now fear is a motion of the appetite away from an impending evil. Hence, the knowledge of the possibility of error which is an intellectual evil arouses fear in the appetite.

On the other hand, the lack of fear of error in the appetite is due to a knowledge that presents no possibility of error because of the determination of the intellect to one object. It is evident then that the exclusion of fear of error is not of the essence of certitude. Rather this lack of fear results as the property of a knowledge that is certain. Firmness of adherence to the object of knowledge, that is to say, the determination of the intellect to one and only one object, seems to be the essential note of certitude.

Doubt:[26] There are two kinds of doubts. The first leaves the mind in suspense between two contradictories so that there is no

---

[26] By doubt we mean, of course, a positive, a reasonable doubt, that is, one founded on some positive evidence or a lack of sufficient objective evidence needed for an assent of the mind that is certain. We do not mean a negative doubt or scruple, since these are not based on reasonable evidence but are irrational doubts. We should never allow any negative doubt to interfere with our moral actions.

assent of the mind, no adherence to an intelligible object.[27] The second is such that the mind inclines more to one object than to the opposite although knowing the possibility of error. This second type of doubt is the disposition of one who forms an opinion.[28] The following text explains clearly the true significance of doubt.

> As to the parts of a contradiction, our possible intellect is disposed (*se habet*) in a different manner. Sometimes the intellect is not inclined more to one than to the other, either because of the lack of motives (ignorance) as in other problems regarding which we have no evidence (*rationes*), or because of the apparent equality of evidence which moves us to either part of the contradiction. Such is the disposition of one who doubts; he wavers between two parts of a contradiction.
>
> Sometimes our intellect inclines more to one than to the other; the evidence, however, does not sufficiently move the intellect so that it determines itself entirely to one part (of the contradiction); hence it accepts one part although it *constantly doubts* (as to the truth) *of the opposite*. This is the disposition of one who opines (has an opinion), that is, of one who accepts one part of the contradiction with fear of the other. (*De Veritate,* XIV, 1, *c.*)

Opinion: The judgment which results from the second type of doubt is called an opinion. It is, as we have just remarked, an assent of the mind, but it lacks the necessary firmness which is needed for certitude. Such a judgment, obviously, must suppose some evidence, since no rational assent of mind can be based upon complete ignorance. The intellect adheres to its object, not, however, in such a perfect manner as to exclude the knowledge and fear of possibility of error.

In short: *Certitude* is the determination of the mind to one; it is the firm adherence of the mind to its object. It is founded on knowledge of such evidence that the adherence of the mind to its object is sufficiently firm to exclude knowledge of the possibility of error. We form a judgment endowed with certitude when this perfect determination of the intellect exists.

---

27 This type of doubt can be called ignorance. It is a lack of knowledge.

28 "He who inclines to one part, yet with fear of the other, is said to opine" (*S. Th.,* II–II, 2, 1, *c*).

Doubt is a lack of certitude. The first type of doubt is based upon evidence which keeps the mind in suspense and prevents the determination of the intellect to one. The other type of doubt is based on evidence which is not sufficient for the firm adherence of the mind to one object. There is in the intellect because of this doubt knowledge of the possibility of error. From the incomplete, the limited evidence which is not sufficient to obtain the firmness of assent necessary for certitude, we may form an opinion. For "if this (assent of the intellect) be accompanied by doubt and fear of the opposite side, there will be an opinion."[29]

Opinion is a judgment in which the adherence of the mind to an object lacks the necessary firmness to exclude knowledge of possibility of error.[30]

Ignorance is merely a lack of knowledge. As a result of the state of ignorance, there is no evidence sufficient for any rational assent of the mind, not even for an opinion.[31]

From this exposition we infer that:

To act with a doubtful conscience is morally evil. This inference is established thus: The first principle of the moral law is that good is to be done and evil to be avoided. Now when we act with a doubtful conscience, we do not exclude but accept the possibility that the action may be morally evil. We do not, therefore, will to avoid evil. Hence, such an act is evil, since the object which specifies the internal act of the will, the understood object, is *understood as not excluding evil.*

Consequently, as long as conscience remains in doubt as to the objective morality of an act, we must refrain from placing such an action. Indeed, if we must act, we are bound morally to embrace the safer course.

How to Remove Doubt and to Form a Safe Conscience: Some-

---

[29] *S. Th.,* II–II, 1, 4, c.

[30] "It is of the very nature of an opinion that the thing assented to (*opinatum*) be thought possible to be otherwise" (*S. Th.,* II–II, 1, 5, ad 4[m]).

[31] Ignorance which is the lack of knowledge cannot be the foundation for any rational opinion. For, to give an example, while I may state with the spoken word that the number of stars is even or that it is odd, there can be no mental assent, no opinion because of the lack of evidence.

times, however, it is possible to remove our doubt so that the judgment of conscience, which looks to the morality of placing an act, is no longer an opinion but becomes an assent which obtains certitude. There are three possible approaches to the certain judgment of conscience necessary for a good act. First, we may directly arrive at certitude by analyzing carefully the premise (the judgment) in which the doubt occurs. Should this analysis fail to give us the evidence required for certitude, we should, if possible, have recourse to a trustworthy authority. When, however, neither of these means can be realized, or, in other words, when our doubt cannot be removed directly, it is sometimes possible, by having recourse to a *reflex principle,* to obtain the certitude needed for a good moral act. Thus we are enabled to remove the doubt indirectly. It is true, such a reflex principle may not remove the speculative doubt, but sometimes it will dispel the practical doubt which impedes the placing of the moral act.[32] Let us exemplify this statement. We shall suppose that I am in doubt as to the existence of a certain law and have no way of removing this doubt that such a law exists. In this state of doubt, I am morally bound to refrain from placing a moral act at variance with the law. I can, however, by having recourse to the reflex principle that a doubtful law does not oblige in conscience, dispel my practical doubt as to the morality of an action contrary to this same law. For I am certain that this law, because it is a doubtful law, has no binding force;[33] unless, of course, there is a possibility of harming the rights of another. These rights, however, should not be doubtful, but certain and definite, as for example, the right to life. For to endanger the certain rights of others is to go against a fundamental precept of the natural law.

---

[32] The speculative doubt regards the law itself. The practical doubt looks to the moral act. As long as the practical doubt remains, the object of the act as known includes the possibility of evil. Hence, unless the practical doubt is removed, the moral act is evil.

[33] *"Nullus legatur per preceptum aliquod nisi mediante scientia illius precepti"* (*De Veritate,* XVII, 3). *"Preceptum non obligat antequam sit divulgatum"* (*In IV Sent.,* dist. 3, art. 5, sol. 3). In the chapter on law we shall show that a law, when not properly promulgated, is not a true law.

The principle is applicable not only to the law in general but to any particular case comprehended under that law. Let us suppose, for example, that I am in doubt (positively) and have no means of discovering whether I have paid a certain debt. In such a case, I am not bound to pay the debt since I am in doubt as to whether the law applies. There is no question of the possible creditor having rights that are definitely and certainly established. There is no question, therefore, of harming the definite and certain rights of another. Consequently, I am not bound to pay the doubtful debt, because a law which is not applicable with certitude does not oblige.

We said advisedly "unless there is danger of harming the definite and *certain* rights of another." In such a case, no reflex principle could dispel the practical doubt; hence, we would be obliged in justice to follow the safer course. For to act otherwise would be an evil act, since the object of the act, the understood good, does not in this case exclude the will to harm another. An example will make this point clear. One cannot shoot to kill a deer when there is a positive doubt that the "deer" might really be a man. In this instance, the doubt regards neither the law, which is absolute ["Murder is an evil act"], nor the comprehension of any individual case under the law, since everyone has a natural right to life. The doubt here is concerned only with the actual presence of the individual. This doubt, obviously, cannot be dispelled by having recourse to a reflex principle.[34] Hence, because of the possibility of harming the certain rights of another, we are obliged to follow the safer course, and in this case, we are bound not to act.[35]

We conclude: Whenever a doubt occurs solely regarding the existence of a law and not regarding the definite and certain rights of another who might be harmed by my action, I may obtain, by

---

[34] One possible exception is had when I have to choose between endangering the rights of another or my own. In such a case, I may act either way. An example will bring out the point. Should someone rush at me with a gun with a possible intention of killing me, although his right to life is certain and I am in doubt of his intention, nevertheless, I may in an effort to defend myself kill the possible aggressor.

[35] In theology this principle is of great practical importance in the use of the matter for the sacraments, since there is a possibility of harming the salvation of souls.

the consideration of a reflex principle, the certitude in a judgment of conscience required for a good moral act.

Let us state by way of summary:

1. A moral act placed with a doubtful conscience is an evil act.

2. The practical doubt regarding the morality of placing an act which results from the speculative doubt as to the existence of a law, or the comprehension of an individual case under a law, may be dispelled by a reflex principle.

3. When the doubt connotes and implies the possibility of harming the *definite* and *certain* rights of another, we are bound in conscience to follow the safer course.

ARTICLE IV: Degree of Objective Goodness or Malice of the Internal Act and Conformity to the Divine Will

Following the order of the *Summa Theologica,* we shall close the question of the internal act with the presentation of two interesting problems. The first of these inquires into the objective reason for a greater or lesser degree of goodness or malice in the same specific internal act. The second is concerned with the necessity and the true meaning of the conformity of the moral act with the Divine Will.

I. Degree of Goodness or of Malice

After studying the nature and causes of the specific determination of good and evil in the moral act, we logically focus our attention on the nature and causes of the varying degrees of this same specific moral determination. Why, we ask, can two will-acts of the same specific determination possess diverse degrees of objective goodness or of malice? St. Thomas explains that the degree of goodness and malice of a moral act depends largely upon two factors: the quantity of the object and the intensity of intention.

This question may seem at first similar to the problem of voluntariness which is concerned with the degree of guilt or merit of the moral act. There are, however, profound differences. The problem of voluntariness is rather psychological, subjective, and negative. Our question here is moral, objective, and positive. The treatise on voluntariness studies the *psychological* nature of an inclination of the will. It explains why various degrees of guilt or merit are imputable (*subjective* aspect) to the agent. It determines the degree of this merit or guilt *negatively* by considering the obstacles to the perfection of this inclination of the will which we call voluntariness. In this present question, on the contrary, what we want to know is quite different. First, we are endeavoring to analyze the *objective morality* of an act, not a subjective imputation of guilt or merit to the agent. Secondly, we want to determine the *positive* factors of the varying degrees, not of the guilt or of the merit, but of the *moral* goodness or malice of the same specific human act. Finally, as regards the internal act, there can be no problem of voluntariness, since the object of the will-act is the object *as known,* not the object *as it is.* Hence, there can be no lack of the perfect knowledge necessary for voluntariness.

St. Thomas lists two positive factors of objective morality. They are the quantity of the object willed and the quantity, or rather the degree, of intensity of the intention. The first depends upon the object chosen; the second looks to the end and depends upon the agent.

1. *Object:* It is sufficiently evident that the quantity of the object desired and willed affects the degree of goodness or malice of the same moral act. Thus the will to steal a larger rather than a lesser sum — all other things being equal — will increase the objective malice of the crime of theft in the will-act.

2. *Intensity of the will-act:* The intensity of the intention, although directed to the end, redounds upon the act of choice. The reason is that "in things voluntary, the intention of the end, and the will to do those things which are ordered to the end (i.e., choice), are one and the same motion."[36] "For the intention, in a certain manner, belongs to the act of the will (willing the means), since it is its essence (*ratio*). Consequently, the quantity (that is, the intensity) of a good intention flows into (*redundat*) the will (willing the means)."[37] For the will is able to will these means only in so far as it wills the end.

---

[36] *S. Th.,* I–II, 12, 4.   [37] *S. Th.,* I–II, 19, 8.

Briefly, then, the increase of moral goodness or malice of the internal act depends (1) upon the quantity of the object willed, and (2) upon the intensity of the intention.

II. Conformity With the Will of God

Finally, to anyone who has thought about the matter, it is evident that in order to be morally good the will of man should be conformed to the Divine Will. There are many reasons why this should be so. Perhaps the most profound is that, since man is a part of the perfect community of the universe, his will should always be directed to the common good, which is the good of the universe. Now the good of the universe is precisely the *object of God's will,* for the will of God is in accordance with His wisdom which is the supreme knowledge (*ratio*) and *exemplar* of the order of the universe. It follows that in order to be morally good, the will of man must always be conformed to the Divine Will. Any human act, therefore, which fails in this conformity is an unreasonable act. It is evil.

The real problem in this matter, however, is not found in establishing formally that man's will should always be in agreement with and never opposed to the divine law, which is communicated to us by the Divine Will. The difficulty, rather, is *how* can this conformity be discovered? For, as it occurs not infrequently, we may not be able to ascertain the true relation of some individual actions — whose objects are not evil — to the common good. Consequently, we may remain in the dark as to their conformity with God's will. In such a case, it may happen "that a certain will is good from a particular aspect, and this aspect God does not will universally."[38]

The solution to this problem is that *man should refer all such actions to the will of God,* willing them in so far as they are in accordance with the Divine Will. In this fashion, the human will is always formally conformed with the will of God. Thus man

---

[38] *S. Th.,* I–II, 19, 10. One excellent example is given of a judge who wills to condemn a criminal, while the thief's wife naturally wishes him not to be put to death.

formally wills the common good which is the will of God. The reason is that God not only moves the will in the order of exercise but also gives to the action itself its "to be" (*esse*).

Hence, although ignorant of God's will in this or that particular matter, man wills formally what God wills by referring his act to the Divine Will. Indeed, even materially, "a man's will is conformed to the Divine Will, because he wills what God wills him to will."[39]

> In both these respects, the human will is in some manner conformed to the Divine Will. According as it is conformed with the Divine Will in the common note of the thing willed, it is conformed with it in respect to the ultimate end. On the other hand, according as it is not conformed to the Divine Will materially in the thing willed, it is conformed with it according to the note of efficient cause. For a thing has from God, as from the efficient cause, this proper inclination following upon nature or upon a particular apprehension of this thing.[40]

SUMMARY

PART II. The Morality of the Internal Act

Article I: *Object (Object-End) Is Sole Determinant of Morality of Internal Act.*

Object of will-act is end. It includes circumstances. It is in the order of knowledge as apprehended by reason. The objective morality of the internal act, its goodness or malice, is caused (specified) by the object *as understood,* not as it exists.

Article II: *Erroneous Conscience and Moral Act*

Conscience is a judgment (judging) by which we apply our knowledge of the moral law to a personal action done or to be done. The judgment of conscience is the conclusion of a syllogism (a reasoning) in which the major is a judgment of the law, and the minor a personal action done or to be done. The judgment of conscience is erroneous when it is not in accord with objective moral truth.

---

[39] *Loc. cit.* Cf. *The Philosophy of God,* pp. 156–161.
[40] *Loc. cit.*

Distinguish between:

Judgment of norm — objective, universal, impersonal.

Judgment of conscience — subjective, particular, personal.

Judgment of specification — subjective, particular, personal which specifies the will-act. It may or may not be in accord with conscience.

Obligation is a moral necessity which results from the finality of rational nature to the last end. It is a "must" inferred from this finality as regards the means which dispose to the end, and a "must not" as regards those which detract from it. Moral necessity does not coerce the will.

Distinguish between:

General or universal, impersonal obligation expressed by precepts of law (right reason).

Particular, individual, and personal obligation expressed by judgment of conscience.

1st Problem: Is the will evil when at variance with an erroneous conscience?

Solution: Yes, because the object of the will-act is evil since the object is the good *as understood,* not necessarily *as is.* In this case, the object of the will-act as understood is opposed to the good as presented by judgment of an erroneous conscience. Hence, the internal act is specified by an evil object as understood.

2nd Problem: Is the will good if it abides by an erring conscience?

Solution: Yes, for the will-act is specified by the good as understood. The external act, however, is specified by an evil object. It is objectively evil but not known to be evil. Hence, it is not a voluntary act, since the object is not known in its objective reality to be evil. There is, therefore, no inclination of the will toward the object as it actually exists. The objective morality of the external act is not imputable because it is involuntary.

Article III: *Doubtful Conscience*

Certitude is the determination of the intellect to one. It consists in the firmness of adherence of the intellect to the object of knowledge; no possibility of error is seen. When such determination of intellect exists, the judgment is certain.

Doubt is the lack of certitude. Two types: (1) prevents the mind from making an assent, (2) results from lack of sufficient evidence for firmness of adherence of intellect to one object; possibility of error is known.

Opinion is a judgment in which the adherence of the intellect lacks firmness. "It is accompanied by doubt and fear of the opposite side."

Ignorance is a lack of knowledge.

Doubtful Conscience: Judgment of conscience in which there is no certitude as to whether an act is good or evil morally.

Problem: Are we justified in placing a human act with a doubtful conscience?

Solution: No, we are not justified in placing a human act with a doubtful conscience, because the object as known does not exclude the possibility of evil. The will-act is specified by an evil object. The act is evil. Doubt can sometimes be removed because a doubtful law does not oblige in conscience. For a law, to be a true law, should be promulgated so as to be known with certitude. If no practical doubt remains as to the goodness of the action, we may act unless there is danger of harming the certain rights of another.

Article IV: (*a*) *Degree of Objective Morality;* (*b*) *Conformity to Divine Will*

a) Degree of goodness and malice of internal act depends on quantity of object as understood and on intensity of the will-act.

b) Conformity with the will of God. Man should conform all actions to the will of God, willing them in accordance with the Divine Will.

PART III. THE MORALITY OF THE EXTERNAL ACT

Prologue

Problem: What is the place of the external act in the scheme of the objective morality of the human act? In itself, that is, leaving out its dependence upon the act of the will, an external action is not a moral act and therefore is neither good nor evil in the moral order.[41] For the moral order consists in the free intention of the will as related to the end. Consequently, an external action can be in the moral order only in so far as commanded and controlled by the will. All this is obvious. We may state at once, therefore, that we

---

[41] While the *object* of the external act may be intrinsically good or evil as compared with rational nature, nevertheless, the action itself is not a moral act unless controlled by the internal act of the will.

are dealing here with only those external acts which are commanded and controlled by the free will of man. The point to be examined, the problem to be solved, is this: Does the external act affect the morality of the whole human act? This we shall study from two points of view by proposing two queries. First, is the objective morality, that is, the goodness or malice of the external act, identical with that of the internal act? Secondly, does the placing of the external act in any way add to the degree of goodness or malice of the internal act?

ARTICLE I: Is the Objective Morality of the External Act Identical With That of the Internal Act?[42]

Meaning of the Problem: In the human act the internal act of the will and the external act are two distinct realities, each possessing a certain goodness or malice of its own. The problem is whether the objective morality of the external act, in its specific determination, differs from that of the internal act.[43] St. Thomas assures us that these two goodnesses or malices are not only the same specifically, but even numerically identical (*specie et numero*). They possess one and the same morality.

And yet the elements which determine the morality of the will and those of the external act are often distinct. The will is determined by the end which is its object, while the external act is specified by an object which is distinct from the end. How then can the respective morality of these operations be one and the same?

Unity of the Human Act: To solve this question properly, we must first of all analyze the unit which results from the union between internal and external act. The human act, we have noted before, is one because of the singleness of the will-act called *intention*. For it is the intention which by its continued influx moves and directs the subsequent operations of intellect and will as well as

---

[42] The supposition here is that we have true knowledge of the external act in its objective morality.

[43] This problem occurs only in the supposition that we have a true knowledge of the objective morality of the external act.

those of the external members. For that reason, we may compare the union between the internal and the external act to that union discovered in corporeal substances between matter and form. "For," explains Aquinas, "just as in the genus of natural things (order of nature) a certain whole (*totum*) is composed of matter and form, as man who is one natural being, although he has many parts, is composed of soul and body, so also in human acts, the act of a lower power is as matter in relation to the act of a higher power, in so far as the lower power acts in virtue of the higher power moving it; for thus also the act of the first mover is as the form in relation to the act of its instrument. Hence, it is evident that command and the commanded act are one human act, just as a certain whole is one, but is many according to parts."[44] Let us add, however, that the unity of the human act is not in the order of nature; it is not, therefore, a perfect ontological unit resulting from a single "to be." Rather, the human act is one analogously; that is, it is a unit in this way, that the direction and control of the external act is effected by the act of the will. Hence, this unity is not really that of matter and form; rather, it is *like* the unity which results from the union of matter and form. "The act of the will is *as* form to the exterior act. From a formal and material principle, however, result one."[45]

What, then, are the relations which exist between these two acts, internal and external? In other words, what is the causality which lies between these acts? Only by pointing out what this causality is, can we hope to explain why the objective morality of both acts is one and the same.

Reciprocal Causality: Let us recall, first of all, that although the end and object of the act are identical in the internal act, they are distinct in the external act. The fact of the matter is that, while the end as willed is from the will, the object as known is from reason.[46] The object of the external act must first be known, then proposed to the will by the reason. We must say, then, that the

---

[44] *S. Th.*, I–II, 17, 4, *c.*
[45] *S. Th.*, I–II, 20, 3, *c.*
[46] The object here includes circumstances.

object is prior in the order of knowledge to the willing of the end, for reason must know before the will can desire. Willing the end, on the other hand, is first in the order of execution. Hence, in the order of knowledge, the object of the external act, as known by the intellect, is included in the *formal* cause of the internal act of the will.[47] For the specification of the act of the will is from the effect as known and desired. On the other hand, in the order of execution, the external act is placed and the effect produced because of the *efficiency* of the will which has been actuated in the order of intention by the desire of the end. Consequently, "the goodness of the act of the will is the (extrinsic) form of the external act as existing in the agent."[48] "If the goodness of the external act is considered according as it is in the ordination and apprehension of reason, it is prior to the goodness of the act done; but if it is considered in so far as it is the execution of the act done, it follows the goodness of the will, which is its principle."[49] In short, the causal relations between internal and external acts are the following:

1. The external act as known by reason in its objective morality is the formal cause of the internal act. "The external act is the object of the will in as much as it is proposed to the will by reason."[50]

2. Not only is the *will* the efficient cause of the external act, but "the goodness (morality) of the act of the will is the (extrinsic) form of the exterior act as existing in the agent."[51]

Clearly, the placing of the external act in the order of execution does not add a new element to the morality of the internal act, since the effect is found in the act of the will as known and willed. "There is *one* goodness of the internal and external act."[52] For, on the one hand, it is the external act as known and desired which determines formally the internal act of the will; and on the other, it is the will as actuated by the desire of the known end which not

---

[47] "The external act is the object of the will inasmuch as it is proposed to the will by reason" (*S. Th.*, I–II, 20, 1, ad 1[m]).

[48] *Ibid.*, ad 3[m].

[49] *Ibid.*, c.   [50] *Ibid.*, ad 1[m].   [51] *Ibid.*, ad 3[m].   [52] *Ibid.*, 3, c.

only efficiently causes the external act, but formally determines it.

Distinct Source of Objective Morality: If we ask, however, whether the elements (*rationes*) of the goodness and malice found in the acts are derived from the same sources, the answer is: no, not always. For sometimes the object of the external act is good or bad in its own right. In this instance, the morality of the external act results from two distinct elements, one of which, the object, is the formal cause; the other, the end, is received through the efficient causality of the act of the will. Accordingly, sometimes the goodness which comes from the will is not the same as that which comes from the external act. In other cases, the specifying object of the external act is indifferent in the order of morality as referred to right reason; such, for example, is the act of walking. In this instance, the external act has its entire morality from the end which comes from the act of the will.

We should not conclude, however, that because the sources of the elements of morality sometimes are distinct, the *morality* of the interior act and that of the external act are really distinct, at least numerically. St. Thomas is definite on this point. It is true, he points out, that the internal and external acts are distinct in the order of nature (*secundum genus naturae*), that is, as distinct operations; but in the order of morality (*secundum genus moris*) they are one. For, and this should be noted carefully, "from the goodness of the act of the will is derived the goodness of the external act and vice versa." Consequently, just as in the analogy of attribution it is the same identical perfection (*specie et numero*) which is attributed to both secondary analogates, so here the goodness of one act is attributed to the other.[53]

Our conclusion stands.

If we consider the sources of goodness and malice of the internal and external acts:

1. In the order of knowledge: The morality which is derived from the external act (when the object is not indifferent) is first, because this object has to be known in order to be desired.

---

[53] Cf. *S. Th.*, I–II, 20, 3, ad 3ᵐ.

2. In the order of execution: The morality which is derived from the will willing the end is first.

3. In the moral order (*in genere morum*): The objective morality of either internal or external act is one and the same, not only specifically but even numerically (*specie et numero*).

Solution: We are now able to give a complete solution to our initial problem. To the question, "Is the objective morality (the goodness or malice) of the external act identical with that of the internal act?" we answer unequivocally: yes. For whatever distinct elements of morality may be derived from either of these acts, these elements are formally communicated to the other act. There is only one objective morality of the human act, and it is found to be the same specifically and numerically in both acts, internal and external.

ARTICLE II: Does Placing or Not Placing the External Act Increase or Decrease the Goodness or Malice of the Internal Act of the Will?

This may seem an idle question, since we have just shown that the objective morality of the internal and the external act is one and the same. Indeed we might infer immediately that placing or not placing the external act can in no way indicate or cause an increase or decrease in the goodness and malice of the internal act. The fact of the matter is, that man is a substance composed of form and matter, whose external operations are in time and space. Accordingly, certain conditions pertaining to space and time may sometimes cause the internal act to be renewed and even increased in its morality when the external act is placed. These occurrences, however, do not destroy the truth already established in the preceding article that the objective morality of the internal and the external act is one and the same. They merely indicate certain changes which occur accidentally because of the corporeal element in human nature. Even in those cases when the morality of the internal act is increased by placing the external act, the final outcome will prove an identity of objective morality of both actions.

Problem: Our present problem is this: Does the actual placing of the external act in the order of existence perfect in any way the already-specified act of the will, which not only is elicited first, but must continue its influx in order to move the members of the body toward the placing of the external act? Does this placing of the external act increase the degree of goodness or malice of the internal act?

Solution: We have pointed out in the previous article that both end and object enter into the constitution of the internal as well as the external act, but in a different manner. For this reason, to the query, "Does the external act increase the morality of the internal act?" we must, in answer, first distinguish between the morality of the end and that of the object.

I. **End:** If we speak of the morality which the external act derives from the will as it tends *to the end,* the answer is: "No," the placing of the external act *of itself* adds nothing, for the external act depends absolutely upon the will for its end. There are, however, three exceptions to the general rule, (1) because of the number of internal acts, (2) because of the duration of the internal act, and (3) because of the intensity of the internal act.

1. When there has been some interruption, the placing of the external act will necessitate a renewal of the act of the will.

2. When, in spite of difficulties, the will perseveres in its first intention until the external act is placed, the duration of the internal act is lengthened.

3. When there is something painful or delightful in the nature of the external act, the act of the will grows in intensity.

In these three instances "the will is made better in good things and worse in evil things."[54]

II. **Object:** If, however, we speak of the morality which the external act derives from object and circumstances, the answer is that the placing of the external act *of itself* does perfect the will. The reason is that every motion is made perfect by the attainment of its term. Hence, the act of the will, which is a motion, is made perfect when it reaches its term which is the external act. The failure to place the external act would generally indicate a lack of

---

[54] *S. Th.,* I–II, 20, 4, *c.*

perfection in the act of the will. There is, however, one notable exception. It may happen that the external act is not placed solely because of extrinsic factors and through no fault on the part of the will. The will, contrary to its inclination and therefore *involuntarily,* is prevented from causing the external act. In this case, the fact that the action is not placed is in no way due to the lack of perfection in the act of the will. Hence, such omission does not make the will less perfect than it would have been had the external action been placed.[55]

Conclusion: The important inferences drawn from this discussion are, first of all, that the external act is a moral act only because of its dependence in the order of execution upon the internal act willing the end. Secondly, that the external act depends primarily for its species upon its object and circumstances as actually determining this act. Thirdly, that this same object *as known* by reason enters into the determination of the internal act.

Consequently, although the goodness and malice of both operations are specifically identical, nevertheless, it often happens that the placing of the external act will add to the perfection of the act of the will, that is, to its degree of goodness or malice.[56]

APPENDIX

Consequents of the Human Acts by Reason of Their Goodness and Malice

At the end of this lengthy and difficult treatise on the morality of the human act, and by way of integrating the more important

---

[55] St. Thomas is of the opinion that failure to place the external act when it could be placed indicates an inefficacious act of desire. In such a case, because the internal act is imperfect, the complete objective goodness or malice of the object cannot be attributed to the subject of the internal act. Accordingly, the perfect act of desire is had *only* when the failure to place the external act is due solely to causes that are extrinsic to the will. Only in such an instance is the complete morality of the external act attributable to the subject of the internal act. This, we should note, is an extremely important factor in judging the guilt of sins of desire.

[56] A point mentioned previously, but one which logically also belongs here, is that a continuous external act may belong to several distinct moral acts because of the change or renewal of intention.

inferences, St. Thomas proposes what he calls the consequents of the human acts. These consequents, he explains, are certain notions (*rationes*[57]) which result from the human acts by reason of the goodness and malice of the actions. Thus, because a human act is good or evil, (1) it has the nature (*ratio*) of rectitude or of sin; (2) moreover, the good act is worthy of praise and the sin worthy of blame; (3) consequently, a moral action possesses the element either of merit or demerit which implies reward or punishment; (4) finally, the human act, which must be referred to God, the last end, is either meritorious or demeritorious before God according as it is good or evil.

I. *Rectitude and Sin*

The notions of rectitude and of sin are more restricted; they have a lesser extension[58] than the concept of good and evil. To the notion of the good, rectitude adds a relation to a due end; on the other hand, sin indicates a relation to an end which is not proportioned to the agent. Now in human actions the relation to the true end is measured, first of all, by right reason which is the proximate norm, and lastly by the supreme norm which is the eternal law. "When, therefore, a human act tends to the end according to the order of reason and of the eternal law, that act is right" because it is good; "when it swerves from that rectitude, it is a sin"[59] because it is evil.

II. *Praise and Blame*

Just as sin and the good moral act have a more limited extension than evil and good, so guilt and praiseworthiness are more restricted than sin and the righteous act. The notions of guilt and deserving of praise add the note of voluntariness, that is, of imputability of the good or evil of the act to its author. To praise or to blame is to attribute the goodness or malice of the act to the agent; "in

---

[57] The *"rationes"* themselves are discovered in the reality. We analyze these and reflect upon them in our understanding (concepts) of them.

[58] Extension of a notion refers to the possibility of the number of subjects (inferiors) of which the notion may be predicated. Comprehension signifies the intelligibility of a notion. Hence the saying: the lesser the extension, the greater is the comprehension.

[59] *S. Th.,* I–II, 21, 1, *c.*

voluntary acts alone, good and evil constitute the essence of praise or blame; and in such acts, evil, sin, and guilt are one and the same thing."[60]

III. *Merit and Demerit*

The notions of merit and demerit not only flow from the nature of an act that is praiseworthy or blameworthy, but they also add a new intelligible note. For we speak of merit and demerit in relation to retribution rendered according to justice. Hence, a demeritorious act is a sinful and culpable act which calls for the proper retribution or punishment. On the other hand, a meritorious action indicates not only that the action is praiseworthy but adds the right to recompense.

Merit[61] fundamentally is based on strict justice. It is an acquired right to reward because of a good action. Reward, therefore, signifies something bestowed by reason of merit. It is a "retribution" (*retributio*), a sort of price due to the labor involved. The opposite, that is, the retribution called punishment, results from the demeritorious act. Sanctions, therefore, should not be thought of as something depending upon the will of the ruler. Such a notion of sanction is based on an erroneous notion of law which derives the nature of law from the act of the will and not from reason. We should think of sanctions as founded upon acquired right resulting from the human act. The primary purpose of sanction is not to instill fear, but to satisfy justice because of the acquired "right" to reward or punishment. Sanction, to be true, must be based on an intrinsic reality, that is, the meritorious or demeritorious act.

Let us add that retribution of justice rests upon the objective fact that man as a member of society is bound in justice to act for the common good. Hence, retribution according to justice should be meted out to him.

We speak of merit and demerit in relation to retribution, which is rendered according to justice. Now, retribution according to justice is rendered to a man because of his having done something to another's advantage or hurt. It must, moreover, be observed that every individual living in a society is, in a fashion, a part and mem-

---

[60] *S. Th.*, I–II, 21, 2, *c*.   [61] We are not considering supernatural merit.

ber of the whole society. Therefore, any good or evil done to a member of a society redounds to the whole society. So, too, who hurts the hand, hurts the man. When, therefore, anyone does good or evil to another individual, there is a twofold measure of merit or demerit in his act: first, in respect of the retribution *owed* to him by the person to whom he has done good or harm; secondly, in respect of the retribution *owed* to him by the whole of society. Now when a man orders his act directly to the good or evil of the whole society, retribution is *owed* to him, before and above all, by the whole society; secondarily, by all the parts of society. Whereas when a man does that which is conducive to his own benefit or disadvantage, then again is retribution owed to him, in so far as this too affects the community, according as he is a part of society; although retribution is not due to him in so far as it conduces to the good or harm of a person, who is identical with the agent (unless, perhaps, he owes retribution to himself, by a sort of similitude, in so far as a man is said to be just to himself). It is therefore evident that a good or evil act has the note of laudable or culpable, according as it is in the power of the will; the note of rectitude or sin according to its order to the end; the note of merit or demerit according to the retribution of justice toward another.[62]

IV. *With God*

Finally, the notion of merit or demerit, which entails the idea of retribution, that is, of reward or punishment according to justice, brings with it the truth that human actions, because good or evil, have the nature (*ratio*) of merit or demerit in the sight of the Supreme Ruler, God, upon whom all men depend absolutely, and who is the Supreme End of men. It is evident, therefore, that human actions acquire merit or demerit in relation to God.[63]

SUMMARY

PART III. Morality of External Act

Article I: *Objective Morality of Internal and External Act Identical*

The objective morality of the internal act is identical with the objective morality of the external act, because the elements which constitute the objective morality of either act are the same although drawn from diverse sources.

---

[62] *S. Th.,* I–II, 21, 3, *c.*   [63] Cf. *S. Th.,* I–II, 21, 4, *c.*

1. The external act as known by the intellect in its objective morality is the formal cause of the internal act.

2. The end of the will communicates its goodness; it is the form of the external act.

Article II: *Placing or Not Placing the External Act Does Not Ordinarily Change the Goodness and Malice of the Internal Act.*

Objective morality is identical for both; hence, ordinarily no increase.

Exceptions:

Regarding the End: (1) interruption, (2) duration, (3) intensity.

Regarding the Object: When the external act is not placed, this indicates a lack of perfection in the internal act, unless the hindrance is caused by external factors contrary to the inclination of the will.

APPENDIX

CONSEQUENTS OF THE HUMAN ACT

Four Important Notions

Evil: unsuitable to nature; greatest extension of the four notions; may be static or dynamic.

Good: suitable to nature. As a transcendental it has the widest extension and the narrowest comprehension.

The Human Act

(Objective Morality):

Sin: evil action; lacks order to supreme end; dynamic.

Righteous action: looks to end; dynamic.

(Subjective Element):

Guilt (blameworthiness): because voluntary, act must be imputed to agent.

Praiseworthiness: because voluntary, act must be imputed to agent.

(Retribution of Justice, which looks to the common good; results from "acquired" right in the author of the human act):

Demerit (punishable): because the agent is part of society which has suffered harm. The punishment is *due* according to justice, because by the evil act man acquires a *right* to retribution.

Merit (worthy of reward): recompense according to justice is *due* because of an action by which man acquires a *right* to the reward.

This last consideration implies a Supreme Ruler, God,[64] the Supreme End, to whom an account of all human actions is to be given, as the Supreme Dispenser of the punishment or reward which such actions have merited. This important truth is seen as the term of our long discussion of the morality of the human act. "All that man is and can and has must be referred to God; and therefore every act of man, whether good or bad, has the nature of merit or demerit in the sight of God *from the very nature of the act.*"[65]

N.B.: Sinfulness and righteousness in moral action, blameworthiness (guilt) and praiseworthiness, merit and demerit, i.e., a "right" to reward or punishment are not extrinsic imputations; they are *intrinsic* consequents of the human act; they flow from the intelligibility of the act. Sin and righteous act are established by the intrinsic determinants of the act: object, end, and circumstances. Guilt and praiseworthiness are due to the inclination of the will to an evil or to a good act. Right to reward (merit) or to punishment (demerit) results from the rectitude or the turning away of the will as regards the last end.

Question IV

THE PASSIONS AND MORALITY

Prologue

The nature of the passions has been studied at length in the philosophy of man.[66] In those pages we ascertained that passions or emotions are the acts of the sense appetites which man, in common with all animals, must often experience. *A passion is nothing else than a movement of the soul caused by the sensible knowledge of a particular good or evil object and accompanied by an organic mutation.* In itself, therefore, a passion is not a free act,[67] a moral

---

[64] We are not trying to prove the existence of God here. This has been done in the course of metaphysics.

[65] *S. Th.*, I–II, 21, 4, ad 3[m].

[66] Cf. *The Philosophy of Man*, pp. 161–175.

[67] "The movement of the sense appetite is aroused suddenly in consequence of an apprehension of sense. . . . Such movements occur *without the command of reason*" (*S. Th.*, I–II, 17, 7).

act; yet, as we shall observe, it may and often does affect profoundly the morality of the human act.

We have pointed out, moreover, that because the sense appetites are inferior to reason, their operations, the passions, should be controlled by the higher faculties of man, that is, by his reason. The nature, however, of this mastery by intellect and will over the passions is peculiar; it is not a direct, but an indirect control. The reason is that a passion is aroused through knowledge of sense and not immediately and directly by the command of reason. That is why Aristotle as well as St. Thomas describes the rule of sense appetite by reason as indirect and politic rather than direct and despotic. "Reason governs the irascible and concupiscible not by a despotic supremacy which is that of a master over his slave, but by a political rule."[68]

Finally, let us state once more that the passions are not evil in themselves; on the contrary, they belong to the perfection of man's nature, and consequently when properly directed by reason they definitely contribute to the perfection of the human act. Yet it is a common personal experience in all men that the passions can easily overstep the limits set by right reason, and that, at times at least, they entice man to place actions which are opposed to the

---

[68] *S. Th.,* I–II, 17, 1. The control of the passions by reason will be effected by proposing to the sense faculty of knowledge an object which should move the sense appetite in accord with reason. For passion is caused by a *sensible* knowledge of a particular object which is good or evil. There are various ways by which reason may bring this about. The will can move (order of exercise) the intellect so that it will recall definite objects. We discovered in the philosophy of man that the intellect does not act without an accompanying phantasm, so that whenever the intellect, ruled by the will, applies itself to a universal consideration, the accompanying phantasm is brought into focus, for "the apprehension of the imagination . . . is regulated by the apprehension of reason. . . . Consequently, in this respect the operation of the sense appetite is subject to the command of reason" (*S. Th.,* I–II, 17, 7). In this way "the irascible and concupiscible are said to obey reason. . . . Anyone can experience this in himself, for by applying certain universal considerations, anger, fear, and the other passions can be mitigated, or even instigated" (*S. Th.,* I, 81, 3). This is what we call the indirect, political control of reason over the passions. In this manner, not only can reason mitigate the violence of a spontaneous passion, but if it so chooses, it can often cause a passion to be aroused. And this it does not by moving the sense appetite directly, but by presenting the proper object to the faculty of sense knowledge.

moral law. This is an observable fact, whatever the cause of such a disorder may be.[69]

Problem: In the study of the philosophy of morality, a twofold problem concerning the influence of the passions upon the moral act naturally arises. First of all, the philosopher wants to discover the nature of the influence of the passions upon the internal act of the will. Secondly, he wants to ascertain the effect of such influence upon the morality of the act. The first problem is metaphysical; the second, moral.

ARTICLE I: Nature of the Influence of the Passions Upon the Internal Act of the Will

Influence of Passion Possible Because of Unity of Person: Because his substantial act of existing is an intellectual "to live," man is a perfect unit, a rational supposit, a person. Because of this unique existential bond of union, the human person is the one principle of all operations, that is, the principle which acts by means of various and complex faculties. Because of the integration of these faculties in the unity of the supposit, it is the person who senses, who understands, who loves. It is evident then, that owing to this integration, to this perfect unity in the principle of action, the operations of one power will often have an important influence upon the placing of an operation by another faculty. We intend to show that the passions at times exert such an influence upon the will.

Influence of Sense Knowledge Upon the Intellect: Obviously, any influence of the operation of sense appetite upon the will can never be in the order of exercise, since in man the will is the supreme motive power.[70] Such influence must be in the order of

---

[69] To those who accept Christian revelation, this obvious disorder in the nature of man is known as a "resultance" from original sin.

[70] In the order of exercise (efficient causality) the will is moved by God. This natural motion of the will by God is to the absolute good. It is because of this divine motion to the absolute good that the will is able to choose freely the particular good. (Cf. *S. Th.*, I–II, 9, 6; *The Philosophy of Man,* p. 194.) We have noted in the first chapter that the will is necessarily determined to the absolute good by a natural desire for happiness.

specification, that is, of the object. It will be indirect through the instrumental causality of sense knowledge. In the philosophy of man[71] we pointed out that between sense and intellectual knowledge there exists a causal influx, a real determining factor. Indeed, it was established that this determining factor is of such necessity that no intellectual word (*verbum*) can be formed unless some fundamental sense data has previously been obtained. For, before it can place the act of knowledge, the act of understanding, the possible intellect needs to be actuated by the joint action of phantasm and agent intellect.

Sense Appetite and Will: Now the influence of the sense appetite as regards the formation of the moral act is of a different nature. There is no question here of a necessary determining factor of the will by the operation of the sense appetite. The reason is, of course, that the will is never necessitated to the particular good. Moreover, the will, since it is the intellectual appetite, is directly determined in the order of specification not by a sense faculty but by the intellectual judgment. Let us examine the influence of the passions upon the forming of the judgment of reason.[72]

Passions and Judgment of Reason: In the analysis of the moral act, we have noted that the free determination (order of specification) of the internal act of the will is had from the *judgment of reason*. It is in the formation of such a judgment that the influence of the passions may be felt. For, although this judgment depends on a previous act of the will which freely directs (order of exercise) the intellect, nevertheless, in forming such a judgment man depends on data proffered by the sense faculties. Now it is a fact of observation that whenever sense knowledge causes a passion to arise, the resulting judgment of the estimative sense,[73] which looks to action, is necessarily colored by the nature and violence of the passion, whether it be love, desire, anger, or the like. A brute ani-

---

[71] Cf. *The Philosophy of Man,* p. 122 ff.

[72] Let us repeat that the term *judgment* does not signify a logical composition and division but an estimation, a judging of values, that is, a judging of objective morality. All the acts of the intellect throughout the psychological process of the moral act are judgments of reason.

[73] In man, the cogitative sense.

mal is, of course, necessitated to action by this judgment of sense. In man, however, the judging of the cogitative sense does not determine to action, since the will, the supreme mover, is free. Nevertheless, this judgment of sense is necessarily communicated to the intellect and has naturally an important although not necessitating influence[74] upon the formation of the practical judgment of reason.[75] It is evident, therefore, that the influence of the passions upon the internal act of the will is in the order of object, in the order of specification. It is also obvious that its influence upon the formation of the judgment of reason will be greater or less in accordance with the violence of the emotion. A man in the state of violent anger will more easily choose to place an act of violence. Indeed, even though such an action retains an element of freedom, since choice is an action freely caused by the will, nevertheless, had it not been for the aroused passion of anger, this act of violence would not have been placed.

Now it is evident that according to a passion of the sensitive ap-

---

[74] We say "not necessitating influence upon the formation of the judgment of the intellect." The reason is that in the order of exercise the intellectual judgment depends upon an act of the will. In the formation of any judgment of reason which specifies the will-act, there occurs an interaction between will and intellect which is a sort of deliberation. The intellect is moved by the accompanying act of the will to weigh and consider the moral value of the object. There really is no necessary priority in the order of time between the acts of intellect and of will; at best we can speak of priority of nature. It appears then that the passion in no way necessitates the will. It is of course possible, though it rarely occurs, that the violence of the passion is such as to blind reason. In such a case, there is no judgment of reason and consequently no act of the will. Man then is reduced to the status of a brute beast. "When the passions are very intense, man loses the use of reason altogether" (S. Th., I–II, 77, 2). St. Thomas is of the opinion that this happens rarely in the case of a spontaneous passion but more frequently in passions deliberately willed or accepted.

[75] "Now it is evident that the apprehension of the imagination and the judgment of the estimative power follow the passion of the sensitive appetite, even as the verdict of the taste follows the disposition of the tongue; for which reason we observe that those who are in some kind of passion do not easily turn their imagination away from the object of their emotion, the result being that the judgment of the reason often follows the passion of the sensitive appetite, and consequently the will's movement follows it also, since it has a natural inclination always to follow the judgment of the reason" (S. Th., I–II, 77, 1).

petite man is changed to a certain disposition. Wherefore, according as man is affected by a passion, something seems to him fitting, which does not seem so when he is not so affected; thus that seems good to a man when angered which does not seem good when he is calm. And in this way the sensitive appetite moves the will on the part of the object.[76]

Influence of Passions Upon Will: Let us conclude: The nature of the influence of a passion upon the internal act of the will is (1) in the order of the object (specification), (2) indirect, that is, through the formation of the judgment of reason, and (3) in no way necessitating. It is possible, however, that because of this influence a judgment of the intellect may be formed which is not in accordance with right reason. Consequently, the free act of choice which is specified by such a judgment will be against the moral law; it will be an evil act.[77]

ARTICLE II: Effect of Passion Upon the Morality of the Human Act

Problem: Passion, we have seen, may have a definite influx in the formation of the moral act. This influx is indirect and lies in the formation of the judgment of reason which specifies the internal act of the will. Our problem is thus stated: Does such influence increase or decrease the morality of the human act; or, more exactly, does it, first of all, affect the objective moral goodness or malice of the internal act of the will? Does it, moreover, affect voluntariness as regards the external act?[78]

---

[76] *S. Th.,* I–II, 9, 2.

[77] A difficulty may be proposed against the possibility of placing a human act against the moral law. It is this: It is impossible for the intellect to form contradictory judgments. Now the judgment which is against right reason contradicts a principle of the moral law which had previously been proposed by the intellect. Hence, no such judgment can be formed.

In answering this difficulty, let us recall that a principle of law is not only a universal judgment, but at the moment of the enunciation of the specifying judgment it is only an habitual, not an actual judgment. Now there is no contradiction in having successive contradictory judgments if one of them is universal and habitual while the other is particular and actual. (Cf. *S. Th.,* I–II, 77, 2, *c.*)

[78] It is evident that passions cannot affect the objective morality of the external

Relation Between Passion and Will: The first step toward a solution of this problem will be to discover the nature of the relation of dependence which exists between the passion and the will. Does the passion depend upon the act of the will, or is the will-act influenced by a spontaneous passion? In other words, is the passion consequent to the act of the will or, on the contrary, does it precede, is it antecedent to, such an operation? This distinction is of the highest importance in determining the morality of the human act which follows the passion. For, if a passion is in some manner caused by the will, the biased judgment of reason which results and the more or less intense action which follows will undoubtedly be imputable to the subject. On the other hand, a spontaneous passion, which arises independently and antecedently to the act of willing, may to some extent, by obscuring the judgment of reason, diminish the objective morality of the internal act as well as impede the voluntariness of the external act.

Briefly, then, a passion is either antecedent or consequent. If antecedent, because it obscures the judgment of reason, it diminishes the morality of the act. If consequent, it increases the morality of the act which follows. Let us explain.

Antecedent: A passion may arise spontaneously and without being foreseen by reason. Two possibilities follow. First, the passion because of its violence may overwhelm reason. In such a case, man is no longer rational and free, since neither intellect nor will are able to act. Consequently, man is reduced to the status of a brute beast. Hence, whatever actions follow are neither human nor moral. This case, which is of rare occurrence, need not be considered, since it has no connection with morality; there simply is no moral act.[79]

---

act which is determined by the specification from the object. It can, however, affect its voluntariness, as we shall show. It is also evident that there is no question of influence of the passions upon the voluntariness of the internal act, since the object of the will-act is *as known*. The passions, however, can modify the objective morality of the internal act.

[79] "Now this influence of a passion on man occurs in two ways. First, so that he has not the use of reason: as happens in those who through a violent excess of anger or concupiscence become furious or insane, just as they may from some other bodily disorder; since such like passions do not take place without some change in the body. And of such men the same is to be said as is said of irrational

Most frequently, however, at first, reason is not completely over-come by the passion. For, as we have explained, there is a quasi deliberation, an interaction between intellect and will similar to that between counsel and consent. Hence, the specifying judgment of reason is a free, not a necessary, act.[80] The judgment of reason which is being formed is under the control of the will and there-fore retains some of its freedom. Consequently, the act of the will which follows this judgment of reason does not necessarily tend to that toward which the passion inclines it. It is free to follow or not to follow the direction of reason although its freedom has been somewhat affected by the influence of the passion upon the judgment.

Antecedent Passions Diminish Morality: When followed by a moral act, an antecedent passion diminishes the morality of the act, because it obscures the judgment of reason. That is to say, if the passion is inclined toward a moral good, it makes the act less good; if toward a moral evil, it diminishes the sin. For, "since they (the antecedent passions) obscure the judgment of reason on which the goodness of the moral act depends, they diminish the goodness of the act."[81] On the other hand, "a passion that tends to evil and precedes the judgment of reason diminishes sin."[82]

If we ask further, in what manner is the morality of an act diminished by an antecedent passion, we may answer thus:

Antecedent Passion:

a) Internal Act: Antecedent passions affect the object which specifies the internal act of the will. They do so not directly, since the object of the will-act is presented immediately by the intellect

---

animals, which follow of necessity the impulse of their passions: for in them there is neither movement of reason nor, consequently, of will" (*S. Th.,* I–II, 10, 3).

Again, "when, however, the cause (of the passion) is not voluntary but natural, for instance, if anyone through sickness or some such cause falls into such a passion as deprives him of the use of reason, his act is rendered wholly involuntary, and he is entirely excused from sin" (*S. Th.,* I–II, 77, 7).

[80] The judgment of reason which precedes specification of the will-act presupposes and in a manner includes the judgment of the norm and the judgment of conscience. See footnote 74 on interaction between intellect and will.

[81] *S. Th.,* I–II, 24, 3, *c.*

[82] *Ibid.,* ad 3[m].

in the judgment of reason. The influence of the passions is indirect. First of all, the phantasm in the imagination is colored, as it were, by the intensity of the passion. This affected phantasm in turn, through the principal efficient causality of the agent intellect, produces as an instrumental cause the intelligible species. Obviously, the judgment of reason which follows such actuation will be biased by the indirect influence of the passion.[83] The passions, therefore, diminish the objective morality (goodness or malice) of the act of the will in this way: the true knowledge of the object is made less perfect because of the biased character of the judgment which has been formed under the influence of the passion ∙ even though the passion be not evil.

b) External Act: Antecedent passions may affect the true knowledge of the morality of the external act. Consequently, they may diminish voluntariness toward the effect by causing some ignorance of the true and complete morality of that effect. In such a case, the passion diminishes the guilt or merit of the author of the act. "For it is more praiseworthy," explains Aquinas, "to do a work of charity from the judgment of reason than from the mere passion of pity."[84]

Consequent Passions: There are two types of consequent passions. The first accompanies the act of the will and results naturally from the intensity of the operation of the will by a natural redundance. Such a passion has no effect on the morality of the act, since it in no way determines the judgment, neither is it willed deliberately. It is a mere manifestation of the perfection of the internal act of the will. A passion which naturally accompanies the act of the will does not affect morality, and consequently does not concern our present problem. A *concomitant* passion, explains St. Thomas, results from the unity of man, so that "when the higher part of the soul is intensely moved to anything, the lower part also follows that movement."[85]

---

[83] "The judgment of reason often follows the passion of the sense appetite" (*S. Th.,* I–II, 77, 8).

[84] *Ibid., c.* "Preceding passion diminishes sin in so far as it diminishes its voluntariness" (*S. Th.,* I–II, 77, 6).

[85] *S. Th.,* I–II, 24, 3, ad 1^m.

The second type of consequent passion is *by way of choice*. A man may choose to be affected by a passion in order to facilitate the performance of a work by exciting the necessary passion. A consequent passion indicates the intensity of the will-act. It manifests the perfection of the morality of the act, both subjective and objective. It is a sign of the gravity of the moral act.[86]

On the other hand, a consequent passion does not diminish a sin, but increase it; or rather, *it is a sign of its gravity,* in so far as it shows the intensity of the will toward the sinful act; and so it is true that the greater the pleasure or the concupiscence with which anyone sins, the greater the sin.[87]

N.B.: Let us note that when a passion that has been willed overcomes reason by its violence, the action which follows, although no longer under the control of the will, is nevertheless voluntary *in its cause* and therefore imputable to the subject. "A passion," explains St. Thomas, "is sometimes so strong as to take away the use of reason altogether, as in the case of those who are mad through love or anger; and then if such a passion were voluntary from the beginning, the act is reckoned a sin because it is voluntary in its cause."[88]

In short, an *antecedent passion* diminishes the goodness and malice of the internal act as well as the voluntariness of the external act; or, in other words, it diminishes objective morality and the imputability of a human act.

A *consequent passion* manifests the perfection of the act which caused it.

---

[86] It is obvious that the intensity and perfection of the act which follows will be greater as a result of the passion that has been willed. Consequently, the moral act will have greater goodness or malice. A passion, therefore, that is freely willed increases the morality of the human act which follows. Some moralists distinguish between a passion which has been *entirely initiated* by the will-act, and a passion which has been *accepted* after some effort and struggle to reject it. These moralists explain that there is greater voluntariness in the first type.

[87] *S. Th.,* I–II, 77, 6.

[88] *S. Th.,* I–II, 77, 7.

SUMMARY

Question IV

THE PASSIONS AND MORALITY

Article I: *Nature of Influence of Passion Upon Will-Act*

This influence cannot be in the order of exercise since, in that order, God alone can move the will. It must be in the order of specification, that is, of the object.

Genesis: Sense knowledge causes passions. Passions have influx upon phantasm. Affected phantasm as elevated by agent intellect causes intelligible species. Biased judgment of reason results. The will, however, is never necessitated to a particular good.

Conclusion: Influence of passion upon will is:
1. In the order of specification,
2. Indirect through phantasm and judgment of reason,
3. In no way necessitating.

Article II: *Effect of Passion Upon Moral Act*

Antecedent Passion

a) Internal act
  — Diminishes objective morality because it affects objective morality of object *as known.*
  — Does not affect voluntariness.

b) External act
  — Diminishes voluntariness because it affects knowledge of morality of effect.
  — Does not affect objective morality.

Consequent Passion
  — Manifests perfection of act of the will which caused it.
  — Increases intensity of internal act which follows.
  — Increases voluntariness of external act which follows.

Question V

HABITS AND THE MORAL ACT

Prologue

In the philosophy of morality we study habits only in so far as they are principles of the moral act. To do this with profit, we should recall, first of all, some of the fundamental facts regarding habits which were studied in the philosophy of man.[89] The habits, we saw, are qualities which complete the operative potencies and enable them to perform certain actions with greater perfection and ease. The subjects of these qualities are those faculties which can place human acts or influence such acts. They are, therefore, the will, the intellect, and the sense appetites. These habits are acquired and are caused and increased by repeated actions. They can be diminished and ultimately destroyed by actions that are directly opposed to them, that is to say, actions which tend to produce a contrary habit.

A virtue is a good habit which perfects man's nature. We found that for the perfection of man's nature eight fundamental virtues are required. Of these, five are in the intellect and are therefore called intellectual virtues. The other three are called moral virtues and are in the appetites. (See diagram on page 172.)

Division: Since some virtues are principles of the good moral act, and, moreover, since morality depends primarily upon the will, it follows that the virtues which either are in the will or are necessarily related to and dependent upon the act of the will, will be the main subject of our discussion. We shall need, first of all, to distinguish between those intellectual virtues which are not necessarily connected with the act of the will, and, on the other hand, the moral virtues together with prudence which either cause directly, or necessarily influence, the act of the will. Consequently, the first article will examine the difference between these two types of virtues; it will establish which of these virtues are principles of good moral actions. In the second article we shall present an analy-

---

89 Cf. *The Philosophy of Man*, pp. 198–227.

DIAGRAM OF VIRTUES

Virtues are *good* habits. They dispose man to actions that are suitable to his nature. Now the perfection of the nature of man is to be rational. A rational nature, however, is in potency to know all beings, to attain all truth, and to love the good. The good of man is the absolute good. The actions of man which are suitable to his nature will dispose him to attain his end, that is, to know the true and love the good. These actions, therefore, will need to be ordered to understanding the true and to loving the good. The following habits will enable man to place such actions with relative **ease, constancy, and delight.**

					INTELLECTUAL VIRTUES	MORAL VIRTUES

The diagram structure:

UNDERSTANDING THE TRUE — Intellect

- *Speculative* (contemplation of truth)
  - Principles that are immediately evident — Habit of Principles[90] — { Habit of understanding = Purely speculative; Synderesis = Connects with the practical order }
  - Principles which result from reasoning regarding
    - (a) Highest truths — *Wisdom*
    - (b) Lower truths — *Science*
- *Practical* (looks to action, tends to specify the act of the will according to the good presented by the intellect)
  - True knowledge of things to be made — *Art*
  - True knowledge of things to be done — *Prudence*

LOVING THE GOOD

- Will — Looks to the good due to others — Tempers inordinate desires in accordance with the good of reason — *Justice*
- Sense Appetites
  - Concupiscible — Tempers inordinate desires in accordance with the good of reason — *Temperance*
  - Irascible — Strengthens courage, controls fear, enables us to place difficult acts for the good of reason — *Fortitude*

Conclusions:

1. In the intellect there are three speculative virtues: Habit of Principles, Wisdom, and Science.
2. In the intellect there are **two practical virtues: Art and Prudence.**
3. In the appetites there are three moral virtues: Justice (in the will), Temperance, and Fortitude (in the sense appetites).
4. "The intellectual virtues **are** those by which reason of itself is perfected; the moral virtues are those by which the appetitive powers are perfected in order to obey reason."[91]

---

[90] The habit of principles is not an acquired habit. It is the intellect itself necessarily tending to know being and to form the first principles of the speculative and of the practical order. Without such an innate disposition, man could never come to an understanding of the real.—"Our intellect naturally knows being and those things which belong of themselves to being (*ea quae sunt per se entis*). In the knowledge of these, our understanding of the first principles is founded" (II, C.G., c, 83, adhuc).

[91] *S. Th.*, I-II, 68, 8.

sis of the functioning of the moral virtues and of prudence. The third article will study the relations between the moral virtues and the passions in so far as these relations affect the moral act. In the fourth article we shall discuss briefly the mean of virtue.

ARTICLE I: Which Virtues Are Principles of Good Moral Actions?

The only virtues which of themselves affect the act of the will, and consequently are in some manner connected with the good moral act, are the moral virtues and prudence. It is therefore necessary to distinguish sharply between the moral virtues together with prudence on the one hand, and on the other, the remaining intellectual virtues. In establishing this distinction, it will be made evident why the former, namely, moral virtues and prudence, are necessarily principles of good moral actions, while the others are not.

Moral Virtues: Moral virtues are the principles of the good moral act, because their subject is either the will or a sense appetite as controlled by reason. For the moral act is primarily an internal act of the will.[92] Consequently, (*a*) a virtue such as justice whose subject is the will is directly a principle of good moral action, while (*b*) a virtue which is radicated in a sense appetite affects the moral act indirectly only, that is, by moderating the passions in accordance with right reason and thus preventing those same passions from obscuring the judgment of reason. In this way, the virtues of temperance and fortitude become, indirectly at least, principles of good moral operations.

Intellectual Speculative Virtues: The intellectual speculative virtues, on the other hand, do not look to action but to contemplation. In themselves, therefore, they do not necessarily influence the

---

[92] A virtue is a good habit which disposes a faculty to place a good act. Hence, a virtue of an appetite disposes the will (directly or indirectly, mediately or immediately) to place a good act. Now a good act of the will is a good moral act. The reason is that the will-act depends here and now upon the last end as desired. Consequently, a good act of the will must dispose the subject toward the attainment of the last end.

moral direction of the act of the will to the last end. They are not necessarily principles of the good moral act.[93]

Prudence: The virtue of prudence, which is in the practical intellect, looks to the specification of the moral act of choice in accord with right reason.[94] In this way, that is, in the order of formal causality, it becomes a principle of the good moral act.[95] Because of this causality prudence is sometimes termed a moral virtue. For prudence "is a good counselor (*est bene consiliativa*) regarding the things that pertain to man's entire life. Prudence looks to the last end of man."[96]

Art: On the other hand, art, although a virtue of the practical intellect, which looks to action and specifies the act of the will, cannot be termed a principle of the good moral act. The reason is that "Art counsels regarding the things which pertain to the end proper to art."[97] It does not of itself look to the end of man's life but to its own end, for art is concerned with the right way of making things, not with the direction of the will as regards the last end of human life. Art in itself, therefore, is not necessarily a principle of the good moral act.

Speculative Virtues and Art: These virtues affect the good moral act indirectly. In brief, with the exception of the understanding of principles and of prudence, the virtues of the speculative intellect

---

[93] By the intellectual speculative virtues we mean the *acquired* virtues of wisdom and of science. The innate tendency of the intellect called habit of principles is subdivided into the habit of understanding as regards the fundamental principles of thought and the habit of synderesis as regards action. Synderesis, which is the foundation for the acquired habit of right reason, is necessary for judging the objective value of any thought or action in the order of morality.

[94] Cf. *S. Th.*, I–II, 58, 2, ad 4ᵐ.

[95] The specification of the act of choice by a prudential judgment is necessary in order that the act of choice may be morally good. Hence, the virtue of prudence is necessary to a good life. "To that which is suitably ordained to the due end man needs to be rightly disposed by a habit in his reason, because counsel and choice, which are about the things ordained to the end, are acts of the reason. Consequently, an intellectual virtue is needed in the reason to perfect the reason and make it suitably affected toward the things ordained to the end; and this virtue is prudence. Consequently, prudence is a virtue necessary for a good life" (*S. Th.*, I–II, 57, 5, *c*).

[96] *S. Th.*, I–II, 57, 4, ad 3ᵐ.

[97] *Ibid.*

together with the practical virtue of art do not of themselves necessarily enter into the determination of a good moral act. *It is only in so far as they are controlled by a will which is good and rightly ordered to the end of man that the actions which result from these virtues are morally good.*[98] Such actions would be morally evil if controlled by a will that is not rightly ordered to the last end of human life. Quite the contrary is true of the moral virtues as well as of prudence. These are necessarily of themselves principles of good moral actions.

Qualified and Unqualified Perfection in Man: In order to clarify this distinction, that certain virtues are of themselves principles of the good moral acts while others are not, we must add that the virtues which are the principles of the good moral act perfect man unqualifiedly (*simpliciter*),[99] while the others do so only qualifiedly (*secundum quid*).

First, let us explain these two terms, *qualifiedly* and *unqualifiedly*. By *unqualified* perfection in man we mean, of course, that by acquiring such a perfection man *as man* is made more perfect. Now man as man is a rational creature ordered to complete happiness as to his last end. Hence, those habits will perfect man as man which will dispose him to place good moral acts, acts which of themselves are ordered to man's last end. The moral virtues and the virtue of prudence thus perfect man unqualifiedly, for the acts placed in accordance with these virtues are necessarily ordered to the end of man. On the other hand, "to perfect man *qualifiedly*" means that man is made more perfect, not necessarily as regards the attainment of his last end, but according to some perfection which has no necessary relation to that end. Let us amplify this.

---

98 "A virtue which perfects the will, as charity or justice, confers the right use of the speculative virtues" (*S. Th.,* I–II, 57, 1, *c*). "In order that a man make good use of the art he has, he needs a good will, which is perfected by moral virtue" (*ibid.,* 3, ad 2[m]).

99 We know from revelation that the existential order, that is, the order in which man finds himself, is that of a nature ordered to a supernatural end. Hence, prudence, in order to perfect man unqualifiedly in the order of existence, would need to be the supernatural infused virtue of prudence which presupposes charity as its form. This question is theological. (Cf. *S. Th.,* II–II, 23, 7 & 8.)

A man who acquires the science of mathematics or the art of music is made more perfect as a mathematician or a musician, but not necessarily more perfect in relation to his last end. The perfection here is qualified, limited.

N.B.: The distinction between the perfection which results in man's nature from moral virtue and that which is acquired by the speculative virtues is of the greatest importance. Because they failed to take cognizance of this distinction, many philosophers from Socrates down to the American idealists and pragmatists of the present day have thought erroneously that knowledge is identical with moral virtue, since knowledge perfects man. It would follow from this assertion that by acquiring knowledge one is made unqualifiedly better. Indeed, according to these thinkers the only cause of evil, moral or otherwise, is ignorance. The necessary inference which these philosophers make is that the most important factor in the development of a child is not to form good moral habits, but to acquire learning, science, and the like. This is a very great error, since these intellectual virtues of themselves perfect man only qualifiedly.[1]

Why is it that the moral virtues as well as prudence perfect man unqualifiedly, while the others do so only qualifiedly? Why is it that the former virtues necessarily dispose man to his true end, while the latter do so only accidentally? The reason is that the intellectual speculative virtues together with art, since they are ordered to their own peculiar ends, do not of themselves tend to produce an action which is necessarily ordered to the last end of man. Prudence and the moral virtues, on the other hand, by their very nature are in accord with right reason. Consequently, they are ordered to the last end. Hence, all actions which flow from these virtues are good moral acts.

Aptness and Use: The fundamental difference between these two types of virtues is succinctly expressed thus: The intellectual speculative virtues and the virtue of art give *aptness*[2] but not

---

[1] Cf. *S. Th.,* I–II, 58, 2. This important article should be read by the student.

[2] Aptness means facility to place the act. Use means direction of action toward the last end.

use. The reason is that of themselves these speculative virtues are not principles of the good moral act; of themselves, they are not ordered to the supreme end of man. Hence, vast knowledge, even wisdom, could be used by an evil will for evil purposes, for it does not necessarily dispose the will to a good action as related to the last end.[3]

The opposite is true of the moral virtues and prudence. These do not merely give *aptness* but also *use;* that is, they do not only make it possible to place the act of the virtue, but they determine the true relation of the action to the last end. Consequently, any action which results from the virtue of prudence, of justice, of fortitude, of temperance is necessarily a good moral act. In other words, the operation of the will which results from a moral virtue could never be an evil act. For the end of an evil will-act must be evil. Now the end to which the moral virtues are ordered is the true end of man. Hence, an evil act could never flow from any of the moral virtues. That is why St. Augustine states in his definition of a moral virtue that, "Virtue is a good quality . . . of which no one *can make bad use.*" We must conclude that a virtue which perfects man as man "must be in the will itself or in some power moved by the will."[4]

Difficulty: One obscure point remains. Why is it that the virtue of prudence which is not in the appetite perfects man unqualifiedly? It would seem that any action of the intellect is not necessarily of itself ordered to man's last end and therefore need not of necessity be morally good.

In solving this difficult problem, St. Thomas points out that in so far as the intellect is moved by the will (order of exercise) it can become the subject of a virtue that is unqualifiedly good. The reason is that the will is the supreme mover in man, and therefore the will can move other faculties to action. Hence, if certain opera-

---

[3] Art, like the speculative habits, is not concerned with the disposition of the rational *appetite* toward man's ultimate end. Consequently, neither art nor a speculative habit tends to make a work good as regards the use, that is to say, as ordered to the last end. Such a disposition is the property of a virtue which perfects the appetite either directly, as the moral virtues, or indirectly, as prudence. Art, therefore, perfects man only as regards the ability to work well. (Cf. *S. Th.,* I–II, 57, 3.)

[4] *Ibid.*

tions of the intellect depended upon a will that is properly ordered to the last end, it would follow that the intellectual virtue thus established in the intellect would make man good unqualifiedly.

This is obviously the case regarding prudence; for, "since prudence is the right knowledge of things to be done, in order to have prudence it is necessary that man be properly disposed to the principles of this knowledge of the things to be done. These principles are the ends to which man is properly disposed by the rectitude of his will. . . . Hence, the subject of prudence is the practical intellect but in relation to a right will."[5]

N.B.: In an analogous manner we may speak of a prudential judgment in the order of the end, that is, when volition or intention is the term of the elicited act. That is why St. Thomas states that in such cases some sort of consent takes place; there is deliberation, and a prudential judgment is formed. The will-act which terminates the process, whether it be volition or intention, can be considered as a sort of choice.

Conclusion: In this article we have shown why prudence and the moral virtues, unlike the speculative virtues and art, are principles of the moral act. They are dispositions to act toward the true end. Hence, they perfect man unqualifiedly. They give not merely aptness, that is, facility of action, but use, that is, direction to the last end of man.

ARTICLE II: Functioning of Moral Virtues and of Prudence

We shall examine, first of all, the interrelations between prudence and the moral virtues; secondly, we shall inquire whether intellectual and moral virtues need to coexist.

I. Interrelations Between Prudence and Moral Virtues

Let us now analyze the interrelations between the moral virtues and prudence in the moral act of choice and examine their recipro-

---

[5] S. Th., I–II, 56, 3. The same is to be said "mutatis mutandis" of the intellect as subject of the virtue of faith. "For the intellect is moved by the command of the will to assent to what is of faith" (ibid.).

cal influence upon the internal act of the will. "In choice there are two things: the intention of the end which belongs to moral virtue and the disposing of the means to the end. This latter belongs to prudence."[6]

Order of End: The disposition of the will to the end is caused by the habits that are in the will itself — good or bad habits — and from the judgment of reason which specifies the act. Now this judgment of reason may or may not be darkened or biased by a rising passion. The control of the passions, and consequently of their influence upon the judgment of reason, depends largely upon the dispositions established by the basic virtues of temperance and fortitude which are in the sense appetites.

From the above we perceive why the act of the will called intention will be more easily elicited toward a good end than toward an evil end according to dispositions resulting from good moral habits. Hence, it will generally happen that the act of intention will be morally good if good moral habits inform the will as well as the sense appetites.

N.B.:   This does not mean that a man who lacks good habits both in the will and in the sense appetites cannot place a good act of intention. Quite the contrary, for the will is never necessitated to any particular object. All that is indicated here is the importance of such a disposition and therefore the great need for developing good habits. For, as St. Thomas wisely remarks, if virtue were not developed by repeatedly placing good actions, man would grow weary and discouraged because of the constant struggle required to act contrary to the disposition of the faculty, and after a while he would probably give up his endeavor to live a good life. It is, therefore, extremely important for all men to acquire good habits at an early age, to keep a vigilant watch over their growth, and to develop them by repeated actions.

Order of Means; The Prudential Judgment: The intention of the will to a good end which is attainable moves the intellect to deliberate regarding the means about which there is to be a choice. It is at this point that the virtue of prudence enters; it is here that

---

[6] *S. Th.*, I–II, 56, 5, ad 4[m].

a prudential judgment is needed. Prudence, we have explained, is the true knowledge of the things to be done. It looks to the means, that is, to placing an action that will enable us to reach the intended end. It is obvious that the will should be rightly disposed toward a good end and should, moreover, intend this same end before there can be any question of an act of prudence. For prudence deals with the means, not with the end. Now the disposition of the will-act to a good end is generally a resultant of the moral virtues. Hence, prudence ordinarily presupposes the moral virtues, and by moving the will to a good moral act (prudential judgment, order of specification) it directs, conserves, and increases these same moral virtues. That is why prudence is called the regulator of the moral virtues. Indeed, without prudence the moral virtues would soon disappear; for without a prudential judgment which specifies the act of choice in accord with right reason, the moral act which would follow would be evil, and in time the repetition of such action would destroy the opposite moral virtues which are in the appetites. The prudential judgment, therefore, may be defined as a moral judgment which specifies choice in accord with right reason.

Let us apply to prudence what has been already stated about the moral virtues: It does not follow that we can never place a good choice unless we already possess the virtue of prudence. We are always free to form a prudential judgment in spite of the lack of virtue, whether it be a lack of prudence or any moral virtue. The reason is that the intellect is controlled by the free will; it is moved efficiently by a previous act of the will to enunciate freely the last practical judgment. As a matter of fact, we are born without any virtues and first need to place acts of virtue before the habit can be acquired. What we mean to say is that without the virtue of prudence and without the moral virtues it is much more difficult to act virtuously because of the lack of the proper disposition of the intellect and will.

Analysis of Prudence: Let us examine the functioning of the virtue of prudence as it forms the judgment which will specify the good choice. There are three distinct operations necessary for a complete, a perfect act of the virtue of prudence. (1) There is the intellectual operation called *counsel* which examines and deliberates about the things that are related to the end. (2) Then man judges what is better for the attainment of the end. (3) This judgment is followed by the precept (*ratio praeceptiva*) which consists in the application of the things counseled and judged in accordance with right reason. This precept is properly an act of the practical intellect for it looks to the work to be willed, to be done. It is the principal, the perfect act of the virtue of prudence.[7]

Difficulties: 1. If a habit is specified by its act, it would seem that prudence is not one but three distinct habits, since the acts are three distinct operations: counsel, judgment, and precept. To answer this difficulty, we should recall that a habit as well as its actions is basically specified by the formal object of the operation. Now the formal object of these operations belongs to the same virtue of prudence.

The minor premise, namely, that the formal object of these three operations is one and the same, can be easily established. The formal object of prudence is the specification of the act of the will, the moral act, in accordance with right reason. This appears from the definition of prudence which is the *"recta ratio agibilium."* In other words, the formality of the act of prudence consists in this, that the judgment which is formed by the intellect under the guidance of prudence tends to specify an act of the will in accordance with right reason. It is obvious that the three operations, counsel, judgment, and precept (*ratio praeceptiva*), tend to do just that: (1) counsel, of course, in a more remote manner by weighing and considering what means is more in accord with right reason; (2) practical judgment by stating definitely that this is the better according to the true norm; and (3) lastly, the most perfect expression of that judgment is proposed by the precept, "Do this." By this act the intellect specifies the act of choice. These three distinct operations obviously complement one another; they flow naturally from one another; they have the same formal object; therefore, they belong to the same virtue of prudence.

2. The question is sometimes raised whether St. Thomas in the

---

[7] Cf. *The Philosophy of God*, p. 137.

Secunda Secundae, 47, 8, and elsewhere places the second act of prudence, the judgment, in the speculative intellect.[8] This is not the case. The problem in the various articles where this difficulty occurs is to show that the precept (*ratio praeceptiva*) is the most perfect act of prudence, because it is the only one which is proper to such a virtue. This he solves by explaining that "to judge" is not limited to acts of the practical intellect, but is found as well in the speculative. Hence, "to judge" is not the perfect act of prudence because not proper to it. On the other hand, the *ratio praeceptiva,* whose function is to specify immediately the choice, cannot be formed except by the practical intellect which looks to action. Hence, of the three operations, command is the most perfect and the only one proper to prudence.

From this discussion we perceive why this same precept (*ratio praeceptiva*) of prudence necessarily takes place before and not after the act of the will called choice. For since choice is the moral act *par excellence* as regards the means, if the specification of such an act were had without a prudential determination, the act of choice would not be in accord with right reason. It would be an evil act.

> Now there are three acts of reason in respect of anything to be done by man: the first of these is counsel; the second, judgment; the third, precept (*praecipere*). The first two correspond (*respondent*) to[9] the acts of the speculative intellect which are inquiry and judgment, for counsel is a kind of inquiry; but the third is proper to the practical intellect in so far as the practical intellect is ordained to operation, for reason does not have to command in things that man cannot do.[10]

---

[8] *"Secundus est iudicare de inventis; et hoc facit speculativa ratio"* (S. Th., I–II, 47, 8). Judging (*iudicium, iudicare*) the objective values, whether ontological or moral, may occur in the speculative as well as in the practical intellect. Hence the act of judging cannot be the *proper* act of prudence, since prudence belongs to the practical intellect. On the other hand, a precept or command has no place in the speculative intellect. The reason is that the speculative intellect is not concerned with action, whereas a precept or command specifies the act of the will.

[9] Counsel and judgment which pertain to prudence are not acts of the speculative intellect. They correspond to, that is, they are like certain actions of the speculative intellect.

[10] S. Th., I–II, 57, 6, c.

How do these three acts fit into our psychological analysis of the free act? In the philosophy of man[11] we noted that counsel is followed by the last practical judgment. No mention is made of precept. As a matter of fact the last practical judgment contains a judgment which terminates in the precept. There are really two operations. The first states that this is the best means. The second is the command, "do it." Now whenever these three acts of the intellect, counsel, judgment, and precept are in accordance with right reason, we speak of a prudential judgment which specifies the moral act of choice.

Summary: By way of summary we may state that to place good moral actions:

1. The three moral virtues are needed in order to dispose the will to a good end. This disposition is obtained immediately in the will by *justice,* and mediately by *temperance* and *fortitude,* that is, through the forming of the judgment of reason under the influence of the sense appetites which are disposed in accord with right reason by these virtues.

2. Following the intention to a good end, the virtue of prudence, by enabling the intellect to form a prudential judgment which specifies the act of choice, disposes the will toward willing the proper means.

II. *Must Intellectual and Moral Virtues Coexist?*

The interrelations between prudence and the moral virtues bring up the question of whether intellectual and moral virtues must coexist; whether it is possible for one type of virtue to develop without the other. There are, therefore, two distinct problems.

1. **Problem:** *First of all, can moral virtues exist without intellectual virtues?* The solution will be based on this, that the inclination which results from a moral virtue is *"with choice."*[12] Moral virtue is the disposition to make a good choice between various possible means. Such disposition supposes intellectual knowledge. Hence,

---

[11] *The Philosophy of Man,* p. 187 ff.

[12] *"Inclinatio virtus moralis est cum electione . . ."* (*S. Th.,* I–II, 58, 4, ad 1[m] *et passim*).

the moral virtues cannot be without some intellectual virtues, at least, not without prudence. Moreover, prudence presupposes the habit of principles, for to be able to counsel, to judge, and to command according to right reason, man needs the true knowledge of principles. On the other hand, the other intellectual virtues, wisdom, science, and art, are not necessary in order to place a good moral act. The reason is that there is no necessary connection between knowledge obtainable by means of these intellectual virtues and the choice of the proper means toward the last end.

Solution:

a) Moral virtue cannot exist without the intellectual speculative habit of principles and the intellectual practical virtue of prudence. The reason, as we have stated, is that a moral virtue is a choosing habit (*habitus electionis*); it disposes to a choice. Now two things are necessary for a good choice: (1) the right intention to the due end, hence, a knowledge of the first principles of the moral law (right reason); and (2) a correct view (*ut accipiat recte*) of those things that are related to the end. This latter is had by means of a prudential judgment.

b) Moral virtue can exist without some of the intellectual virtues — e.g., wisdom, science, art — because the act of choice does not necessarily require the knowledge which results from these intellectual virtues.

2. **Problem:** *Secondly, can intellectual virtues exist without moral virtues?* There are two points to be examined: (*a*) Prudence cannot long exist without moral virtues; (*b*) speculative virtues and art can exist without moral virtues.

Solution:

a) Prudence (as a habit) cannot exist without moral virtue. "The reason is that prudence is right knowledge about the things to be done, and not merely in the universal sense but in the particular which is the order of actions. . . . Consequently, just as by the habit of natural understanding or of science, a man is made to be rightly disposed in regard to the universal principles, so, in order that he be rightly disposed with regard to the particular principles of action, viz., the ends, he needs to be perfected by certain habits, whereby it becomes connatural to man, as it were, to judge rightly about the end. This is done by moral virtue, for the virtuous man judges rightly of the end of virtue because such as a man is, such does the end seem to him. Consequently, the right reason about things to be done, viz., prudence, requires man to have moral virtues."[13]

N.B.: When we say that prudence cannot be without the moral virtues and that the moral virtues cannot be without prudence, we mean that there cannot be one without the other *habitually;* that is, the disposition which is designated as habit will not endure without the coexistence of the other dispositions. On the other hand, it is quite possible to place a virtuous act without the disposition due to the other habits. This seems obvious, because man is free. Moreover, were it impossible to place a virtuous action without the coexistence of the other virtues, since man is born without such innate dispositions, it would be quite impossible to acquire moral virtues and prudence.

b) Speculative virtues and art can exist without moral virtues: A true understanding, a correct judging in matters of art and science, does not depend on the disposition of the will toward the last end of man. In these matters our inferences depend on reason which can judge in accordance with the principles of science and art. Now these principles are not necessarily connected with right living. Hence, art and the speculative virtues do not require a moral virtue which perfects the appetite.

ARTICLE III: Moral Virtue and Passion

The moral virtues of temperance and fortitude are concerned with the rational control of the passions. Passions and virtues are

---

[13] *S. Th.,* I–II, 58, 5. ". . . one cannot have prudence unless one has the moral virtues, since prudence is *true knowledge about things to be done,* and the starting-point of reason is the end of the thing to be done, to which end man is rightly disposed by moral virtue. Hence, just as we cannot have speculative science unless we have the understanding of principles, so neither can we have prudence without the moral virtues" (*S. Th.,* I–II, 65, 1).

both situated in the sense appetites. We should like to inquire, (1) how they differ, (2) whether they can coexist, and (3) in what manner the objective morality of a virtuous act is affected by the passional disposition of the individual.

1. **Difference Between Moral Virtue and Passion:** There is a vast difference between virtue and passion. Virtue is a disposition to a reasonable act; passion is the act of a sense appetite and may or may not be in accordance with reason. Passion is a motion of the soul, while virtue is a principle of motion. Passion begins in the appetite and, when tempered by virtue, terminates in a reasonable act. Virtue, on the other hand, begins in the reason, since it is educed by means of reasonable acts and remains in the appetite. For moral virtue is a habit of choosing the means *appointed by reason.*

2. **Moral Virtues of Sense Appetite Do Not Exclude Passion:** Since the passional act can be in accordance with reason, that is, since it can by control of the virtues be a reasonable act, it follows that virtue and passions can coexist. Indeed, it is a grave error to think that the rational life of man means a complete destruction of the passions. If the passions are inordinate, that is, if they tend to lead man to place actions that are against right reason, then they should be controlled, subdued, muzzled, but not destroyed, even if that were possible. Acts of virtue do not indicate impassivity and perfect quiet; rather, such actions imply a control of *those* passions "which *are* as they should not be and *when* they should not be." It is not the function of virtue to deprive the sensitive appetites of their proper activities — which belong to the perfection of a rational animal — but to make them execute the commands of reason by exercising their proper acts.[14]

Moral Virtue of the Will Is Not Directly Connected With Passion: We should add that not all the moral virtues are connected with the control of the passions, but only those whose subjects are the sense appetites. The virtue of justice, which is in the will, is concerned not with passions but primarily with external operations. It is true, however, that often a passion will result, follow, and even

---

[14] Cf. *S. Th.,* I–II, 59, 2.

accompany an intense act of justice. This arousing of a passion is caused by a sort of redundance, a flowing over from the higher to the lower faculties because of the perfection and intensity of the act of the will and the unity of the supposit. Moreover, "it may happen that sometimes in operations which are directed to another (such as the operations pertaining to justice) that the good of virtue is lost sight of because of an inordinate passion."[15] When a man, for example, in violent anger will strike another unjustly and perhaps injure him unjustly, the good of the virtue of justice is neglected because of the passion of anger.

3. **Is the Objective Morality of a Virtuous Act Affected by Passional Disposition of the Individual?** The objective morality of the actions which flow from the virtue of justice is determined by the object without any consideration of the passional dispositions of the individual who places the operation. On the other hand, the objective morality of the moral acts of temperance and fortitude will vary in accordance with the passional state of each man, and consequently will have to be gauged accordingly. As regards justice, therefore, the goodness of the act will be entirely determined by the object, no matter how an individual man may be affected toward such an action. A classical example is the operation of buying and selling. Obviously, the justice or injustice of this transaction will be determined by the formal object without direct consideration of one's personal emotions. The opposite holds as regards the virtuous actions of temperance and fortitude. Because these virtues are directly concerned with the passions of each individual, the good and evil of an act will not depend solely on the relation of the object to any rational principle, but to this individual agent. The reason is that the objective morality of each action will be affected by the personal disposition of the agent. An object, for example, which proves a source of anger or lust to one who is given to these passions may not be a danger to another individual. Consequently, as regards fortitude and temperance, the good and evil of the object of the action is to be gauged not only in itself but also according as the individual is well or ill affected toward such

---

[15] *S. Th.,* I–II, 60, 2.

an object. Hence, what is good for me (supposing an object good or indifferent in itself) may be evil for another.

In Short: Justice is properly and solely related to operations as to its proper matter; that is, the acts of justice depend solely upon the object of the operation for their objective morality. Acts of temperance and fortitude must be referred also to the internal affections and passions of the individual.

Cardinal Virtues: The three moral virtues of justice, temperance, and fortitude, together with the intellectual practical virtue of prudence, are called cardinal or principal virtues because of the manner in which they perfect man, that is, by giving not only the aptness, but the use, as was explained. These virtues, therefore, because they imply the rectitude of the will, are called cardinal or principal virtues.

They are principal virtues, because they embrace the good of man as man according to four distinct formalities. Hence, all virtues will be classified under them according to their formality in causing the good of man as man. "In this way they are called principal, being general, as it were, in comparison with all the virtues; so that, for instance, any virtue that causes good in reason's act of consideration may be called prudence; every virtue that causes the good of rectitude and the due in operations may be called justice; every virtue that curbs and represses the passions may be called temperance; and every virtue that strengthens the soul against any passions whatever, be called fortitude. . . . It is in this way that the other virtues are contained under them."[16]

They are also called *perfecting* virtues, because they are "virtues of men who are on their way and tending toward the divine similitude. Thus prudence, by contemplating the things of God, counts as nothing all things of the world, and directs all the thoughts of the soul to God alone; temperance, so far as nature allows, neglects the needs of the body; fortitude prevents the soul from being afraid of neglecting the body and rising to heavenly things; and justice

---

[16] *S. Th.,* I–II, 61, 3, *c.*

consists in the soul's giving a whole-hearted consent to follow in the way thus proposed."[17]

ARTICLE IV: The Mean of Virtue

Conformity with a rule signifies a mean between extremes, that is, between excess and deficiency; e.g., the goodness of an artifact will be measured according as it conforms with its rule, so that if it exceeds the measure or falls short of it, the artifact is said to be bad or to lack perfection. Now a habit to be a virtue must conform with the rule of right reason. Virtue, therefore, consists in a mean between excess and deficiency from that rule. Hence, we must admit that the act of a moral virtue, which is an elective habit, must lie, in respect to its object, in a mean between excess and deficiency from right reason.

From this it appears that the mean of a moral virtue is not always determined solely by the object of the act, but by applying the true norm to individual conditions, so that the concrete personal action will be in accord with right reason. This is not to be taken to signify that the object itself should be determined to a mean between extremes, but rather that the measure established by right reason is a mean between excess and deficiency. In determining, for example, the true mean in giving alms, one should be guided by his own financial responsibilities and the needs of those who receive the alms.

It should be noted, moreover, that in the act of justice the mean set by reason is determined entirely by the object. The reason is that justice is not concerned with passions but with operations. Now the measure of the operations of justice, whose objects are exterior things, is established in the operation itself, no matter how one may be affected toward it. Hence, the mean of the act of the virtue of justice is the same, whether we look at the measure set by reason or that set by the object.

---

[17] *S. Th.*, I–II, 61, 5, *c.* This text evidently considers the state of human nature elevated by grace to a supernatural end.

On the other hand, with respect to the other moral virtues, we must observe that the mean of reason is not necessarily identical with the mean set solely by the object. For the goodness or evil of the action which results from the passion is had according to the commensuration not with the object alone but as related to the individual agent. By that we mean that the good and evil is had according as a man is well or badly affected toward the object, right reason being the judge. That is why St. Thomas wisely remarks that the mean to be observed in the virtues which are concerned with the passions rather than with operations cannot be judged only by the matter or object alone, but by reference to each individual, because men are differently disposed to various passions.[18] Because of this varying disposition to passion, an action which might be reasonable, and therefore right for one man to perform, might be quite wrong for another, for the violence of the latter's passions might lead him to place an unreasonable action.

The theory of the mean of virtue will be made clear by an illustration. The mean of temperance as regards food and drink, for example, is established not solely by the object, that is, by the amount or kind of food and drink, but by the object as referred to the disposition of the individual subject here and now toward such an object. On the other hand, the mean of justice is determined by right reason in accordance with the value of the thing or object bought and sold.

In Short: The mean of justice is established by right reason according to the thing or object. The mean of temperance and fortitude is set by right reason by referring the object to the individual disposition of the subject.

---

[18] *"Propter hoc quod homines diversimode se habent ad passiones"* (S. Th., I–II, 64, 2).

SUMMARY

I. DISTINCTION BETWEEN INTELLECTUAL SPECULATIVE VIRTUES AND ART, ON THE ONE HAND, AND, ON THE OTHER, THE MORAL VIRTUES AND PRUDENCE

Moral Virtues and Prudence

They look necessarily to the last end of man. The reason is that, on the one hand, a good appetitive habit disposes the will to place a good moral act, one which is directed toward the attainment of the last end. On the other hand, prudence specifies the will-act according to right reason. Hence:

1. They are necessarily principles of the good moral act. Their influx, however, upon the will-act differs:

   a) In general — they are either in the will or have influx upon the act of will.

   b) In particular:

   Justice is in the will, immediately affecting the act of the will.

   Temperance and *fortitude* are in the sense appetites, affecting the will-act only through the judgment of reason.

   Prudence, which is in the practical intellect, specifies the act of choice.

Intellectual Speculative Virtues and Art

They do not necessarily look to the last end of man. The reason is that these virtues do not necessarily dispose the will to place a good act since they have an immediate end of their own which may or may not be subordinated to man's last end. Hence:

1. They are not of themselves principles of the good moral act. Actions of these virtues, however, can be directed by the will, either toward the last end or away from it.

2. They perfect man *unqualifiedly* because the acts of these virtues are ordered to the last end. Hence, these virtues give not only *aptness* (facility), but *use* (direction to last end).

2. They perfect man *qualifiedly* because they are not necessarily ordered to the last end; they are ends in themselves. They give only *aptness,* not *use.*

II. Functioning of Moral Virtues and Prudence

A. *Interrelation Between Prudence and the Moral Virtues.*

1. The three moral virtues are needed in order to dispose the will to a good end.

2. Following the intention to a good end, the virtue of prudence by means of a prudential judgment specifies the will toward willing the proper means.

B. *Must Intellectual and Moral Virtues Coexist?*

1. Moral virtues:

   a) Cannot exist without the habit of principles and prudence.

   b) Can exist without wisdom, science, and art.

2. Intellectual virtues:

   a) Prudence cannot exist without moral virtues.

   b) Wisdom, science, and art can exist without moral virtues.

N.B.: The moral virtues and prudence are acquired by repeated actions. We are free to place good moral actions even when we do not as yet possess the virtue.

III. Distinction Between Moral Virtue and Passion

1. *Moral virtue differs widely from passion.* Passion is a movement beginning in sense and terminating in reason. Virtue is a principle of movement, beginning in reason (or established by reason) and terminating, in the case of fortitude and temperance, in the sense appetites.

2. The moral virtues in the sense appetite, i.e., temperance and fortitude, do not exclude passions, but coexist with them. The moral virtue of justice, which is in the will, is not directly concerned with passion.

3. Not all moral virtues are connected directly with passions:

   a) Temperance and fortitude directly affect the passions.

   b) Justice looks directly to operations.

4. *a*) Objective morality of an act of justice is determined solely by the object of operations as referred to a rational principle.

b) Objective morality of an act of temperance or fortitude is determined by the object as referred to *this individual* rational principle viewed with his own *individual* passional disposition.

IV. THE MEAN OF VIRTUE

1. Conformity of the act of a virtue with the measure of reason signifies a mean between excess and deficiency.

2. With fortitude and temperance — the mean is established in accordance with right reason, not solely by the object, but according to dispositions of subject. With justice — the mean set by reason and by the object are identical.

CHAPTER III

LAW

Prologue

The most common notion of law is that it is the rule and measure of human actions.[1] The philosopher inquires into the meaning of this notion; he tries to discover a metaphysical foundation for such a rule; he wants to know why law imposes a "must," an obligation to do what it commands, and why such an obligation implies a right to the things necessary for the observance of the law.

Natural Law: According to St. Thomas, law in man, the natural law as it is called, is from God; *it is a participation of the rational creature in the eternal law.*[2] For the law in any creature is an impression of the eternal law by which the creature is inclined according to its natural capacity to its due actions and end. This explains why a precept of law binds. It does so from necessity to the end. Law, therefore, implies order to the end. Indeed, the natural law is fundamentally the finality of human nature to its last end.

"A precept of law, since it is binding, is about something that must be done. That a thing should be done results from the necessity of an end. It is obvious, then, that the very nature of a precept implies an order to the end, in so far as that is commanded which is necessary or expedient to the end."[3]

---

[1] The rule and measure of human actions which we call law can be viewed as it exists: (1) in the ruler or lawmaker: law is a knowledge of government; (2) in the ruled: true law in the ruled is a radical inclination of nature to its end which founds a true obligation to due acts.

[2] Eternal law is the knowledge (*ratio*) of Divine Wisdom directive of all actions and motions of creatures to their proper end.

[3] *S. Th.*, I–II, 99, 1, *c*.

"All (creatures) in some manner participate in the eternal law in so far as from an impression of it (eternal law) they derive inclinations to acts and ends that are proper to them. . . . Consequently, the (rational creature) has a share in the Divine Reason, deriving therefrom a natural inclination to due act and end. This participation of the eternal law in the rational creature is called the natural law."[4]

Finality: These texts are illuminating. Man, like any being, is ordered to his last end by a necessity of nature. The obligation, the moral necessity to reach the end is absolute; and, since nature is a principle of action to its end, to fail in the fulfillment of this obligation is to frustrate nature absolutely. Unlike other natures which are necessarily determined to operation, man is free to place actions which will dispose him toward his last end or cause him to deviate from it. He is bound, therefore, not by a natural necessity, not by coercion, but by a moral obligation to place those actions which, because they dispose him to the end, are good for his nature. Likewise, he is obliged to avoid those actions which frustrate nature. This is the first principle of the natural law: *do good and avoid evil.* This principle expresses man's most fundamental obligation. From the discovery of this first principle of law, we infer that obligation, any obligation, to be true, must be founded ultimately on the finality of nature. Let us repeat: obligation of the law in man is the "must" which results from the finality of nature to its last end. To attain the end, man is obliged to observe the law. Because of this general obligation, man is bound to place acts that are suitable to his nature and to avoid their contraries. This obligation is not a physical necessity, but only moral. For man is free as regards the particular good.

Finality Is Foundation for Obligation and Right: The impression of the divine power, by which the rational creature is inclined to the due act and due end, results in a desire of nature for those things (means) that are necessary for the end. Consequently, this participation in the eternal law establishes in human nature an inclination to place the operations necessary for the attainment of those means.

---

[4] *S. Th.,* I–II, 91, 2, *c.*

That is why St. Thomas states that the rational creature is inclined not only to the due end, but to the "due acts." Because of these inclinations of nature to place certain actions, we infer that these operations are for the good of nature and therefore that they should be done, and on the other hand, that the contrary actions should be avoided. The expressions of these fundamental inclinations of nature to the necessary means are the primary precepts of the natural law. They manifest man's essential obligations. Moreover, because of these obligations, which are expressed in the precepts of the law, it becomes obvious that in man there are definite rights; that is to say, certain things are owed man in justice as complements of his nature. These are the good things which are necessary for his observance of the law; they are the necessary conditions for the fulfillment of his obligations. Indeed, without these he could never dispose himself toward his ultimate end. Hence, if he has an obligation to observe the law, he must have the right to those things which are necessary for such observance. The finality of human nature to the last end, which is fundamentally the natural law, is the foundation for every right and every obligation. Consequently, right and obligation are not related as effect and cause. Neither one causes the other. Both depend immediately on law which is the finality of nature.

Obligation: Obligation — we have shown — signifies that something should be done from the necessity of the end. In man, the obligation of law is expressed by a definite command or precept of law. The binding force of law is only moral, not physical, since it results from the finality of a rational free nature to its last end. This obligation entices man to act so as to dispose him to attain happiness.[5] The obligation of law, therefore, is not a constraint, a limitation of the subject; rather it is perfective of nature.

Rights: Philosophers distinguish two types of rights: objective and subjective. Objective right is the "object of justice." Now

---

[5] There is a profound difference between this objective obligation which flows from the radical finality of human nature toward the possession of the absolute good, and the subjectivism of Kantian "duty" which is founded upon the irrational voluntarism of a categorical imperative.

the virtue of justice is that virtue by which one renders to another that which is owed him, the *"debitum."* This adequate *"debitum"* (that which is due) is the right thing to do; it is the term of justice, the *"justum."*

St. Thomas limits himself to a consideration of objective right.[6] Objective right, he explains, is founded on law, whether that law be the knowledge of the wisdom of God, the principles of the natural law, or the accidental determination of those principles by human law. Law in its most profound aspect of *finality of nature* establishes the rights of nature, namely, the right to the things necessary for the attainment of the end. A right, therefore, is the object of justice; it is that which is due.

Many modern jurists, having founded law on the will of the legislator rather than upon the finality of nature, find it necessary to approach the notion of right, not from the point of view of the law, but from a consideration of the subject of the right. For, if law is not necessarily a thing of reason, if law is not founded on finality of nature, it may impose an obligation that is not perfective but destructive of nature. Hence, there is need of something positive in the subject to counteract the law. Consequently, while St. Thomas does not bother to inquire about subjective right, and in fact considers that the only right which has meaning must be implied by the law, the emphasis today is generally placed on subjective rights. Now subjective right is defined as an inviolable moral power of acting (*facultas moralis agendi inviolabilis*). Clearly, such a definition has no relation to a law which is formed by the will of the legislator; in fact it is obvious that there could easily be opposition between such law and right.

We are of the opinion that true right is based upon law whether it be the eternal law, the natural law, or even the human law. This is true only of objective right which is the object of justice and which rests upon the finality of nature. This seems the only firm foundation for right. For, as remarks P. Fourneret, if we place the basis for right in the subject, whether individual or collective, as the

---

6 Cf. *S. Th.*, II–II, 57.

state, and not in the law, eternal, natural, or human, the outcome could easily be tyranny.[7]

Conclusion: A profound understanding of the true nature of law brings out the correct notion of obligation and of right. The natural law, which is a participation in the eternal law, consists in the finality of human nature to the last end. From this finality we infer the nature of obligation and of right in this way: (1) because of the necessary order to the last end, man is bound by a moral necessity, an obligation to place freely those actions which will dispose him to the end; (2) because he is bound to place those actions in order to attain his last end, there is in man a right to the goods necessary for placing good moral acts commanded by law. Law, therefore, manifests obligation and implies right.

Human Law: When we attack the problem of law from such a radical point of view, it becomes evident that any man-made law, to be a true law, will have to be subordinated to this finality, that is, to the necessary tendency of human nature to its last end. Human law will have to be in accord with right reason, which is the expression of the natural law. To be sure, the ultimate purpose of human law should be to help man fulfill the natural law by the practice of virtue, thereby disposing him to his last end. For, although the immediate end of the law of the commonwealth is that common good which is the good of the State, namely peace and material prosperity, nevertheless, human law should promote this common good because it can be a means to man's last end. This the human law should endeavor to accomplish in so far as the common good of the state is essential or helpful to the attainment of the ultimate end. For human law, by making it possible or easier for man to practice virtue, enables each citizen, each person, to attain more easily his supreme happiness.

Viewed from this angle, the problem of law is not too difficult to approach and even to solve along general lines. On the other

---

[7] This is true of natural right; it is also true, at least indirectly, of positive right (*ius positivum*). For positive right is implied by the positive law that is just; it should be the object of the just act. (P. Fourneret, Droit, *Dictionnaire de Théologie Catholique*, T. 4, II Partie, Col. 1831.)

hand, if we approach law only from a consideration of the good of the state or as flowing arbitrarily from the will of the legislator, we prepare the way for the nefarious doctrines of Marxism and Nazism.

Division: There will be two questions: (1) law in general, and (2) various types of law.

Question I

LAW IN GENERAL

This question will have three articles: (1) the nature of law, (2) the diversity of laws, and (3) the effects of law.

ARTICLE I: The Nature of Law

Since law is generally accepted as the rule and measure of human actions, it is of importance to the philosopher to study the nature of law as such, in order to discover why the observance of true law is essential to right living. It will be necessary, therefore, by an analysis of the notion of law, to examine how and why law is formed. In doing so, we shall come to understand the essence of law, which we shall express by a definition.

In our search for the true definition of law, four essential points will be examined: (1) Does law belong to the will or to the reason? (2) What should be the end of a true law? (3) Who has the right to make laws? (4) Is it necessary that a law be promulgated in order to have the binding force of a true law? Obviously, the first three problems have reference to the various causes of law: formal in the first, final in the second, and efficient in the third. In solving the last problem, namely, promulgation, we shall examine, not a cause, but an essential property of law, that is, the necessity that a law be made known to those who are bound to observe it.

1. Law in Man Is a Dictate of Practical Reason: The first notion of law is that it is the rule and measure of human actions, and, consequently, that it implies a "must," a moral obligation which binds one to act accordingly. Now the immediate measure and rule of human actions is reason. For reason is that which specifies the act of the will. In this sense, reason is the first immediate formal principle of human actions. This is made evident because reason itself by a last practical judgment and by a precept orders the human act toward or away from the end. "For it properly belongs to reason to order to the end."[8]

How does reason rule and measure the human act and actually direct it toward the last end? Reason does so, first of all, by forming the various judgments which express the precepts of the natural law. These judgments compose the intellectual habit called right reason. Secondly, reason actually measures and rules the human act in the following manner. First, by judging the objective morality of a human act, it measures the act. In the second place, reason rules the act by forming the practical judgment: "this must be done," and the command: "do it," which specify the moral act. Clearly, if law is to be a true measure and rule of human actions, it must essentially be from reason and not from the will. This then is our first and most important inference as to the nature of law: *Law is something which belongs to reason.*

Argument: Law is the rule and measure of human actions. But the immediate rule and measure of human actions, that is, the formal determination of human actions to the end can only be from reason. Therefore law is a thing of reason; it belongs to reason.

Major: Law binds; it indicates a "must." Hence, it induces us to act by having an influx on the formal determination of the human action.

Minor: Reason is the formal principle of human acts. For a human act proceeds from the "deliberation of reason."[9] This deliberation consists in judging the objective morality of the act by comparing it to the law. Hence, (1) by referring the act to the

---

[8] *S. Th.,* I–II, 90, 1. The end (final cause) is the first principle of action. Now the final cause is in the order of intention. It must first be known by the intellect in order to be desired by the will.

[9] *S. Th.,* I–II, 1, 1, ad 3[m].

precepts of law, reason measures the morality of the human act; (2) by specifying the free will-act, reason rules the human act.

Law, therefore, is a thing of reason. It is a command of practical reason.

Inferences:

A. Law as a rule or measure exists:

    a) In the one who rules and measures, as a knowledge of true government. Law in the lawgiver is in the reason of the lawgiver.

    b) In the measured and ruled, as the finality of nature which results in natural inclination to due acts and end.

        1) In man the obligation to place due acts is moral and therefore observed freely.

        2) In nonrational beings the obligation is physical and therefore observed necessarily.

B. Law is expressed in man by propositions formed by *acts* of reason. These propositions are retained in the memory as *habits* of the intellect.

C. We *grant* that reason, when framing a human law, depends on a previous act of the will loving (willing) the end. Moreover, some will-act must follow the framing of law in order to promulgate and enforce the law. We *deny* that a true law depends formally on the arbitrary will of the legislator.

2. Law Must Be Directed to the Common Good: Law, because it is the rule of human actions, is a dictate, a command, of practical reason. In the order of action, which is the order of practical reason, the first principle is the last end. Now the attainment of the last end is happiness, the possession of the absolute good. Hence, law should be concerned primarily with the attainment of the good. We ask, what is this good which is the purpose of all true laws? To answer this, we must consider that man is a part of the perfect community of the universe. Consequently, law necessarily looks most of all to the attainment of the common, universal good, which is universal happiness.[10]

---

[10] The common good of the universe signifies primarily the possession by rational

In a lesser degree, a properly organized state is a perfect community since it is self-sufficient in the attainment of the common good of its citizens. In what does the common good of the state consist? The commonwealth is not concerned directly with the ultimate end of man, which is his perfect happiness in the next world. It can only promote an imperfect or relative happiness attainable in this life. The state does this by directing its citizens in the practice of virtue, in living the good life. Hence, the laws of the state should first of all preserve internal peace, and establish — in so far as it is possible — a reasonable degree of prosperity among its members. Man-made laws should, moreover, direct the members of the commonwealth to live virtuous lives. They should make it easier for the citizens to render justice to God and men, thereby attaining a degree of imperfect happiness which is a preparation for the possession of the ultimate end. Clearly, the common good of the republic is necessarily subordinated to the supreme good of the universe.

Briefly: (1) Since the last end (as desired) is the first principle of practical reason, law which is a dictate of practical reason must look to the last end. (2) Because man is a part of a perfect community, his actions should be directed (by law) to the common good. Law, therefore, which is a dictate of practical reason, is the rule and measure of our actions in their relation to the common good which is the ultimate end of the universe.

The important doctrine, that law to be a true law must be ordered to the common good, is found in a celebrated page of the *Summa Theologica*, I–II, 90, art. 2. We propose an analysis of this difficult article.[11]

---

creatures of the supreme good which is God. To this end all other created things are subordinated. The reason is that only a rational nature is ordered to such an absolute happiness. The ultimate purpose of any true law, even of civil law, must be either directly or indirectly to help men attain their last end through the practice of virtue.

[11] It will help the student to recall some fundamental notions regarding the nature of the last end of man.

The end of man is complete happiness, i.e., the possession of the absolute good. This is had primarily by means of an act of the intellect (knowledge) accompanied

Analysis of *S. Th.*, I–II, 90, 2

Must Law Always Be Ordered to the Common Good?

Three distinct steps can be noted in the argument: (1) Law (true law) looks to the attainment of man's last end, his complete happiness. (2) Since man is a part of a perfect community, the law which rules his actions should be ordered to the last end of all, their common happiness, that is to say, the common good. (3) It follows that every true law must be ordered to, subordinated directly or indirectly to, the common good.

a) **Law looks to the last end of man:** Since it is the rule and measure of human actions, law belongs to the principle of human acts which is practical reason. Now reason in ruling human actions depends on the first principle of action which is the last end (as desired). Therefore, a true law must be ordered to, must look to, the attainment of the last end. Now the last end of man is complete happiness. Consequently, law should direct human actions toward the attainment of happiness.

b) **Law looks to the common good which is the happiness of all men:** Every part should be ordered to the good of the whole (i.e., the common good). But man is a part of a perfect community.[12] Therefore man, in his actions, should be ordered to the common good. Now the common good is the happiness of all men. Therefore, law which rules the action of man should be ordered to, should look to, the happiness of all men.

The common good in its perfection is the perfect happiness of all men, that is to say, the complete attainment of the absolute good in the next world. To this end, therefore, must all laws be ordered directly or indirectly so that a true law may never contradict or

---

by love and fruition of will. Complete happiness is attained only in the next life. On the other hand, imperfect happiness may be reached in this world. Now true but imperfect happiness consists in the subordination (direct or indirect) of all human actions to the knowledge and love of God. All this was discussed at length in the first chapter.

[12] A perfect community is one that is self-sufficient. The state, and most of all the entire human race as established by the Creator, are perfect communities. The family is not a perfect community.

impede the common good. Although this supreme good is not attainable in this life, we can nevertheless reach a certain degree of imperfect happiness by ordering our actions to the knowledge and love of God, that is to say, by the practice of true virtue. Hence, the immediate end of the laws of the state should be to promote this imperfect and relative happiness. This the state endeavors to do by securing order, peace, and prosperity which are necessary or helpful for the good, the virtuous life.

c) **Subordination of all laws to the common good:** That which is supreme in a given order is the principle of all others which belong to that order. Now the common good is supreme in the order of law. It follows that any true law should be subordinated directly or indirectly to the common good, the happiness of men.

This last argumentation is an inference already implied in the demonstration that law looks to the common good.

N.B.: A precept which looks merely to the individual good is not a law. Hence not every command is a law.[13]

Why must every human action be ruled by a law which is ordered to the common good and not by an individual precept? Because *every human action is related to the common good* (the good of human nature) *as to a common end* (final cause).

In its ultimate analysis, the absoluteness of the moral order is due to the finality of human nature to its last end. That end is the good of *human nature,* that is, the common good. Hence, every human action must be ruled by a true law, a law which directs men to their last end.

This conclusion brings out the importance of establishing that every human act depends actually upon an influx from the first final cause which is the last end. Hence, if a law is opposed to the attainment of the last end, the good of human nature, it is not a true law, but lawlessness.

It is precisely this relation, whether direct or indirect, to the

---

[13] The good of the body politic is truly a common good; it is for all who are members of the state. The common good of the state is, however, a limited good and consequently must be subordinated at least indirectly to the supreme good of man, his eternal happiness.

common good of the universe, the complete happiness of all men, which establishes the firmness, the absolute truth, and the moral force of law. Without such an essential relation to the last end of all men, which is the common good of the universe, a command would have no force of law.

3. **To Whom Does the Power to Make Laws Belong?** The answer to this question flows from the preceding discussion. If, in order to be a true law, the command of practical reason must be directed to the common good, it follows that only those have the power to make laws to whom the end, the common good, properly belongs. Hence, most of all, God, who is not only the efficient cause but also the end of His creatures, is the Supreme Legislator. For, in His infinite wisdom, God ordains all things to their proper end, which is a communication of His goodness. This He does, first of all, by impressing in all creatures a natural inclination (appetite of nature) to their appointed ends. Secondly, He does this in a special manner as regards His rational creatures, by giving to their intellect a natural tendency to discover and enunciate the principles of the natural law.[14] Consequently, the eternal law, which is the knowledge of the wisdom of God, is the supreme norm. It follows that no man-made law has any value if it is contrary to this norm. God, therefore, is the supreme legislator; indeed in an absolute sense God is law.

This, however, is not precisely the point of our discussion. Our problem here pertains rather to the making of human laws. Let us begin our solution by restating a principle: The power to make laws belongs to those to whom the end of law, that is, the common good, properly belongs. The question here then will be to determine to whom the common good of the body politic properly belongs. Now the common good belongs most properly to the whole people or to those who represent the people, for the simple reason that the common good of the body politic is the primary purpose of their existence as a unified social body. Consequently, we can conclude,

---

[14] This natural inclination of the intellect is called synderesis. Those who accept revelation know that, besides a natural inclination to discover the natural law, God has communicated to man His divine law by some form of revelation.

the power to make human laws belongs most of all to the whole people, and secondly to him or to those who represent the people.[15]

To Conclude: No individual in his own right has the necessary power to make laws, since the common good does not belong properly to him. This is also evident from the fact that the individual has not the coercive power necessary to enforce the law. Now a law that is not upheld by sufficient coercive power for its enforcement falls from the high estate of a true law and becomes mere advice with only persuasive, not coercive, power. It is not a law. For the coercive power, the power to inflict punishment and penalties, is an essential property of law, and therefore must accompany every true law. Such power is, of course, vested in the whole people or in those to whom this power has been communicated. In short: the framing of a true human law belongs to the people or to those who represent the people.

4. A True Law Must Be Promulgated: The rule or measure of human action can bind a rational being only when known. For the object of the will is the good as known. Hence, a command does not oblige, it is not a true law, unless the proper care has been taken by the lawmaker to make it known to the people. This is what is meant by saying that the law must be promulgated.

There are, of course, various ways of promulgating a law. "The promulgation of the natural law is from this very fact, that God has instilled it into the minds of men so as to be known naturally."[16] The divine law was given directly in revelation to man by God. Human law is generally communicated by newspaper, radio, and books.

Definition: We are now able at the close of our analysis to propose the true definition of law. *Law is an ordinance* (a command) *of reason for the common good, promulgated by him who has the care of the community.*

---

[15] From this declaration, that law must be directed to the common good, we can infer that the various commands and precepts of a father to his household, of an employer to his employees, do not have the force and meaning of law, since they do not look to the common good of a perfect community.

[16] *S. Th.*, I–II, 90, 4, ad 1[m].

ARTICLE II: Diversity of Laws

We distinguish four types of law: eternal, natural, human, and divine. We shall indicate their diversity by analyzing the nature of each.

Eternal Law: Law in the ruled (creatures) is fundamentally the finality of nature, the natural inclination to the end impressed by the Creator.[17] In the ruler, law is in the reason; it is the knowledge of government. In God the knowledge of governance of the universe is called Eternal Law. This law is not restricted to any type of creature but pertains to all creation. Hence, it is in accordance with the eternal law that all creatures are ordained to their end, which is the good of the universe, and are governed in their operations either directly or through the instrumental mediacy of other creatures. "The knowledge in God of the government of all things has the nature of law."[18] "Eternal law, therefore, is the knowledge of divine wisdom as it directs all actions and motions."[19]

Natural Law: All creatures, in so far as they are ordered to the common good of the universe, share in the eternal law. This participation in the eternal law, however, is diversified in accordance with the nature of each creature. For it consists in a divine impression upon the created nature which inclines it to tend naturally by proper actions toward its end. This natural appetite in non-rational creatures results in a necessary determination to each action. Man, however, because of his rational nature shares in the eternal law in an altogether different and superior manner. He alone is able to provide freely for himself as well as for others. This superior participation of man in the eternal law is called the natural law. Because the natural law is the finality of nature inclining man not only to his last end but also to due acts, human reason[20] is capable of discerning between that which is good and

---

17 We suppose as already established the truth that the world is ruled by Divine Providence (cf. *The Philosophy of God*, p. 175).

18 *S. Th.*, I–II, 91, 1, *c.*

19 *S. Th.*, I–II, 93, 1, *c.*

20 The profound trust of St. Thomas in the natural rectitude of the intellect as

that which is evil for human nature. The knowledge of what is good and what is evil enables man to form the principles of the natural law which should guide his free operations.[21] "The natural law is nothing else than the rational creature's participation in the eternal law."[22]

Human Law: The precepts of the natural law are indemonstrable principles. The reason is that, like the principles of the speculative intellect, they are first in the moral order, since they flow from a consideration of the good as referred to human nature. These general precepts of the natural law need to be particularized by a consideration of the varying conditions and problems peculiar to time and place. Definite and detailed regulations will result from such considerations. These detailed regulations are human laws which must be drawn up and promulgated by those who have the necessary legislative power. Human laws, therefore, to be true laws, must never be opposed to the natural law which should be their true foundation. For human laws are the particular determinations of the common primary precepts of the natural law, which are formed by man's reason.

Against this argumentation for the need and nature of human laws, one might object that man does not need such addition and multiplication of laws. For the natural law, which is the reasonable participation in divine wisdom, should be quite sufficient to guide man in his free actions. St. Thomas answers this difficulty with a comparison. Just as in man the knowledge of the first speculative principles, which are a participation in the divine intellection, do not suffice for the understanding of the various sciences, so the common principles of the natural law do not formally express the particular determinations needed in all individual instances. We often need a definite human law to proceed with security in par-

---

regards the moral law is expressed in the following manner. First he speaks of a "participation in Eternal Reason"; then he adds: " . . . the light of natural reason, whereby we discern what is good and what is evil, which belongs to the natural law, is nothing else than an imprint of divine light in us." (Cf. *S. Th.*, I–II, 91, 2, *c*.)

[21] "Each operation of reason and will in us is derived from that which is in accordance with nature" (*ibid.*, ad 2ᵐ; cf. *S. Th.*, I–II, 10, 1, *c*).

[22] *Ibid.*

ticular cases. It is true, however, that human laws do not have the inerrancy nor do they attain the certitude of the first precepts of the natural law, since they deal with contingent facts. That is why a human law should not be observed if it is opposed to the natural law.

Divine Law: Why does man need a divine law, that is, a law given to him by revelation? It would seem that such a law, to say the least, is unnecessary. For man is capable of discovering the first principles of the natural law. Moreover, human law unfolds and particularizes the natural law, enabling man to face the contingencies of the day.

There are two reasons which indicate the need of such God-given law. The first is that man is ordered to a supernatural end. This truth cannot be attained by unaided human reason; it depends upon our acceptance of revelation. We cannot discuss it in a treatise of philosophy.[23] The second reason can be ascertained by an observation of the weakness of the human intellect, whatever may be the cause of such weakness. We find that man not only is subject to error, but that he sometimes errs even in forming some of the secondary precepts of the natural law, and most of all in applying these precepts to his actions. That is why a divine law which is definite and known to be absolutely true will help man greatly to act in accordance with truth and morality. The divine law, therefore, is a participation in the eternal law which is revealed to man in order to guide him to his supernatural end.

ARTICLE III: The Effects of Law

The end of law is the common good. Every true law, then, must be directed to the good of the whole community. Now the good of the whole cannot exist unless the parts themselves are good. Hence, the proper effect of law should be to make individual men good, that is, to make it easier for them to practice virtue.

---

[23] The revealed fact is that man is ordered to a supernatural end. Hence, in order that he may be guided with security to this supernatural end, man needs a God-given law, a law which is higher and more extensive than the natural law.

A law is nothing else than a dictate of reason in the one by whom subjects are governed. Now the virtue of any subject is that it be well subordinated to him by whom he is governed, as the virtue of the irascible and concupiscible appetites consists in this, that they are obedient to reason. In this way the virtue of any subject is that it is well subjected to its ruler. . . . Now any law is ordered to this, that it should be obeyed by its subjects. Consequently, it is evident that it is proper to law to lead subjects to the proper virtue. Therefore, since it is virtue "which makes the one having it good," it follows that the proper effect of law is to make those to whom it is given good, either unqualifiedly or in a certain respect. For if the intention of the one giving the law tends to the true good, which is the common good regulated according to divine justice, it follows that through this law men become unqualifiedly good.[24]

Observance of Law Develops Virtue: Virtue, we know, is a good habit, that is, an intrinsic disposition of the faculty to place a good action. We may wonder how law, which is extrinsic to the act, since it is first proposed by the lawmaker, can cause man to acquire the habits, the virtues, which make him good. In order to solve this problem, let us recall that a habit is acquired by repeated operations.[25] Now a true law expresses a moral obligation to place certain actions that are good because ordered to the common good according to divine justice.[26] The repetition of such good actions will eventually form in the subject habits that are good, because they dispose the soul to act in accordance with the dictate of right reason, which is law. In this way, law causes men to become good.[27]

---

[24] *S. Th.,* I–II, 92, 1, *c.*

[25] Cf. *The Philosophy of Man,* p. 213.

[26] The supreme common good is eternal happiness of all men. To such a good must all human laws be directed, at least implicitly.

[27] St. Thomas, the theologian, distinguishes sharply between acquired and infused virtues. The former are caused by the good actions of man; the latter can only be infused by God's direct action. Hence, the infused virtues are not caused by the actions which are placed in accordance with the law. The operations which belong to acquired virtues, although not causes, may be termed dispositions for the reception of the infused virtues, and safeguard for their conservation.

"Virtue is twofold, . . . namely, acquired and infused. Now for both, the repetition of the act (which belongs to an acquired virtue) does something but diversely; for this repetition causes the acquired virtue, whereas it disposes for the infused

LAW 211

Difficulty: It may be objected that law cannot develop virtue because it is obeyed through fear of punishment and not through love of virtue. It is often true, we grant, that the determining motive in the observance of law is one of fear. We shall observe, however, that while fear is not the highest motivation for action, nevertheless, if the fear be reasonable, that is, founded on truth, such motivation is good, not bad. Hence, by repeatedly placing good acts, even when motivated by a reasonable fear, an individual should in time develop habits that are proper to man, and thus perfect his nature.[28]

Perfection Attainable: What is the nature of the perfection which the observance of law entails? To answer this, we must distinguish between the natural and the positive law. The observance of the natural law brings with it every perfection of which man is naturally capable, since it is the law of his nature. On the other hand, the positive law of the republic does not propose to develop such perfection among the citizens. The reason is that the immediate end of human law is the good of the body politic, which does not necessitate the observance of the entire law of nature, but only of those particularizations of the natural law which make for the good of the commonwealth. "Hence, it is enough for the good of the community that the citizens be virtuous to this extent, that they obey the law of the land."[29]

---

virtue, and it conserves and fosters the infused virtue when it is already had. And because law is given for this, that it direct human acts, in so far as human acts conduce to virtue, in so far does law make men good" (*S. Th.*, I–II, 92, 1, ad 1^m).

[28] There is a false notion abroad among men that any fear is an evil and must be done away with because unworthy of a courageous man. This is absurd. True love is consonant with *filial* fear toward those who have rightful authority and power over us. Indeed, it is proper for a child to fear and to love his father. Most of all, we should fear God. We should fear damnation. Hence, to fear punishment which upholds the law is not necessarily an evil motive, although not the most perfect. On the other hand, a *servile* fear, because unreasonable, is an evil.

[29] *S. Th.*, I–II, 92, 1, ad 3^m.

Question II

THE VARIOUS LAWS

This question will have three articles: (1) the eternal law; (2) the natural law; and (3) human law.

ARTICLE I: The Eternal Law

In a philosophy of law, a discussion of the reality of eternal law is fundamental. Indeed no intelligible metaphysics of law can stand without such a foundation of truth. For all other laws, and indeed all true knowledge in man, are a radiation, a participation of the eternal law.

Division: Five problems will be examined in this article: (1) Is there an eternal law? (2) What is it in itself? (3) Is the eternal law known? By whom? How much of it? (4) Why must every true law be derived from the eternal law? (5) Are all beings subject to the eternal law?

1. There is an eternal law: The following demonstration paraphrases an article of the *Summa Theologica:*[30]

Law is a command of practical reason in the one who governs a perfect community. Now the universe is ruled by Divine Providence in this wise. The actual execution of divine government presupposes the knowledge of the things to be governed.[31] Hence, the universe is governed in accordance with the Divine Knowledge. But this knowledge of governance has the nature of law. Therefore, there is in God the law which is the knowledge of governing the universe. Now whatever knowledge the Divine Reason conceives is eternal. Therefore in God the law of the universe is eternal.

2. What is the eternal law in itself? Eternal law is the knowledge of divine government. It is, to use the magnificent language

---

[30] Cf. *S. Th.,* I–II, 91, 1.

[31] Cf. *S. Th.,* I, 22, ad 2ᵐ; *The Philosophy of God,* p. 175. The knowledge of the things to be governed is Divine Providence.

of Aquinas, the knowledge (*ratio*) of Divine Wisdom, inasmuch as it is directive of all acts and motions of creatures to their appointed ends. This definition gives rise to a difficulty.

How can we distinguish eternal law from providence? Providence, properly speaking, we saw in the philosophy of God, is the "knowledge (*ratio*) of the things to be ordered toward an end."[32] This definition of providence, one might conclude, indicates that law and providence are identical. This is not so; indeed, in a well-known text of the *De Veritate,* the Angelic Doctor states definitely that providence in God is not the eternal law, but rather flows from law. Law, he states, is the principle of Providence.[33]

The problem is not merely textual, it is real. The difficulty perhaps lies in a failure to distinguish between knowledge (*ratio*) and exemplar, between law, providence, and government, between a command of reason, a formal determination of the will-act, and an exemplary cause of the effect. The word "ratio" here is restricted to a knowledge which is not viewed as the exemplary cause of a creature. "Ratio," therefore, differs from exemplar in this, that although a "ratio" of the practical intellect looks to action, it is not the exemplary cause of the existing effect. For, as was shown in the philosophy of God, the exemplary cause in God is an existential cause which, through the action of the agent (the Divine Will) determines here and now the nature of the creature.[34]

The knowledge (*ratio*) which belongs to the practical reason can be considered either as Law or as Providence.

a) Law is the knowledge (not exemplar) of directing creatures to their end. It is not government itself. For government in God implies an existential exemplary cause which specifies the effect through the agent (Divine Will).

b) Providence is the knowledge (not exemplar) of Divine Wisdom. It is like the command (*ratio praeceptiva*) of prudence in

---

[32] *S. Th.,* I, 22, 1, *c.*

[33] Cf. *De Veritate,* V, 1, ad 6^m: "*In Deo, lex aeterna non est providentia, sed principium. . . .*"

[34] The *Fourth Way* for the proof of the existence of God rests on this that a true exemplary cause has to be existential.

man, which specifies the act of the will of the agent, not the effect.
In Short:

a) The knowledge (*ratio*) of Divine Wisdom directive of all
actions and motions of creatures to their proper end is the *Eternal
Law*.

b) The knowledge (*ratio*) of Divine Wisdom in so far as it is
joined with (*coniuncta*) the act of the Divine Will is called
Providence. Hence, Providence is the "knowledge (*ratio*) of the
things to be ordered to their end."

c) The idea (exemplar) in the Divine Intellect which through
the act of the agent (Divine Will) actually determines, that is to
say, specifies the nature of the effect (creature) is called exemplar.
Such an idea in God is an existential exemplary cause for every
creature, not only as regards creation and conservation, but for
every motion and action of the creature (government). Divine
government, therefore, is the actual moving and directing of all
creatures to their end by Divine Providence.[35] Law in God is the
knowledge of government, not the governing itself.

To Conclude: Although law looks to action, it does not specify
the act of the will; Providence does.[36] Law, therefore, is a different
function of the knowledge (*ratio*) of Wisdom than Providence.
Law belongs to the intellect of the lawmaker; Providence specifies
the will-act of the governor; it looks to the things for which pro-
vision must be made. Law is the knowledge of Wisdom of the *one*
who governs all things, whereas Providence is the knowledge of
Divine Wisdom of the *things to be ordered*. We conclude: Law is
not identical with Providence. "Law," in the phrase of Aquinas,
"is related to Providence as its principle."[37]

3. **Knowledge of the Eternal Law:** Is the eternal law known to
all rational creatures? Certainly not in itself, for the Wisdom which
is the truth of God is beyond the comprehension of any created intellect; such knowledge is simply incommunicable. Nevertheless,

---

[35] Cf. *The Philosophy of God*, p. 211.

[36] In man, providence belongs to prudence. It specifies choice; it is a cause
(formal) of the good act. Law does not specify the will-act.

[37] *De Veritate*, V, 1, ad 6m.

any true knowledge in man is a certain radiation from the eternal law. Most of all, the understanding of moral truth which the creature attains is a participation in the eternal law. Now all those who have the use of reason, because they are able to form the common principles of the natural law, have attained some knowledge of moral truth. In this manner, all rational beings arrive at some limited understanding of the eternal law.

4. **Every True Law Must Be Derived From the Eternal Law:** All laws, in so far as they are true and good, that is, in so far as they are in accord with right reason, must be derived from the eternal law. The truth of this inference appears clearly from consideration of human government. For, just as the virtue of secondary causes must depend necessarily upon the First Mover, so in good government the direction of a subordinate administration must follow the direction (*ratio,* plan) of the highest; otherwise, a state of confusion and anarchy would prevail. "Now since eternal law is the knowledge of governance in the supreme governor (*ratio gubernationis in supremo gubernante*), it is necessary that all plans (*rationes*) of governing in the secondary governors be derived from eternal law. These plans (*rationes*) of inferior governors are all laws other than the eternal law. Hence, all laws in so far as they participate in right reason are derived from the eternal law."[38]

It should be noted that the comparison of human government offered in this argumentation is not a demonstration from parity, but a mere analogy, an example (*manuductio*). For in divine government of the universe, the plan or exemplar which is communicated by the divine impress of finality and by actual divine motion, directs creatures here and now to the common good of the universe. Hence, the true demonstration is founded upon an exemplary causality that is *existential*. Let us present the argument with its metaphysical content.

Argument: In existentially subordinated causes the power (*virtus*) of the secondary causes is derived, here and now, from the first.

Now the eternal law in God is the knowledge of the plan of

---

[38] *S. Th.,* I–II, 93, 3, *c.*

His efficacious government. It is a knowledge of a plan directive of the finality and actions of creatures to their end.

Consequently, all finality found in creatures[39] is necessarily derived from the eternal law. A striking example of such plan for government is the finality of human nature inclining man to due end and due actions. This plan of government (finality) in man is the natural law.

We infer that human laws which are true and just, in so far as they are a further determination of the precepts of the natural law, ultimately depend for their virtue upon the eternal law.

Conclusion: Therefore, all plans of government in creatures have the power of law (i.e., are true law) only in so far as they are derived from the eternal law.

N.B.: This actual derivation or dependence of any true secondary law upon the eternal law in God is had through an exemplary causation communicated by the operation of the agent (Divine Will). The Divine Exemplar specifies the creature by an impress of finality to end and by successive divine motions. Hence, whenever a man-made law participates in, or is derived from this finality, that is to say, is in accordance with the finality of human nature, it is a true law. Whenever the command of the legislator is opposed to this radical finality, it is not a law, but lawlessness.

5. All Things Are Subject to the Eternal Law: All created things are subject to the eternal law, for the eternal law is the *ratio,* the knowledge or plan, of divine government. Hence, anything created by God is subject to His government and, therefore, to His law. Only the absolute realities which belong to the Divine Nature are not subject to His law because they really are the law itself.

Rational Creatures Are Subject to the Eternal Law in a Special Manner: The eternal law, unlike human law, is not limited to

---

[39] St. Thomas speaks of *"rationes gubernationis quae sunt in inferioribus."* This could be rendered as the plans of governance in creatures. By this phrase the Angelic Doctor does not mean merely the plans which human legislators form in accordance with right reason. The signification of this statement is far more extensive. *"Rationes gubernationis"* includes the participated finality of all creatures to the end of the universe. Such participated finality is the foundation for the natural law, for laws of nature, and for human laws.

rational beings, but extends itself to the whole of creation. To be sure, the manner in which rational creatures and irrational creatures are subject to the eternal law will differ in some respects. In the first place, the law is common to all created beings in this manner, that they are moved by Divine Providence as a result of a divine impress upon their natures which orders them to their proper end. This is the way of "action and passion," and this way is common to all creatures. But on the other hand, besides the way of action and passion, all rational beings are subject to the eternal law in a special manner which is the way of knowledge and freedom. Alone in creation, rational creatures attain to a knowledge of the law which they must freely observe by co-operating both with the divine impress received in nature, and with the various divine motions.

Difficulty: The truth that rational creatures are free to co-operate with the divine motion brings up an ever recurring difficulty: since men are free to obey the law, they are free to disobey. Consequently, those who choose not to observe the law are not really subject to it. The answer is that although free not to observe the law, wicked men remain subject in this way, that a punishment will be meted out to them by the Supreme Ruler and Lawgiver. In this manner, while for a time they do not observe the law by way of freedom, they are absolutely subject to it by way of passion.

Accordingly, the good are perfectly subject to the eternal law, as always acting according to it. But the wicked are subject to the eternal law, imperfectly as to their actions, in so far as their knowledge of what is good and inclination thereto are imperfect; but what is lacking on the part of action is supplied on the part of passion, in so far as they suffer what the eternal law decrees concerning them, according as they fail to do that which is in accord with the eternal law.[40]

ARTICLE II: The Natural Law

In a philosophical treatise, by far the most important page in the chapter on law is the one devoted to the natural law. For the natu-

---

[40] S. Th., I–II, 93, 6, c.

ral law is man's participation in the eternal law; it is a share in the knowledge of the wisdom of God. Because of his knowledge of the natural law, man is able to direct his actions with security toward the end for which he is made.

What It Is: What is the natural law? We have discussed this point before. Let us recall some of our conclusions. The natural law is the participation of the eternal law in the rational nature. Radically, it consists in the finality of human nature, which results in a natural inclination to the ultimate end and to due acts. Because of that finality, the intellect of man is disposed by its natural inclination to enunciate the primary precepts of the natural law.[41] Hence, although the natural law is not a habit, but a participation in the eternal law and an impression of finality upon human nature by its Maker, nevertheless, the judgments or precepts of law, once they have been elicited by the intellect, can be retained in the memory and consequently become an intellectual habit. This habit is called right reason. For, as we have seen, right reason is the true knowledge of the first precepts of the natural law.

How the Natural Law Is Discovered: The natural law, therefore, consists neither in propositions nor in judgments (moral universal judgings). This law, however, becomes known to man by means of judgments which are expressed by propositions.[42] These judgments, which are called precepts of law, may be inferred almost immediately from the consideration of the good of nature, that is, from the consideration of man's natural inclination to the end and to the means. For the natural law is "an impression of the external law . . . by which the creature is inclined to the due act and end." Accordingly, the primary precepts of the natural law, at least, are attainable by all who have the use of reason. This we intend to show by a metaphysical inference from the knowledge of the good. Of course, we do not pretend that all men attain the true knowledge of these primary principles by a personal analysis of the good

---

[41] The natural inclination of the human intellect to enunciate moral principles is called the habit of principles and, more immediately, synderesis.

[42] A judgment or "judging" is the knowledge of reality (truth), ontological or moral. It is expressed by an enunciation, a proposition. We communicate our judgments by propositions, oral or written.

of nature. Most of the members of the human race, we know, are taught by their elders some principles of the moral law. The point we make is that, first of all, such analysis is possible. Secondly, by this analysis we establish, beyond doubt, the objective truth of the fundamental precepts of the moral law. This we shall do by showing that the propositions which express those primary precepts are self-evident. It is our purpose, therefore, to give a full exposition of the genesis and complete enunciation of these precepts.

GENESIS OF OUR KNOWLEDGE OF THE PRECEPTS OF THE NATURAL LAW

In presenting our analysis we can do no better than to paraphrase a famous page of the *Summa Theologica, Prima Secundae*, XCIV. For the purpose of study, we may divide St. Thomas' treatment into three parts, followed by a conclusion and two inferences.

The three parts are: (1) meaning of self-evident propositions; (2) formation of the first principle of the moral law; and (3) formation and enunciation of the primary precepts of the moral law.

The conclusion is: These judgments of the law are self-evident; they can be attained by anyone having full possession of reason.

The inferences are: (1) These precepts propose moral obligations and presuppose moral rights. (2) The natural law is the same for all men with these distinctions: (*a*) Regarding the common principles — it is the same for all both as to objective truth (rectitude) and as to knowledge. (*b*) Regarding particular conclusions — it is the same for all in the majority of cases, but in some few cases it may vary both as to knowledge and as to objective truth (rectitude).

1. Meaning of self-evident propositions:

The precepts of the natural law are to the practical reason what the first principles of demonstrations are to the speculative reason, because both are self-evident principles. Now a thing is said to be self-evident in two ways; first, in itself; secondly, in relation to us. Any proposition is said to be self-evident in itself, if its predicate is contained in the notion of the subject; even though it may happen that to one who does not know the definition of the subject, such a proposition is not self-evident. For instance, this proposition, *man is a rational being,* is, in its very nature, self-evident, since he who says *man,* says a *rational animal;* and yet to one who does not know what a man is, this proposition is not self-evident. Hence, it is, that, as Boethius says, certain axioms or propositions are universally self-evident to all; and such are the propositions whose terms are known to all, as, *Every whole is greater than its part,* . . . and . . . *Things equal to one and the same are equal to one another.* But some propositions are self-evident only to the wise, who understand the meaning of the terms of such propositions. Thus to one who understands that an angel is not a body, it is self-evident that an angel is not circumscriptively in a place. But this is not evident to the unlearned, for they cannot grasp it.[43]

Self-Evident Proposition:[44] A proposition is self-evident in itself when the predicate belongs to the essence of the subject, as for example, immaterial beings are not circumscribed in space. Now, although this statement is self-evident in itself, it might not seem so to an ignorant person. Why? Because the terms of that proposition, that is, its subject and predicate, are not understood by him. Such is not the case as regards the first principles of the natural law. Our contention is that these principles are not only self-evident in themselves, but self-evident to all men who have the proper use of their intellectual powers. The reason is that the terms of these principles are known to all and, consequently, all are able to understand that the predicate is of the essence of the subject.

2. Formation of the first principle of the moral law:

A definite order is to be found in these things that are apprehended by men. For that which first falls under the apprehension is *being,* the understanding of which is included in all things whatsoever a man apprehends. Therefore the first indemonstrable principle is that *the same thing cannot be affirmed and denied at the same time* which is based on the notion of *being* and *non-being;* and on this principle all others are based, as is stated in Metaph., iv. Now as being is the first thing that falls under the apprehension unqualifiedly, so *the good* is the first thing that falls under the apprehension of the

---

[43] *S. Th.,* I–II, 94, 2, *c.*

[44] The phrase of St. Thomas is *"propositio per se nota."* In the philosophy of being we spoke of such propositions as analytic, because they become self-evident to us by analysis. (Cf. *The Philosophy of Being,* pp. 123–127.)

practical reason, which is directed to action; for every agent acts for an end, which has the nature of good. Consequently, the first principle in the practical reason is one founded on the nature of good, and this is that the good is that which all desire. This, therefore, is the first precept (principle) of law, that *the good should be done and promoted, and evil must be avoided.* All other precepts of the natural law are founded upon this; so that all the things which the practical reason naturally apprehends as man's good belong to the precepts of the natural law under the form of things to be done or avoided.[45]

Order of Understanding Truths: How do we arrive at a true knowledge of the judgments which express the natural law?

a) **Speculative Intellect:** First of all, we apprehend being in this way, that the understanding of being is included in whatever we know intellectually. The reason is that the formal object of the intellect is being as being. From the apprehension of being, knowledge of the principle of contradiction enables us to infer the other fundamental principles of the speculative intellect.

b) **Practical Intellect:** In a manner similar to the knowledge of being in the speculative intellect, the knowledge of the good as desirable[46] follows upon our apprehension of being and is had by the practical intellect which looks to action. Why does the knowledge of the good as desirable belong to the practical rather than to the speculative intellect? The reason is that the speculative intellect is ordered to the contemplation of truth, and unlike the practical intellect, it does not look to action. We do not deny that the speculative intellect can and does speculate upon the nature of the good, but the apprehension of the good as desirable looks to the appetite and, therefore, looks to action at least as a remote possibility.[47] Now every agent must act for an end, and the end must be viewed as good and desirable. For in so far as it is the formal aspect of the end, the good is perfective of nature.[48] Hence, action

---

[45] *S. Th.,* I–II, 94, 2, *c.*

[46] Being becomes known as *desirable good* because known as suitable to the nature of the subject of knowledge. This is because the "object of the will is the end and the good." (*S. Th.,* I–II, 1, 1.)

[47] *S. Th.,* I–II, 9, 1, ad 2ᵐ.

[48] *"Dicitur bonum ens perfectivum alterius per modum finis"* (*De Ver.,* XXI, 1).

presupposes knowledge of the desirable good. From this knowledge of the good as desirable, the intellect forms the first principle of practical reason. This first principle of practical reason is expressed thus: *The good is that which all desire and seek.* The inference by which we form this first principle of practical reason is immediate, since anything desired and sought is sought under the formality of good. Hence, "the good is that which all seek"; it is the object of the appetite, for it is the perfection of nature. Nothing is desirable, nothing is sought except under the formality of good. This first principle of practical reason is true of all beings which are distinct from their last end; that is to say, it is applicable to all creatures.

c) **First Principle of the Moral Law:** Now, when we apply the first principle of practical reason to a rational nature, that is, to a nature which is free to choose or to reject the particular good, a moral obligation to seek the good and to avoid its contrary evil is immediately perceived. Consequently, the human intellect is necessitated to enunciate and at the same time to apprehend the absolute truth of the first, the most universal principle of the natural law: *The good must be done, must be sought; evil must be avoided.*

d) **Principle Is Self-Evident:** This first principle of the moral law is self-evident to all, for the terms of the proposition, "good" and "must be done," are understood by all men; the same is true of "evil" and "must be avoided." Moreover, the knowledge that the predicates, "must be done" and "must be avoided," belong to the nature of the subjects, "good" and "evil," is explained in the following manner.

Reason naturally understands that the good is that toward which nature tends by its appetite, for the good is that which is suitable to human nature, that which disposes man toward his last end. Evil, on the other hand, is that which causes human nature to deviate from the end. Evil, therefore, is the contrary of good. Hence, reason understands that the good must be sought, precisely because it is the perfection of nature. For "to seek" is the action of a nature toward its end or good. On the contrary, evil which is opposed to good must be avoided.[49] This metaphysical analysis, of course, al-

---

[49] Obviously this first principle of the moral law, indeed, the whole approach

though within the reach of all who have the use of reason, is not actually evoked by all in the formation of the first principle of the natural law. Nor is it necessary, since everyone is aware by a natural and immediate inference that the appetite naturally desires and seeks its good and naturally avoids evil. The first principle of the natural law, "good is to be done and evil must be avoided," is not only absolutely true, but self-evident.

3. Formation and enunciation of the primary precepts of the moral law:

a) From a general application of the first principle.

Because good has the nature of an end, and evil, the nature of the contrary, hence it is that all those things to which man has a natural inclination are naturally apprehended by reason as being good, and consequently to be sought by action, and their contraries as evil, and objects to be avoided. Consequently, the order of the precepts of the natural law is according to the order of natural inclinations. For there is in man, first of all, an inclination to good in accordance with the nature which he has in common with all substances, inasmuch, namely, as every substance seeks the preservation of its own existence, according to its nature; and by reason of this inclination, whatever is a means of preserving human life, and of warding off its obstacles, belongs to the natural law. Secondly, there is in man an inclination to things that belong to him more properly, according to that nature which he has in common with other animals; and in virtue of this inclination, those things are said to belong to the natural law which nature has taught to all animals, such as sexual intercourse, the bringing up of offspring, and so forth. Thirdly, there is in man an inclination to good according to the nature of his reason, which is proper to him. Thus man has a natural inclination to know the truth about God, and to live in society; and in this respect whatever pertains to this inclination belongs to the

---

to the good presented in this analysis, is applicable only to a rational, free nature. When we understand that good must be sought, we are referring to the means which can be freely chosen by man. All irrational beings are necessitated to every action; for unlike man for whom the human act is a means which may dispose to the last end, the animal, the plant, the stone, by every action attain their last end, which is to be and to act necessarily in accordance with the eternal law communicated to them by a necessary impulse of nature.

natural law; e.g., to shun ignorance, to avoid offending those among whom one has to live, and other things which look to this.[50]

Analysis of Text: All other principles are founded upon this first principle of the natural law in this way, that whatever the practical intellect apprehends to be the good of human nature, that must be done; and, on the contrary, whatever the practical intellect understands to be bad for man, that must be avoided.

The principle is clear, self-evident. The real crux of the matter, the point to be established is this: How can we discover in the concrete (1) what the good of human nature is, that is, not the last end, but the true means to the last end in order that we may seek it, and (2) what is evil because contrary to the end, in order to avoid it? St. Thomas answers very simply that the good will be understood from a consideration of the things to which man has a natural inclination. Consequently, the order of precepts of the natural law will be discovered in accordance with the order of natural inclinations. Let us repeat this capital text:

Since the good has the nature of end, while evil has the aspect of its contrary, it follows that reason naturally understands to be good all the things to which man has a natural inclination, and consequently that these things should be sought by action, while on the other hand, the contraries of these are evil and should therefore be avoided.[51]

---

[50] *S. Th.,* I–II, 94, 2, *c.*

[51] *Ibid.* The doctrine that a nature is inclined to acts which dispose it to its end is a fundamental one in the philosophy of St. Thomas. Nature is a principle of action to an end. Hence, a nature which is not inclined to the proper operations which dispose it to attain its due end is a contradiction; it is a *"non-ens."* "Every nature is inclined naturally to an operation that is suitable to it" (*S. Th.,* I–II, 94, 3). The following texts may prove helpful:

"God imprints on the whole of nature the principles of its proper operations . . ." (*S. Th.,* I–II, 93, 5) . . . so that "all (created) beings in some way participate in the eternal law in so far as from the divine impress they possess inclinations to proper acts and ends" (I–II, 91, 2). From this truth, we gather that the "rational creature has a natural inclination to those (actions) which are in accord with the eternal law" (I–II, 93, 6). Indeed "the rational creature receives a share of eternal reason in this manner, that it is naturally inclined to due act and end" (I–II, 91, 2). Consequently, "there is in every man a natural inclination to act according to reason . . . Now everything to which man is inclined according to his nature belongs to the natural law" (I–II, 94, 3).

The argument of St. Thomas is that "reason *naturally* understands" that the good of nature which is the true means to the last end must be manifested by a natural inclination, that is, by an inclination resulting from man's specific as well as generic perfection. Hence, first of all, we must understand — not merely by observation but by a reflection upon man's nature — what these inclinations of nature are. From these inclinations we shall become certain that some actions are good and their contraries evil, and, consequently, that we must do those actions toward which we are naturally inclined in accordance with our nature, because they are good and, at times, necessary means which dispose us toward the last end. On the other hand, we must always avoid the contrary of our natural inclinations, because, being evil, they frustrate nature.

This statement implies an admirable trust in the natural "rectitude" of the intellectual nature of man. It declares that the *natural* inclination must always be toward the good of nature. This position of St. Thomas as regards the rectitude of our rational nature is obviously poles apart from such errors as those of the completely vitiated nature proposed by Luther, of the hopeless predeterminism of Calvin, of the pessimistic tenets of Jansenius, and of the frustrating despair of the modern existentialists. St. Thomas is a realist for whom nature is a principle of action ordered to its last end and, therefore, a principle which must be naturally inclined to the necessary means.

Difficulties: Against this realistic trust in the fundamental rectitude of our intellectual nature in its search for the precepts of the natural law, two objections may be proposed.

1. We find distinct inclinations to evil actions in individual men. Sometimes these inclinations, if followed, would not only cause great social disorder but would affect the very rationality of the individual. Such "natural" inclinations certainly are not indicative of the good of nature, of the actions to be done, of the precepts of the natural law.

The answer is not difficult to find. These are *individual* inclinations which depend on the material cause and are communicated through heredity, education, and environment. Our contention refers only to natural, *specific,* universal inclinations which we discover by an analysis of nature, not merely by the observation of individual tendencies.

2. A universal inclination toward evil actions is observable in all men. This is especially noteworthy as regards an inordinate concupiscence and an insatiable selfishness.

The answer is rather obvious. No man in his right mind is led astray in thinking such an inclination to evil to be a naturally good inclination, since all men who reflect on the matter come to know, at least in a fundamental way, that such inordinate passions are not in accord with the highest specific perfection of man, his rationality, and therefore that they are against the good of nature. Right reason indicates that these unnatural appetites should be controlled lest nature be frustrated and even destroyed.[52]

b) *Discovery of primary precepts.*

Let us now examine these fundamental natural inclinations of man in order to formulate the first precepts of the natural law. The end is the good of nature[53] and evil is radically opposed to this good. Now nature, being necessarily inclined to its end, must be naturally inclined to those things which are good, that is, which dispose it to the end. Consequently, the things to which the rational nature of man is inclined must be proposed by reason as good and as something to be sought by action. On the other hand and for the same reason, those things that are contrary to the natural inclinations are opposed to the good of nature and therefore are to be avoided. Hence, the order of the precepts of the natural law will be discovered in accordance with the order of natural inclinations. Now as we examine the natural inclinations of man we distinguish three fundamental urges of nature, not individual

---

[52] To those who accept Christian revelation these inordinate unnatural inclinations are known to result from original sin, from what St. Thomas calls the wound of nature. Certainly, no one has ever thought that we should found our precepts of the natural law upon these evil inclinations.

[53] This statement supposes an understanding of finality. Nature is a principle of action by means of which a being necessarily seeks its perfection which is its end. To deny this truth is implicitly to deny that being is intelligible.

inclinations, but specific tendencies,[54] according as the nature of man is a substance, an animal, and a rational being. From these three inclinations we discover the first three precepts of the natural law:

1. In common with all existing substances, man naturally seeks to preserve his existence which is his life.[55] Hence, it is a precept of the natural law to do what is necessary or reasonably helpful for the conservation of life and to avoid and impede what might destroy life.

2. In common with all animals, there is in human nature a strong inclination to the procreation and education of offspring. Consequently, man must avoid as being against the natural law anything that would be contrary to the *proper* and *natural* use of the procreative power, anything which would tend to misuse directly the generative act.

3. In rational beings alone and in accordance with the nature of reason, we find an inclination to know God and to live peacefully in society. Thus, the highest precept of the natural law establishes our primary obligation to know and to love God and to be just in our dealings with others.

Affirmative and Negative Expression of Each Precept: It should be noted that each of these precepts can be expressed affirmatively and negatively. The affirmative command directs man to the good which must be done; the negative forbids the evil act which harms nature as regards its disposition toward the ultimate end. Thus:

First Precept	*a*) affirmative: Man should take reasonable care of his life.
Substance — (self-preservation)	*b*) negative: Man should not attempt directly to destroy his life (suicide).

---

[54] By these specific tendencies we do not mean only the natural inclination which is founded upon the last specific difference, that is, upon rationality alone, but we include as a foundation for such natural urges all the essential intelligible perfections of the substance, the animal, and the intellectual being.

[55] "To live is the 'to be' (*esse*) of living beings" (*S. Th.*, II–II, 179, 1, ad 1ᵐ; *De Ver.*, IV, 8; *C.G.*, I, 98, *c*).

Second Precept	*a)* affirmative: It is right and good for man to establish a family.
Animal — (propagation)	*b)* negative: It is wrong to misuse directly the generative act.
Third Precept	*a)* affirmative: Man should acknowledge his dependence upon God and his obligation of justice to his neighbor.
Man — (rational life, justice)	*b)* negative: Man should not reject God, or be unjust toward others.

N.B.: The nature of the obligation manifested by the affirmative command necessarily differs from that of the negative. The affirmative binds one always, but not at all times; the negative binds always and at all times.[56] An example will clarify this statement. The affirmative command: "Be just in your dealings with others," is always true, always right; it does not, however, oblige us to place such actions at every moment of the day. On the other hand, the negative law: "Do not be unjust to another," binds me always and at every moment.

The reason for this difference in the extension of the precept as expressed affirmatively and negatively is twofold. First of all, an evil moral act is directly opposed to the attainment of the last end. Hence, it can never be justified; it must be avoided always and at all times. On the other hand, as regards the good actions commanded by the affirmative precept, it is obvious that, first, we are not bound to do that which is more perfect, and, secondly, the placing of all good actions at every moment is simply an impossibility.

Subordination of Precepts: The three primary precepts of the natural law are not in themselves of equal perfection. The reason is that their immediate foundations in nature vary in degree of

---

[56] "Affirmative precepts do not bind for all times" (*S. Th.,* I–II, 100, 10, ad 2ᵐ). The lapidary phrase used by moralists is that such precepts bind *semper sed non pro semper*. The negative precepts, on the other hand, bind *semper et pro semper*.

intelligibility. The third precept is, of course, the most perfect since it results immediately from the rationality of human nature. Now, although the negative aspect of any precept can never be dispensed with, since it is directly opposed to its active rational principle, nevertheless, the affirmative command may be neglected in order to observe more perfectly a higher precept. We may, for example, expose ourselves to danger of death in order to safeguard the family or for the defense of Divine Truth. In like manner, the use of the right to form a family may be relinquished for the service of God, but the highest precept cannot be subordinated since it is connected directly with the last end.

Conclusion

Our conclusion is that the primary precepts of the natural law are self-evident and consequently can be known by all who have the use of reason. This conclusion appears from our analysis in this manner: (1) the first principle of the moral law, good — that which perfects nature by disposing it toward its last end — is to be done, and evil — that which frustrates nature as regards the end — avoided, was shown to be self-evident and implicit in every action. (2) The inclinations of nature according to its specific and generic perfections manifest the goods necessary or useful as means to the last end.[57] Moreover, by means of an immediate inference these natural inclinations indicate the evil — because it is contrary to the good — to be avoided. (3) From this knowledge, the intellect draws the primary judgments of the natural law.

That these three primary precepts are self-evident, and that they can be known by all who have the use of reason, is the definite doctrine of Aquinas, a doctrine fundamental to an objective and realistic theory of morality.[58]

---

[57] A nature is a principle of action to the end. To deny that such a principle is necessarily inclined to place actions which dispose it to its end would be to imply a fundamental contradiction in nature. It would be to state that nature is and is not a principle of action to the end.

[58] The use of reason means precisely a fundamental understanding of human nature. Consequently, one who has attained the use of reason should be able to have some knowledge of the last end and of the necessary means.

First Inference

These precepts propose moral obligations and presuppose moral rights.

Obligation: The precepts of the natural law express obligation or duty.[59] They state what all men must do in order to dispose themselves to their last end. The moral necessity which these precepts establish is not derived from the will of the legislator or from a categorical imperative. Our obligation to observe the moral law flows immediately from the finality of man's nature and ultimately from the eternal law. Obviously, the fulfillment of any obligation declared by the law does not limit and constrain nature, but perfects it by an exercise of the highest freedom of human nature, that is to say, the freedom which consists in seeking the true end, happiness.

Rights: Rights are manifested by the precepts of the natural law, for any objective right is the object of justice. Now nature is ordered to an end; it exists only to place actions that will dispose it to that end. Consequently, those things that are necessary for the attainment of the end must themselves be attainable. They are due in justice to the nature. The precepts of the law manifest these rights. Consequently, a right is not an extrinsic title established by the will of a superior, by a decision of a law court or of a lawmaker. At best, these can recognize and declare a right; they cannot establish it, for a right is the term, the object of the virtue of justice. An example will clarify this point: If I am to fulfill my obligation to know and love God, I have a right to all the things that are essential for such action. No declaration of a law court

---

[59] The word *duty* is sometimes used instead of obligation. In using this term we should strip it of all Kantian connotations. Let us not accept it as something established from without. It does not result from an extrinsic determination of the will of a lawmaker which may well be against the true good of man. Duty is the term of justice; it is the *"debitum."* The fulfillment of our obligation, the doing of our duty, should never mean the restriction or the crushing of nature. On the contrary, it should express man's natural inclination to the good of his nature, to a disposition toward the last end. To do our duty is to perfect nature, to render it its due.

can confer or remove this right. It is a *"debitum,"* that which is due.

The precept of law, obligation, and right are united in the closest bond. They are distinct aspects of the same reality which is the finality of nature, a participation in the eternal law, and the impression of the Creator in the creature. Law, which consists in the finality of nature, is the rule of human acts; obligation, which rests upon finality of nature, is the moral necessity expressed by the law; right, which is presupposed by the precept of the law, is the object of the act of justice, due to nature for the fulfillment of its finality. All three, law, obligation, and right, in their unity and interdependence are perfections of human nature; all three proclaim its finality to the attainment of happiness.

Second Inference

The natural law is the same for all men.

If one grants that the natural law is founded on the common natural inclinations of human nature, the proposition that the natural law is the same for all men will seem a foregone conclusion. Yet, St. Thomas takes great care to indicate exactly how this truth is to be understood.

Knowledge and Objective Truth (Rectitude): We should distinguish, on the one hand, between man's *knowledge* and the *objective truth* of the principles of the natural law, and, on the other, between the common principles (or primary precepts of the law) and the *particular conclusions* which are particular applications of common principles to given cases. These "particular applications" are sometimes called secondary precepts. They are universal judgments based on the primary precepts and express one particular aspect of the first precept. For example, the judgment "to steal is wrong" is a particularized inference from the third primary precept, "Do not be unjust to others." Knowledge, of course, refers to the knowledge man may obtain of these various principles and conclusions. Rectitude looks to their absolute truth. Our twofold problem is to discover, first, whether both, principles and conclusions, have always the same moral truth and rectitude, and consequently whether they must always be observed; secondly, whether both, principles and conclusions, are always known by all men.

Common, Primary Universal Precepts: (1) *Objective Truth:* Are the common precepts which we call the three primary precepts of the natural law always right, always true? St. Thomas affirms vigorously that, since they are founded on the fundamental inclinations of nature, they must be absolutely true. Accordingly, we can never be dispensed from them.

2. *Knowledge:* What is the knowledge which men have of these first precepts? St. Thomas is of the opinion that they are "equally known by all." For it is proper to man to be inclined to act in accordance with reason. Now the first principles of the natural law are nothing else than an expression of this truth, that man should act according to reason, since these principles result from a knowledge of the fundamental inclinations of human nature to the good of nature.

Particular Conclusions: (1) *Objective Truth:* In the application of these first principles, "it may happen in a particular case that it would be injurious and therefore unreasonable" (*S. Th.,* I–II, 94, 4, *c*) to act in accordance with the principle. The reason is that because of a change in the object or circumstances as referred to the rational principle of action, the specification of the act has been so affected that its goodness or malice has been modified. An example will make this evident. It is in accordance with justice that I should return to others what belongs to them. This is a general principle and its rectitude and truth are absolute. A particular application which might seem an exception to this principle is that it would be unreasonable and therefore wrong to return a gun to its owner who in his present wrathful condition would use it to commit murder. Clearly, the present circumstances change the specification of the act. For the object is no longer returning what belongs to its owner, but to its owner who intends to commit a crime with it. What would be just and right generally (*ut in pluribus*) becomes unreasonable and therefore evil because of the change in the specification of the act. The common principle here is not applicable.

2. *Knowledge:* As regards the knowledge of the objective moral truth of the more restricted conclusions, it is an observable fact that, because of the state of civilization, because of prejudice, faulty education, passion, habit, or other obstacles to knowledge, men sometimes err in evaluating properly the rectitude of a particular case. They fail in judging correctly as to the goodness or malice of the act. Hence, a true knowledge of the natural law is not always had by all men as regards the particular applications of the principles of the law.

We conclude, then, that while the first principles of the normal law are always true (right) and known by all men who have the use of reason, it happens that sometimes, though rarely, the particular applications are not in accordance with the truth and *rectitude* of the general principles. It also happens that men may err in their *knowledge* of the rectitude of these particular applications.

N.B.: Accordingly, the natural law as regards its first precepts cannot be blotted from the hearts of men; but as to the particular conclusions of the secondary precepts this may and does happen.

If, then, a further question were asked as to whether the natural law could ever change, the answer in accordance with the preceding discussion would be that regarding the first precepts there can be no change; the natural law is immutable. Regarding the particular conclusions there can be a change in this way, that the general precept no longer applies because of a change in the specification of the act by the object and circumstances.[60]

---

[60] The examples that are generally brought to bear as being exceptions are often taken from biblical history. One of these examples is the case of Abraham being ordered to kill his innocent son. The solution of these problems is that God the Creator has supreme ownership over all things and supreme power over life and death. Hence, if God were to command a father to kill his innocent child, this would not be murder, and the father would be obliged to obey. If God were to order a man to despoil another of his property, such an action would not be against justice since all things belong absolutely to God, and man has only a right to the proper use of them.

ARTICLE III: Human Law

We shall close our treatise on law with a few brief remarks about man-made law. It is sometimes thought that laws are arbitrary commands of the lawgiver which must be obeyed because of fear of punishment. This, of course, is quite false. A true law, one that merits the name of law, is a command of reason, and its purpose is to secure the common good. This common good the law obtains primarily by causing the one who observes the law to become more perfect by placing virtuous actions. The law does so in this wise: a just and true law directs men to place actions that are just and reasonable and which, therefore, must perfect human nature. For, while the law of the state tends primarily to promote the common good of the commonwealth by endeavoring to safeguard peace and prosperity, it must always be subordinated to the supreme good of man which is his eternal happiness.[61] Thus, law, man-made law, is nothing foreign to right reason. It prescribes actions which, because they are good human acts, perfect man's nature and consequently are a means to attain the last end.

Derived From the Natural Law: The statement that a true, i.e., a just law is founded upon reason indicates that human laws must be derived from the natural law. To be just and good, the law must be reasonable, that is, in accordance with the rule of reason. Now the first rule of reason is the natural law. Hence, all human laws to be true laws must be derived from the natural law. Consequently, the true definition of human law is the following: Human laws are the particularized determinations of the common (general) precepts of the natural law, framed by human reason for the common good of the body politic.

There are, however, various ways by which a human law could be derived from the natural law. Some human laws are necessary and almost immediate conclusions from the precepts of the natural law; others are further determinations of the natural law, determi-

---

[61] "The end of human law is the temporal tranquillity of the state. Law effects this end by controlling (*cohibendo*) external actions as regards the evils which can disturb the peaceful state of the commonwealth" (*S. Th.*, I–II, 98, 1).

nations which as such are not formally contained in the natural law. Examples abound: The human law which forbids murder is an immediate inference from the precept of the natural law that we should not harm another. Instances of further determinations of the same precept of the natural law are the various traffic laws which obtain today in our larger cities.

We may add that, since the natural law is a participation in the eternal law, it follows that human laws are true and just in so far as they share in the perfection of the eternal law.

Inferences: St. Thomas discusses various inferences regarding human law. We shall mention the more important of these.

1. Human laws should be framed along general lines and should not be particularized, so that they may be applicable to all cases. It will be for the judge to interpret and apply the law properly to each individual case.

2. Human laws do not pretend to repress all vices, but only those which are more heinous and injurious to the common good of society.

3. Nor does human law prescribe all virtues. Because, however, it seeks to obtain the good of the commonwealth, it can command the practice of any virtue which would help attain this end.

4. Do human laws bind in conscience? St. Thomas is of the opinion that any true, any just human law must bind in conscience.[62] "Laws," he points out, "are either just or unjust. If they are just they have the power of binding in conscience from the eternal law whence they are derived." The reason, therefore, for the moral obligation is that any true law is an ordinance of reason and, accordingly, must be founded upon the eternal law which is the divine reason.[63] Now the eternal law as the supreme norm is absolute.

On the other hand, an unjust law in itself does not bind in conscience. We should distinguish, however, between laws that

---

[62] This opinion is also proposed and defended by two other Doctors of the Church: St. Albert the Great and St. Robert Bellarmine.

[63] Those moralists who accept the definition that law is an act of the will, teach that purely penal laws, as they are called, do not bind in conscience because the lawmaker had no intention to make the law binding in conscience.

are opposed to the divine good and those opposed to the human good. A law, for example, inducing men to idolatry belongs to the first type; excessive taxation belongs to the other. It is obvious that we can never obey the first type of law because to do so would mean to go directly against the law of nature and of God; it would mean committing an evil action. What must we say of the second type of laws which are opposed merely to the human good? It seems that while we are not bound to obey, since the law is unjust, nevertheless, to do so is not necessarily an evil act and therefore may entail no moral fault. Indeed, at times, it may be more prudent to obey such a law, because of the disorder that would result from our action.

St. Thomas explains that in the observance of law we should take account of the purpose rather than the letter of the law. Now, since law is for the common good, a law which fails in this purpose is without binding force. Hence, in a case where the observance of such a law would be injurious to the common good, and, moreover, should there be no time to refer the matter to the proper authority, one is dispensed from such observance. (Cf. *S. Th.*, I–II, 96, 6.)

Conclusion: It has been stated by recent writers that the modern legalistic attitude of mind toward law is that law is a restrictive measure, a burden which has to be imposed upon man; that it is a rule which limits his liberty, peace, and happiness, a norm whose supreme motivation is the fear of punishment. Contrary to this notion, St. Thomas presents law in its true aspect, that is, as resulting from the highest perfection of man's nature, his reason. Law is a thing of reason. It flows from man's reason; it shares in the Divine Reason, and, consequently, its purpose is not to limit, bind, and enslave, but to direct man to the true liberty of his nature, which is to act reasonably, to place good human actions. This is the concept of law we find presented so often in Holy Scripture, especially in the Psalms. There the law is generally presented as a thing of joy and the object of our love. "I have loved Thy Law, Oh Lord" (Ps. 118). Consequently, the observance of the true law is not a restriction but a powerful means of perfecting our nature, without which we can never hope to reach beatitude.

SUMMARY

Common Notion: Law is the rule and measure of action. {
In the ruler, law is in the reason.
In the ruled, law is primarily an inclination of nature to the last end and to due actions.
}

In man: The natural law is fundamentally the finality of nature which consists in a natural inclination to the last end and due acts.

Obligation and right: The expressions of the inclination to end and acts, which are the judgments or precepts of the natural law, (1) manifest "obligation" which is moral necessity resulting from finality, and (2) presuppose "right" which is the object of the virtue of justice.

Question I

LAW IN GENERAL

Article I: *The Nature of Law*

Definition:

Law is an ordinance or command of reason for the common good promulgated by him who has care of the community.

Analysis:

a) Formal cause. Law is a thing of reason because the rule and measure, i.e., the formal determination of a human act, is from the intellect, not from the will.

b) Final cause. Law must look to the common good.

1) The rule of human acts should flow from the first principle of practical reason which is the last end, the absolute good as desired (happiness).

2) Because man is part of a perfect community, his actions should be directed to the common good (happiness of all men).

3) The laws of the state should be subordinated to this supreme common good.

c) Efficient cause. The power to frame human laws belongs to the people or its vicegerent. The reason is that such power is vested in those to whom the common good belongs.

d) Property of true law. Law should be promulgated. A rule of action binds a rational being only when known. For the object of the will-act is the good as known.

Article II: *Diversity of Laws*

Eternal law in God is the *knowledge* of government. In other words, it is the knowledge of divine wisdom directive of all actions and motions of creatures to their end.

Natural law is the rational creature's participation in the eternal law. It consists in a divine impress upon human nature which inclines it to tend naturally toward the last end and to due actions. Fundamentally the natural law is the very finality of man.

Human laws are the particular determinations of the common precepts of the natural law to the varying conditions of time and place.

Divine law is a participation in the eternal law which is revealed to man in order to guide him to his supernatural end.

Article III: *Effects of Law*

The end of law is the common good which is universal happiness. Hence, the proper effect of law is to make men good by directing them to practice virtue. For the practice of virtue is a necessary means to the attainment of happiness.

Question II

THE VARIOUS LAWS

Article I: *The Eternal Law*

Importance of treatise: No intelligible metaphysics of law can stand without it.

Basic Notions:

1. Existence: There is an eternal law. In God, the knowledge of government of the universe, which has the nature of law, is eternal.
2. Essence: What is the eternal law in itself?
   a) Not providence, which is the knowledge of the things to be ordered to their end.
   b) Not government, which is the actual moving and directing of all creatures to their end.
   c) Eternal law is the knowledge of government. Eternal law is not the actual governing in which the exemplar actually specifies

the effect; it is not providence in which the knowledge directs the divine will. It is the knowledge of government. "The knowledge of Divine Wisdom directive of all actions and motions of creatures to their proper end is the eternal law."

3. Knowledge: The eternal law is not known in itself but in the various participations observed in creatures. Most of all, a limited understanding of the eternal law is had in the discovery of the precepts of the natural law.

4. Derivation: Every true law is derived from the eternal law:

   a) Already shown:

   1. Law in the legislator (ruler) is in the reason. It is the *knowledge* of true government.

   2. Law in the ruled is fundamentally a natural inclination to the last end and to due acts. It is the finality of nature.

   b) Argument: In existentially subordinated causes, the power (*virtus*) of the secondary causes (movers) is derived here and now from the virtue (power) of the first, so that the second does not move (itself or another) except in so far as it is here and now moved by the first.

   Now the eternal law in God is the knowledge (*ratio*) of His efficacious government, that is, knowledge of the motions of creatures to their end, a knowledge of their finality.

   It follows that all finality found in creatures (*rationes gubernationis quae sunt in inferioribus*) is necessarily derived from the eternal law. Such, for example, is the natural law which is man's finality to his end and to due acts.

   We must infer that human laws, which are true and just laws in so far as they are particularized determinations of the natural law, are derived from the eternal law. Every true law, therefore, is derived from the eternal law.

5. Application: *All creatures are subject to the eternal law:*

   a) Nonrational beings — all motions and actions in the whole of nature are subject to the eternal law in so far as they are moved by Divine Providence.

   b) Rational creatures are subject in two ways:

   By way of action and passion, in so far as they are inclined naturally to the last end and to acts.

   By way of knowledge of the natural law which is a participation of the eternal law.

N.B.: Although not coerced to observe the law, men remain subject to the law by way of passion through retribution of justice.

Article II: *The Natural Law*

What it is: The natural law is the participation of the eternal law in the rational creature. It consists in the finality of human nature which is a natural inclination to ultimate end and to due acts.

Man is able to elicit judgments which are the precepts of the natural law. These judgments, which are expressed by propositions, are retained in the intellectual memory as the habit of right reason.

Genesis of our knowledge of the natural law.

1. Knowledge of being and formation of first speculative principles (by means of habit of understanding).
2. Knowledge of good and formation of the first principle of practical reason: "The good is that which all seek (by action)."
   Application of the first principle of practical reason to a rational free nature. The intellect (synderesis) enunciates the first principle of the moral law: "Good should be done; evil must be avoided." (The good here refers to proximate ends, not to the last end.)
3. Application of this first principle. We discover the fundamental goods of human nature by an analysis of its specific (essential) inclinations.
4. There are three essential inclinations:
   a) As substance: to live.
   b) As animal: to form a family.
   c) As rational: to recognize dependence upon God and to be just to neighbor.
5. There are three primary precepts. In their negative expressions, they are as follows: It is evil:
   a) To commit suicide.
   b) To misuse sex.
   c) To fail in justice toward God and neighbor.

Conclusion: These three precepts are self-evident truths. A self-evident proposition is one in which the predicate is somehow contained in the subject. But in each of these precepts the predicate is contained in the subject.

1. It is evil to commit suicide. Evil is that which is unsuitable to nature. Self-destruction is unsuitable (evil) to any *substance*.

2. It is evil to misuse sex because unsuitable (evil) to *animal* nature.
3. It is evil to fail in justice toward God and man. Injustice is opposed (evil) to *rational* nature; it is unreasonable not to give to others what is their due.

Inferences:

1. These precepts propose obligations and suppose rights.
   a) These primary precepts state definite obligations (moral necessity).
   b) These primary precepts presuppose rights. The "must" (obligation) of the law indicates that all things necessary to the observance, the fulfillment of my obligations, are due (*debitum*) to me. I have a right to them. Otherwise, nature is not intelligible.
2. The natural law is the same for all.
   a) Common (primary) precepts:
      1) Truth — always morally true because immediately rooted in finality of nature.
      2) Knowledge — equally known by all who have the use of reason because self-evident.
   b) Particular applications (secondary precepts):
      1) Truth — the secondary precepts may vary because object and circumstance change.
      2) Knowledge — man may err in applying the precepts to more particularized instances.

Article III: *Human Law*

Definition: Human laws are the particularized determinations of the precepts of the natural law for the common good of the body politic.

Derived from the natural law: In order to be just and reasonable, a law should be in accordance with the rule of reason. Now the rule of reason is the natural law. Therefore a human law is just and good in so far as it is derived directly or indirectly from the natural law.

Inferences:

Human laws should not be too particularized.

Human laws do not pretend to repress all vices or to prescribe all virtues.

Human laws when just bind in conscience, because derived from the natural law and ultimately from the eternal law.

EPILOGUE

THE PHILOSOPHY OF MORALITY is an effort to establish a system of morals from an examination of the finality of the nature of man, the rational animal. It was pointed out that our approach to the problem of morality, as well as the solution, was along essential rather than existential lines of thought. By this statement, we indicated that our inferences did not proceed from a philosophical reflection founded upon an experience of man as he actually exists. Our science of morals began with an abstract study of man's nature; it envisaged the end of that nature to be an actuation, a perfection whose attainment depended on the natural powers of man in placing moral actions; it analyzed these actions only in so far as they are caused by and flow from the operative potencies of human nature. The law, expressed by moral judgments, was viewed as the very finality of that rational animal to its last end, an end necessarily proportioned to the natural inclinations of man. From this we gathered that the rules of human acts, which we call the precepts of the natural law, were capable of perfect observance by the rational animal, since these rules expressed the most profound urges of that nature. Finally, the obligations manifested by the law, as well as the rights which these obligations implied, appeared easy of fulfillment and within the reach of all, because they are founded on the finality of nature.

When, however, we look at man, not in an ideal state of philosophical abstraction, but as we actually find him in reality, that is, as he exists, we are filled with wonder as we observe that, in his actual exercise of life by moral actions, man differs not a little from what we reasoned him to be. Two fundamental discrepancies will bring this problem to focus.

According to our science of moral philosophy, man, the rational animal, is a composite of body and soul. The existential union between these essential elements results in the human person whose supreme actions are intellectual knowledge and love. So intimate is this existential union that, although the soul is a subsisting and therefore a spiritual form whose highest acts transcend matter, nevertheless, this same soul must obtain its data, even for intellectual knowledge, from the operations of sense before it can begin to place the act of understanding. The body is for the soul; the soul needs the body.

Yet, man must die; his body must corrupt; that is the law of living corporeal natures. What then will be the status of the soul after its separation from the body? Because it is immaterial, it will continue to exist. We ask: How can the soul, a disembodied spirit — still retaining its transcendental relation to the body, still retaining its need for operations of sense in order to understand and love — attain the natural happiness of man which is the last end of human nature?[1] It would seem that, in the present existential conditions in which man finds himself, the end is not attainable without special help from God. Such special help, however — as for example, the resurrection of the body or the needed infused species[2] — would seem to indicate that the order of man to his last end is not a natural order, that is, that it transcends the natural capacities and powers of man. For, although man is made for a lasting happiness, this happiness is never attained in this life, and in the next it does not seem attainable by man's natural powers.

Another radical disorder, and this time one that is immediately evident even from personal experience, can be stated thus: Even from a casual observation of human actions viewed in the

---

[1] We grant that man could have been created in the state of pure nature, and, moreover, had he been placed in such a state, that the natural end would have been possible of attainment by man's natural powers. As a matter of fact, in an earlier chapter, we established what this natural end would have been. The point we make here is that, in his present existential status, the ultimate end seems to be unattainable by man's natural powers. We conclude, therefore, even from reason, that man does not seem to be in the state of nature.

[2] "The separated soul . . . understands . . . by means of species participated from the influx of divine light" (S. Th., I, 89, 1, ad 3ᵐ; cf. ibid., art. 2, ad 2ᵐ; art. 3, c; art. 4, c; art. 7, c).

order of existence and not as inferred from an abstract analysis of nature, we note a fundamental disorder in man, a disorder unwarranted by nature, a disorder which could easily frustrate nature. It is this: the finality of a nature to its last end demands that the various fundamental inclinations of that nature, its strongest and most constant tendencies, should be toward the operations and the objects most necessary and useful for the attainment of that end. Yet we observe that in man there seems to be an ineradicable inclination to do the things that are against right reason, the things that will undoubtedly frustrate nature, the things that will cause human nature to deviate from its natural rectitude to the last end; in short, we observe in man an inclination to things that are morally evil.

Now it is true that a rational nature is capable of choosing deliberately and of placing freely a good or an evil act. Nevertheless, it is also true that in any nature — and the more perfect the nature, the more perfectly so — there should be a fundamental urge not to evil but to the good of the nature.[3] A nature, because it is a principle of action to an end, must naturally tend to turn away from the things which will impede its natural appetite to the last end. A nature must naturally tend to place actions that perfect it, that dispose it toward its end. Such a state of nature does not seem to be the case in existential man.

In man's nature we find not infrequently that the powers of the soul seem to lack the true inclination to the virtuous acts necessary to dispose man's nature to the attainment of the last end.[4] Reason, for example, finds it difficult to seek truth and is easily satisfied with error; the will wavers constantly in its quest after the true good of nature, and instead, often finds its delight in the things of earth; man at times lacks courage and weakens in facing the hardship which he must courageously accept in order to reach his happiness. Moreover, in the order of sense, there is

---

[3] ". . . God imprints on the whole of nature the principle of its proper actions" (*S. Th.*, I–II, 93, 5).

[4] "If man's appetite inclines to evil, this is due to the corruption or disorder in some one of the principles of man" (*S. Th.*, I–II, 78, 1).

a lack of moderation, of proper accord with reason in seeking the pleasurable. The passions are inclined to be inordinate even as regards objects that are good and useful. Now these evil tendencies of the soul are observable even in children who could not as yet have developed vicious habits by repeated evil actions. These evil inclinations, therefore, are not acquired. The individual is born with them; they are innate. Truly, in the existential order, man is quite different from what our philosophical analysis of human nature has led us to surmise.

What, then, is the true nature of man, his true end? What is the law which must govern his actions in the order of existence? And lastly, what is the worth of a science of morality which fails to present a true picture of the moral act? What is the value of a science which fails to give a complete solution to the problem of morality?

The answer is that man is not in the state of pure nature. We who accept the truth of revelation know that the first man received an elevated nature ordered to a supernatural end through the infused gift of sanctifying grace. This supernatural end is the intuitive vision of God. Because of the sin of Adam, man's nature fell from that high estate. Although retaining its ordination to the supernatural end, the elevated nature was wounded deeply.[5] This wound of nature which resulted from original sin is now found in all the children of Adam. It is the reason, the foundation for the innate inclination to evil acts found in all men.[6]

Obviously, the complete solution to the problem of morality in the existential order can be given only after we have accepted and studied and understood the true meaning of the revelation given to man. This revelation proclaims to us man's elevation, fall, and redemption; it indicates the extent of the wound of

---

[5] "A fourfold wound was inflicted upon human nature by the sin of our first parent" (S. Th., I–II, 85, 3). "This wound of nature consists, as regards the soul, in a disorder (deordinatio) of the powers" (ibid., art. 5). For "from the turning away from God (aversione a Deo, which is sin) there followed a disorder in all the powers of the soul" (I–II, 82, 3).

[6] "A certain inclination to an inordinate act follows from original sin" (S. Th., I–II, 82, 1, ad 3ᵐ).

nature, and the true significance of the supernatural gifts of God which we call grace, infused virtues, and gifts of the Holy Ghost. The revealed word declares the finality of our elevated nature to a supernatural end and as a consequent founds a divine law. The philosophy of morality which studies human nature from the light of reason cannot therefore pretend to solve completely the problem of man's existential act. A complete solution can be given only by a philosophy of Christian conduct which, having accepted the philosophical data obtained by the philosophy of morality and having received the revealed truths regarding man's elevation, will by philosophical inference establish how man can act, how he must act in order to reach his perfect beatitude in the intuitive vision of the Divine Essence.

The philosophy of morality, while it does not give a complete answer to the problem of the existential moral act, establishes a true foundation for its solution. For man, although ordered to a supernatural end, although hurt by a wound of nature, is still the rational animal. The reason is that the wound in no way impaired the essential elements of his nature. Hence, the existential act of man, in its fundamental objective morality, is truly determined and specified by the object as referred to the rational active principle. In like manner, the subjective morality, that is to say, the imputability of the act, is gauged in accordance with the natural processes of the rational animal. It is true that the law which man must now follow has greater extension because of man's ordination to a supernatural end. It is no longer merely a law of justice, but of faith and love, *"fides quae operatur per dilectionem."* On the other hand, all the free actions of man, even in his elevated state, are still the actions of the rational supposit, and, therefore, the natural law will always be the foundation, the essence of the rule which must govern man's actions. The divine law which is revealed to man will not contradict the natural law; rather, it will confirm the law of nature and open new horizons of perfection, of love, and of happiness. "Grace does not destroy but perfects nature."

The philosophy of morality is only a preparation, but an essential preparation to the understanding of man's destiny, of his aspirations, his hopes, his joys and sufferings, his sins and his happiness. It is an extremely important foundation in helping us not only to understand but actually to live a moral life which is the core of a supernatural life, the foundation and bulwark of a life of real sanctity. The true application of the philosophy of morality will be a remote preparation for the attainment of the supernatural end which is the beatitude of man,

"WHEN . . . WE SHALL SEE HIM AS HE IS."

INDEX

249